Taxcafe.co.uk Tax Guides

Salary versus Dividends

& Other Tax Efficient Profit Extraction Strategies

By Carl Bayley BSc FCA
and
Nick Braun PhD

Important Legal Notices:

Published by:
Taxcafe UK Limited
67 Milton Road
Kirkcaldy KY1 1TL

Email: team@taxcafe.co.uk

ISBN 978-1-911020-79-0

23rd edition, November 2022

Disclaimer
Before reading or relying on the content of this tax guide please read the disclaimer.

Disclaimer

1. This guide is intended as **general guidance** only and does NOT constitute accountancy, tax, investment or other professional advice.

2. The authors and Taxcafe UK Limited make no representations or warranties with respect to the accuracy or completeness of this publication and cannot accept any responsibility or liability for any loss or risk, personal or otherwise, which may arise, directly or indirectly, from reliance on information contained in this publication.

3. Please note that tax legislation, the law and practices of Government and regulatory authorities (e.g. HM Revenue & Customs) are constantly changing. We therefore recommend that for accountancy, tax, investment or other professional advice, you consult a suitably qualified accountant, tax adviser, financial adviser, or other professional adviser.

4. Please also note that your personal circumstances may vary from the general examples provided in this guide and your professional adviser will be able to provide specific advice based on your personal circumstances.

5. This guide covers UK taxation only and any references to 'tax' or 'taxation', unless the contrary is expressly stated, refer to UK taxation only. Please note that references to the 'UK' do not include the Channel Islands or the Isle of Man. Foreign tax implications are beyond the scope of this guide.

6. All persons described in the examples in this guide are entirely fictional. Any similarities to actual persons, living or dead, or to fictional characters created by any other author, are entirely coincidental.

About the Authors & Taxcafe

Carl Bayley is the author of a series of Taxcafe guides designed specifically for the layman and the non-specialist. Carl's particular speciality is his ability to take the weird, complex and inexplicable world of taxation and set it out in the kind of clear, straightforward language taxpayers themselves can understand. As he often says himself, "My job is to translate 'tax' into English."

In addition to being a recognised author, Carl has often spoken on taxation on radio and television, including the BBC's It's Your Money programme and the Jeremy Vine Show on Radio 2.

A chartered accountant by training, Carl is a former Chairman of the Tax Faculty of the Institute of Chartered Accountants in England and Wales and is also a member of the Institute's governing Council.

Nick Braun founded Taxcafe.co.uk in 1999, along with his partner, Aileen Smith. As the driving force behind the company, their aim is to provide affordable plain-English tax information for private individuals and investors, business owners, accountants and other advisers.

Since then Taxcafe has become one of the best-known tax publishers in the UK and has won several business awards.

Nick has been involved in the tax publishing world since 1989 as a writer, editor and publisher. He holds a doctorate in economics from the University of Glasgow, where he was awarded the prestigious William Glen Scholarship and later became a Research Fellow. Prior to that, he graduated with distinction from the University of South Africa, the country's oldest university, earning the highest results in economics in the university's history.

Contents

Introduction

This guide answers the most common question asked by company owners: "What's the best way to take money out of my company if I want to pay less tax?"

In Part 1 we kick off with a plain English guide to how *companies* are taxed.

The main rate of corporation tax will increase from 1st April 2023. Calculating your company's tax bill will also become more complicated. As a result, new tax planning opportunities will arise.

The corporation tax changes are covered in detail in this part of the guide and, throughout the guide, we explain how the changes will affect your profit extraction decisions in the years ahead.

In Part 1 we also explain how *company owners* are taxed. As a director/shareholder you can choose the best <u>mix</u> of salary and dividends. We examine the pros and cons of each type of income.

Company owners can also choose the most tax efficient <u>level</u> of income. We will see how, by smoothing your income or varying it significantly from year to year, you may be able to cut your tax bill considerably.

Tax-Free Salaries & Dividends

In Part 2 we reveal how much tax-free salary and dividend income you can withdraw from your company this year. You'll discover how to calculate the 'optimal' tax-efficient salary and how couples in business together can receive £29,140 this year without paying any income tax.

In Part 3 we explain how much dividend income you can take taxed at just 8.75% and how to avoid paying tax at 33.75%.

This part of the guide also contains important tax saving strategies for parents who want to avoid the child benefit tax charge.

This kicks in when your income exceeds £50,000 but many company owners will be able to avoid it completely or in part.

There is also important tax planning information for high income earners (those with income over £100,000 or £150,000).

Income from Other Sources

In Part 4 we turn to company owners who have income from other sources (e.g. pensions, rental income, interest income, income from another business and stock market dividends).

We explain why you may need to adjust your company salary or dividends to avoid the higher tax rates that kick in when your income reaches certain key thresholds (£50,000, £50,270, £100,000 and £150,000).

We also examine some tax planning techniques that can be used to reduce or eliminate the tax payable on your income from other sources.

Company owners who are also landlords need to be aware of the restriction to tax relief on mortgage interest. Fortunately, company owners have more flexibility than other landlords when it comes to avoiding some of the worst effects of this tax change.

Company owners can also enjoy much more tax-free interest than other taxpayers (up to £6,000 per year).

Splitting Income with Family Members

Part 5 explains how company owners can gift shares in the business to their spouses, partners or children and save over £10,000 in tax this year, with similar savings every year.

We also show how additional savings can be achieved by paying tax-free salaries to family members, including your minor children.

There are, however, many traps to avoid when it comes to splitting income with family members and these are fully covered in this part of the guide. For example, we examine the danger of gifting shares that have fewer rights than ordinary shares and the danger of using dividend waivers to divert income to your spouse/partner.

Alternative Profit Extraction Strategies

Part 6 looks at alternative profit extraction strategies:

- **Directors' loans** – How they can be used to reduce or postpone tax.

- **Rent** – Why getting your company to pay you rent is more tax efficient than a dividend in many circumstances.

- **Interest** – How to receive up to £6,000 of tax-free interest from your company.

- **Charity** – Who should donate: you or the company?

- **Pension contributions** – Why they're better than dividends, who should make them (you or the company), plus a chapter on putting property into a pension.

- **Capital gains** – How to pay 10% tax when you sell or wind up your company; How to pay 0% tax when you sell your company to an employee ownership trust.

In Part 7 we turn to some of the practical issues and dangers that may be experienced when extracting money from your company:

- How to avoid the minimum wage regulations
- How to make sure your salary is a tax deductible expense
- Making sure your company has sufficient distributable profits to declare dividends
- How to declare dividends properly and avoid an HMRC challenge
- When HMRC might try to tax your dividends as earnings

Finally, in Part 8, we look at some other tax saving strategies for company owners, including how they may be able to reduce the amount of capital gains tax payable when assets like rental properties are sold.

In this part we also explain how you may be able to completely avoid tax by emigrating. There is also a chapter explaining how you can reduce your income tax bill by investing in venture capital trusts.

Using This Guide & Limitations

This tax guide deals primarily with the 2022/23 tax year, starting on 6th April 2022 and finishing on 5th April 2023. Unless expressly stated to the contrary, all references, examples, illustrations, etc, are based on the tax rates, thresholds, and allowances applying for 2022/23.

Nonetheless, there are some references to other tax years, for example when discussing the advantages and disadvantages of postponing income to a future tax year.

Following the Chancellor's Autumn Statement on 17th November 2022, we now know the expected tax rates and thresholds for next year, 2023/24, and also have a reasonable idea of many of the key tax rates and thresholds through to 2027/28. However, it is important to emphasise that none of this has yet been formally enacted and while we now have Government announcements regarding the position in future years, this could all be changed in a later statement, so we cannot truly say the tax rates that will apply in future years are known with absolute certainty. Yes, the position for 2023/24 now looks reasonably certain, but the further one strays into the future, the more uncertain the position in later years becomes.

As well as rates and thresholds, tax laws (and HMRC's interpretation of those laws) are also continually changing. The reader must bear all of this in mind when reading this guide.

Please note that, although small company owners are this book's main target audience, this is NOT supposed to be a do-it-yourself (DIY) tax planning guide.

Our purpose in writing this guide is to explain in plain English how companies and company owners are taxed and provide some tax planning ideas that can be taken to an accountant or other professional adviser for further discussion.

We do not recommend 'going it alone' when it comes to this type of tax planning and there are several reasons for our cautious approach.

Firstly, although the guide covers a fair amount of ground, it does not cover every possible scenario – that would be impossible without making the guide much longer and possibly much more difficult to digest.

In other words, in places we have had to sacrifice definitiveness in favour of making the guide a manageable and hopefully enjoyable read for the average small company owner.

Companies come in many different shapes and sizes, as do their owners, so it is possible that the information contained in this guide will not be relevant to your circumstances.

In particular, please note that this guide is aimed mainly at UK resident director/shareholders who own and work for UK resident companies.

Secondly, the main focus of this tax guide is *income tax* planning: helping company owners pay less tax on their salaries, dividends and other income. There are, however, other taxes that often have to be considered, including capital gains tax and inheritance tax.

Steps that you take to reduce one type of tax can have an adverse impact on your liability to pay other taxes. While some mention is made of other taxes in this guide, we cannot guarantee that all interactions are covered.

Thirdly, there are potential risks involved when it comes to structuring your affairs to reduce the tax payable on salaries, dividends and other payments made by your company.

While most of the tax planning ideas contained in this book are widely used by many accountants and other professional advisers, and have been for many years, this does not mean they have the blessing of HM Revenue & Customs!

There are some grey areas when it comes to this area of tax planning and some tax savings may not always be guaranteed.

In other words, we cannot be certain that some of the tax planning ideas contained in this book will not be subject to some sort of attack from HMRC, even if only at some point in the future.

For example, in the chapters that follow we will show that the most tax-efficient mix of income for most company owners is a small salary coupled with a larger dividend. While this is a well-established, reasonable form of tax planning which, if carried out correctly, is generally accepted, even if grudgingly, by HMRC, there are circumstances under which they might seek to tax dividends as earnings.

We'll look at this potential threat further in Chapter 36 but it's also worth pointing out that, *at present*, such attacks are rare and generally only occur where aggressive tax avoidance schemes are involved. For the vast majority of small company owners the danger is remote and lies firmly in the future.

Fourthly, there are also *non-tax* factors that have to be considered when deciding how much money you withdraw from your company and in what form. In some instances other considerations will outweigh any potential tax savings.

For all of these reasons it is vital that you obtain professional advice before taking any action based on information contained in this guide. The authors and Taxcafe UK Ltd cannot accept any responsibility for any loss which may arise as a consequence of any action taken, or any decision to refrain from taking action, as a result of reading this guide

Scottish Taxpayers

The Scottish Parliament can tax most types of income, but not interest or dividends. The vast majority of the information contained in this guide is relevant to Scottish taxpayers and there is quite a lot of information specific to them. However, unless stated to the contrary, all examples, tables and calculations assume that the taxpayer concerned is not a Scottish taxpayer.

Spouses and Civil Partners

Under UK tax law, all legally married spouses and registered civil partners are treated the same. Hence, when we refer to a 'spouse' in this guide, it includes a civil partner. However, for tax purposes, a spouse does not include a common-law partner or co-habitee. Where we are discussing a partner who may either be a legally married spouse or a common-law partner, we will use the term 'spouse/partner'.

Part 1

How Companies & Company Owners Are Taxed

Chapter 1

How Companies Are Taxed

Companies pay corporation tax on both their income and capital gains.

For the current financial year, starting on 1st April 2022, all companies (except some in the oil and gas or banking sectors) pay corporation tax at the same flat rate of 19%.

From 1st April 2023 the main rate of corporation tax will be increased to 25%.

Calculating the Company's Effective Tax Rate

Not only will corporation tax be increased, it will also become more complicated, just like it was a few years ago. From 1st April 2023 there will be two official corporation tax rates:

- Small profits rate   19%
- Main rate   25%

The practical effect is that companies will pay tax as follows:

- **Profits £50,000 or less** – Company will continue to pay 19% tax on all of its profits

- **Profits between £50,000 and £250,000** – Company will pay 19% tax on the first £50,000 and 26.5% on the remainder

- **Profits greater than £250,000** – Company will pay 25% tax on all of its profits

Some sample corporation tax bills and overall corporation tax rates are shown in Table 1.

TABLE 1
Overall Corporation Tax Rates
After the Increase

Profits	Corporation Tax	Corporation Tax Rate
£50,000	£9,500	19.00%
£60,000	£12,150	20.25%
£70,000	£14,800	21.14%
£80,000	£17,450	21.81%
£90,000	£20,100	22.33%
£100,000	£22,750	22.75%
£110,000	£25,400	23.09%
£120,000	£28,050	23.38%
£130,000	£30,700	23.62%
£140,000	£33,350	23.82%
£150,000	£36,000	24.00%
£160,000	£38,650	24.16%
£170,000	£41,300	24.29%
£180,000	£43,950	24.42%
£190,000	£46,600	24.53%
£200,000	£49,250	24.63%
£210,000	£51,900	24.71%
£220,000	£54,550	24.80%
£230,000	£57,200	24.87%
£240,000	£59,850	24.94%
£250,000	£62,500	25.00%

A company with profits of £100,000 will pay 19% on the first £50,000 and 26.5% on the final £50,000. The total tax bill will be £22,750 which means the company will have an overall tax rate of 22.75% (£22,750/£100,000).

A company with profits of £150,000 will pay 19% on the first £50,000 and 26.5% on the remaining £100,000. The total tax bill will be £36,000 which means the company will have an overall tax rate of 24% (£36,000/£150,000).

A company with profits of £20,000 (i.e. less than £50,000) will simply pay £3,800 (19%). A company will profits of £300,000 (i.e. more than £250,000) will simply pay £75,000 (25%).

Non-Resident Companies

Only companies that are UK resident will be able to benefit from the 19% small profits rate. A non-resident company that earns rental income from UK properties, for example, will therefore have to pay 25% corporation tax on all of its UK rental profits.

Accounting Periods vs Financial Years

Because of the way corporation tax is calculated, the corporation tax increase affects some companies from as early as May 2022.

A company's own tax year (also known as its accounting period) can end on any date, for example 31st December, 31st March etc.

Corporation tax, on the other hand, is calculated according to financial years. Financial years run from 1st April to 31st March. The 2023 financial year is the year starting on 1st April 2023 and ending on 31st March 2024.

This matters when it comes to calculating how much tax your company will pay when the corporation tax rate changes.

For example, on 1st April 2023 the main rate of corporation tax will increase from 19% to 25%. A company with profits of more than £250,000 whose accounting period runs from 1st January 2023 to 31st December 2023 will therefore pay corporation tax as follows:

- 3 months to 31st March 2023   19%
- 9 months to 31st December 2023   25%

The company will therefore pay 19% corporation tax on roughly one quarter of its profits (3/12) and 25% tax on roughly three quarters of its profits (9/12). (It doesn't matter at what point during the year the profits are actually made.)

This means the company's overall corporation tax rate for this year will be 23.5%. (Note, in practice corporation tax is calculated using days not months and this will result in a tiny difference in the overall tax rate which largely disappears in the rounding. For example, the above rate correctly calculated using days not months would be 23.52%.)

Smaller Profits

If the company has profits of less than £250,000 the calculation will be a bit more complicated. For example, a company with profits of £150,000 whose accounting period runs from 1st January 2023 to 31st December 2023 will pay corporation tax as follows:

- 3 months to 31st March 2023   19%
- 9 months to 31st December 2023   24%

24% is taken from Table 1 and is simply the new overall tax rate payable by a company with profits of £150,000.

The practical effect is that the company will pay 19% corporation tax on approximately one quarter of its profits and 24% tax on approximately three quarters of its profits.

This means the company's overall corporation tax rate for this year will be 22.75%.

(In practice, the actual calculation must be performed in days rather than months. Also, 2024 is a leap year, which has a further small effect on the calculation for companies with profits under £250,000, which we have ignored for simplicity.)

Another Example

Let's say the company has profits of £100,000 and an accounting period that runs from 1st May 2022 to 30th April 2023. It will pay corporation tax as follows:

- 11 months to 31st March 2023   19%
- 1 month to 30th April 2023   22.75%

22.75% is taken from Table 1 and is simply the new overall tax rate payable by a company with profits of £100,000.

The practical effect is the company will pay 19% corporation tax on approximately 11/12ths of its profits and 22.75% tax on the remaining 1/12th. This means the company's overall corporation tax rate for this year will be 19.31%.

This example shows how the corporation tax increase started to affect some companies from as early as May 2022.

Marginal Tax Rate Planning

The corporation tax increase means many companies will pay more tax on their profits. The good news is companies will also enjoy more corporation tax relief on their spending.

In recent years companies have enjoyed 19% corporation tax relief no matter how much profit they have made or when they have spent their money. A company incurring an additional £1,000 of tax deductible spending would reduce its taxable profits by £1,000, saving it £190 in corporation tax.

When the corporation tax increase is in full force, the amount of tax relief a company enjoys will depend on its profits:

- A company with profits of £50,000 or less will have a marginal tax rate of 19% and will continue to enjoy 19% tax relief on its spending.

- A company with profits of between £50,000 and £250,000 will have a marginal tax rate of 26.5% and will enjoy 26.5% tax relief on its spending. (However, if the company's spending pushes its profits below £50,000 it will start to receive just 19% tax relief on any additional spending.)

- A company with profits of more than £250,000 will have a marginal tax rate of 25% and will enjoy 25% tax relief on its spending. (However, if the company's spending pushes its profits below £250,000 it will start to receive 26.5% tax relief on any additional spending.)

In Table 1 we listed the new overall tax rates companies will face. For example, a company which makes a profit of £100,000 will have an overall tax rate of 22.75%. Note, the overall rate is NOT used for most tax planning purposes, for example calculating the amount of tax a company will save if it spends some more money. Instead it is the company's marginal tax rate.

This makes sense when you consider a simple example. A company which anticipates making a profit of £100,000 and incurs an additional £10,000 of tax deductible expenditure will reduce its taxable profits by £10,000. This will reduce its tax bill by £2,650 (26.5%). The company's overall tax rate of 22.75% does not tell us how much tax the company will save.

Periods Straddling the Date of Change

A company will have a slightly lower marginal tax rate for the year that straddles 1st April 2023, the date corporation tax changes.

In other words, spending in that year will attract more than 19% tax relief but not quite as much as when the corporation tax increase is in full force.

Take a company whose tax year runs from 1st January to 31st December 2023 and has profits of between £50,000 and £250,000. Its marginal tax rate for that year is calculated as follows:

1st January to 31st March	90/365 x 19%	4.685%
1st April to 31st December	275/365 x 26.5%	19.966%
Marginal rate		24.65%

Thus, if the company incurs an additional £10,000 of tax deductible spending between 1st January 2023 and 31st December 2023 its corporation tax bill will be reduced by £2,465.

Note, it doesn't matter when during the year the spending takes place (it doesn't matter whether it's between January and March or between April and December).

If the company has profits of more than £250,000 its marginal tax rate will be 19% for the first three months and 25% for the final nine months. Its overall marginal tax rate for the year will therefore be 23.52%.

Appendix A contains all the marginal tax rates that apply to companies with different accounting periods straddling 1st April 2023, the date corporation tax increases.

Companies with profits of £50,000 or less will continue to have a marginal tax rate of 19% and will therefore receive 19% tax relief on their spending.

The fact that many companies will see their marginal rates of corporation tax increase above 19% raises a number of questions for their owners:

Should My Company Postpone Spending?

At the time of writing many companies are still receiving 19% tax relief on their spending. When the corporation tax increase is in full force some companies will enjoy 26.5% tax relief on their additional spending and some will enjoy 25% tax relief.

Thus a company that postpones some of its discretionary spending will enjoy up to an additional 7.5 percentage points of tax relief, saving it up to £750 for every £10,000 it postpones.

Unfortunately, however, the company may have to wait a while to enjoy the maximum tax relief.

Take a company whose accounting period runs from 1st January to 31st December and has taxable profits of between £50,000 and £250,000 per year. The company faces the following marginal rates of corporation tax:

- Year ended 31st December 2022   19%
- Year ended 31st December 2023   24.65%
- Year ended 31st December 2024   26.5%

Only spending from January 2024 onwards can enjoy 26.5% tax relief, although spending between January and December 2023 can enjoy up to 24.65% tax relief.

Some company owners may be willing to postpone certain types of spending for this amount of time, others will not.

Super Tax Deduction for Companies

The Government was concerned that companies would postpone some of their *investment* spending until after the increase in corporation tax. For this reason the Government also introduced a 'super deduction' of 130% for investment spending that takes place before 1st April 2023, the date corporation tax changes.

Thanks to the super deduction many companies currently enjoy roughly 25% tax relief on their investment spending. For example, a company spending £1,000 on a qualifying asset will see its taxable profits reduced by £1,300, saving it £247 in corporation tax (at 19%).

The super deduction covers things like computer equipment, vans and office furniture. However, only spending on *new* assets qualifies; second-hand goods do not qualify. It also does not cover spending on cars.

For more information about the super deduction see the Taxcafe guide *'The Company Tax Changes'*.

In summary, if you are thinking about postponing any investment spending until your company's corporation tax rate increases, remember that the spending may currently qualify for the temporary 130% super tax deduction.

How Does the Tax Increase Affect Salaries, etc?

If your company pays you a salary, rental income, interest income or makes pension contributions on your behalf these are all tax deductible expenses for the company.

Thus the tax relief the company enjoys on all of these expenses will increase when its corporation tax rate increases.

As far as payments made in the current, 2022/23 tax year are concerned, it's worth pointing out that there are two types of company where the corporation tax increase will generally have no effect and all tax deductible payments will usually continue to attract relief at 19%:

a) Companies with annual profits not exceeding £50,000 (and no associated companies: see further below)
b) Companies with a 31st March accounting date

In the latter case, payments made after 31st March 2023 may be affected by the corporation tax increase where the company has profits over £50,000. Payments made on or before that date may also be affected by the increase if they relate, wholly or partly, to the next accounting period (e.g. rent paid on 25th March 2023 for the calendar quarter commencing on that date).

Apart from companies falling under (a) or (b), the exact amount of tax relief the company will enjoy in respect of payments made during the 2022/23 *income tax* year will depend not only on the company's accounting period and profit level, but also on whether the payments are made monthly, annually, or as a 'one off', and on how the payment is recognised in the company's accounts.

Companies must operate the accruals basis of accounting which means any periodic cost must be spread over the period to which it relates. For example, a company with a 31st December accounting date may make a single annual rental payment of £20,000 to its owner/director, who owns the company's trading premises personally. Whenever the payment is made, the director will have taxable rental income of £20,000 for 2022/23.

But the payment that suffers income tax in the director's hands in 2022/23 will need to be recognised on a time apportionment basis in the company's accounts. Hence £15,000 (9/12ths) of the rent will fall into the company's accounting period ending 31st December 2022 and attract corporation tax relief at 19%; and £5,000 (3/12ths) will fall into the company's accounting period ending 31st December 2023 and attract corporation tax relief at either 19%, 24.65%, or 23.52%, depending on the company's profit level (see Appendix A).

Let's say the company's profits for the year ending 31st December 2023 turn out to be £200,000, so it will have a marginal corporation tax rate of 24.65%. The corporation tax relief for the rent on which the director pays income tax in 2022/23 will be:

£15,000 @ 19% =	£2,850
£5,000 @ 24.65% =	£1,232
Total	£4,082

The overall effective rate of relief is therefore 20.41%. You will find this rate of relief in Appendix B (it's actually 20.413% to be precise), which sets out the effective rate of corporation tax relief for periodic costs incurred by the company in the 2022/23 income tax year.

Sometimes periodic costs are apportioned on a daily, rather than monthly basis, which gives a slightly different result (for example, the corporation tax relief in the case examined above would then total £4,079 or 20.395%).

Either approach is equally acceptable for both accounting and tax purposes, but we'll stick with monthly apportionment in this guide to keep life simple.

The rent of £20,000 in our example might be either a single payment in respect of the twelve months to 31st March 2023 or it might be made up of the appropriate portions of annual payments made in respect of the twelve months to 31st December 2022 and twelve months to 31st December 2023. Either way, the director will pay income tax on £20,000 of rental income in 2022/23 and the company will enjoy corporation tax relief of £4,082 on that amount.

Where something is a periodic cost, it's also important to appreciate that, for corporation tax purposes, it is generally spread over the period to which it relates, regardless of when it is actually paid. Hence, the rent payment above would attract the same amount of corporation tax relief, and in the same accounting periods, even if it was not paid until after 5th April 2023.

There are some exceptions to this rule, however. Companies cannot claim corporation tax relief on:

- Salaries or bonuses that are still unpaid nine months after the end of the accounting period
- Interest charged by the company's owner that is still unpaid twelve months after the end of the accounting period

In these cases, relief can only be claimed when payment is actually made: credits made to the director's loan account count as payment though.

On the other side of the equation, directors are generally only taxed on payments from their company when they receive them (again, a credit to the director's loan account counts as receipt).

This applies to salary, bonuses, and interest paid to the director (as well as dividends, although these do not attract corporation tax relief). The only potential exception is rent, where the position depends on whether the director is taxed on their property income under the cash basis, or under traditional accruals basis accounting (see the Taxcafe guide *'How to Save Property Tax'* for detailed explanations of both methods and when they are available).

So, where does all this leave us with the effective rate of corporation tax relief for payments made to, or on behalf of, directors in 2022/23?

Generally, if something is paid monthly, it will be a periodic cost. Some things are always a periodic cost, even if paid annually.

Rent and interest are always periodic costs and thus will generally attract corporation tax relief at the rates given in Appendix B.

Salaries and pension contributions paid monthly will usually also be periodic costs, attracting corporation tax relief at the rates given in Appendix B.

Salaries or bonuses, and pension contributions, paid annually, or as a one-off, may not be periodic costs, but this depends on the circumstances. The position for salaries is discussed further below and pension contributions are discussed in Chapter 27. Where payments are not periodic costs and thus do not need to be spread over more than one accounting period, they will attract corporation tax relief at the rates given in Appendix A, based on the date of payment, or the date the cost is recognised in the company's accounts.

What about Dividends?

Dividends are paid out of a company's *after-tax profits*. Thus, the total amount of tax paid on dividend income, including the corporation tax suffered by the company, will increase.

However, the effective rate of tax applying depends on what we are comparing the dividend with. For example, if a director takes a dividend instead of a monthly salary, the effective corporation tax rate applying to that dividend will be as set out in Appendix B. Alternatively, if the director takes a dividend instead of a bonus (which is not accounted for as a periodic cost) the effective corporation tax rate applying will be as set out in Appendix A.

Salaries in the Current 2022/23 Tax Year

The current tax year for *individuals* runs from 6th April 2022 to 5th April 2023. It's a tricky one when it comes to calculating the precise amount of corporation tax relief many companies will enjoy on salaries and other regular payments made to the directors.

The amount of corporation tax relief will vary from company to company, depending on how much profit they make, when their accounting period ends and when the payments are made.

Example

Average Company Ltd has an accounting period that runs from January to December. It makes monthly salary payments to the directors.

For the accounting period ending on 31st December 2022 the company will enjoy 19% corporation tax relief on the salary payments it makes.

For the accounting period ending 31st December 2023 the company will enjoy 24.65% corporation tax relief on any additional salary payments, assuming its profits are between £50,000 and £250,000 (Appendix A).

The 2022/23 tax year falls into both of these years, so the company will enjoy the following tax relief on its salary payments:

April to December 2022	*9/12 x 19%*	*14.25%*
January to March 2023	*3/12 x 24.65%*	*6.16%*
Total corporation tax relief		*20.41%*

The company will enjoy a total of 20.41% corporation tax relief on any salary payments made during the current 2022/23 tax year.

The corporation tax relief would be slightly different if the company was making profits of less than £50,000 (19%) or more than £250,000 (20.13%).

The outcome would also be different if the company's accounting period ended on a different date. For example, if the company has an accounting period that runs from August to July it will enjoy a total of 20.67% corporation tax relief on salary payments made in 2022/23.

For a complete picture of the overall effective rate of corporation tax relief enjoyed by companies paying regular monthly salaries throughout 2022/23, see Appendix B.

The outcome may also be different where the director's salary is paid in a single annual lump sum, rather than monthly.

Example

Annpay Ltd makes annual profits of £200,000 and has an accounting period that runs from January to December. Its director, Anne, takes her salary in a single lump sum in March each year. The salary she takes in March 2023 is accounted for as an expense in the company's accounts for the year ending 31st December 2023 and will thus provide corporation tax relief at 24.65% (see Appendix A).

If we compare the results in the last two examples, we can see that a single lump sum payment (as for Annpay Ltd) may produce a different overall rate of tax relief than regular monthly payments:

Average Company Ltd (monthly pay): Relief at 20.41% on average
Annpay Ltd (lump sum): Relief at 24.65%

In both cases, we are talking about salary falling into the same *income tax* year, 2022/23.

However, such single annual lump sum payments are not always accounted for as an expense of the company accounting period in which they are paid.

It would have been equally acceptable for Annpay Ltd to have accrued part of the cost of the salary paid to Anne in March 2023 as an expense of its accounting period ending 31st December 2022, with the remainder treated as an expense of the accounting period ending 31st December 2023. The split would be done on a time apportionment basis, with the end result being that the overall average rate of corporation tax relief for Anne's 2022/23 salary would be the same as for the monthly payments made by Average Company Ltd.

The proper accounting treatment of a lump sum payment like this is really a question of whether Anne's lump sum salary paid in March 2023 is seen as a reward for her efforts as company director over the period from April 2022 to March 2023, or as a bonus paid in recognition of her continuing service to the company.

In most cases, the decision on how to treat the director's annual lump sum salary in the company's accounts will have been made some years ago. If so, it would be very difficult to argue for a different treatment this year, just because the company's corporation tax rate is increasing.

So, why is all this important? As we shall see in the chapters that follow, when deciding how much salary or other income to pay yourself, the amount of additional corporation tax relief your company receives on these payments is an important factor.

In previous editions of this guide the corporation tax relief appearing in many of the examples and calculations has been 19% for all companies. In this edition the precise amount of tax relief in pounds and pence will vary from company to company, making it difficult to provide exact figures for every single company.

Fortunately, however, the overall conclusions will be the same in most cases.

Multiple Companies

Company owners often think about setting up a second company, to keep a new venture separate from an existing business. Often there are sound commercial reasons for using more than one company, including to:

- Reduce risk (limit liability)
- Involve different shareholders
- Enable a stand-alone sale of each business
- Make it easier to borrow money

Using more than one company allows you to reduce your risk – if one business goes bankrupt, the other venture housed in a separate company should be protected because each company has limited liability status.

Using more than one company is also ideal when you want each business to have different shareholders. It's not uncommon for business owners to engage in different projects with different people.

Using separate companies may also make it easier to exit each business. For example, someone who owns an ecommerce business and a restaurant chain may wish to keep them in separate companies to make it easier to sell each business to a different buyer in the future.

When it comes to borrowing money, it's not uncommon for property investors to put their properties in a separate stand-alone company and lenders often insist on this. Mortgage lenders tend not to like companies that have 'trading' activities which are perceived as being more risky than property investment.

Saving Tax

Using separate companies may also be attractive when it comes to saving capital gains tax and inheritance tax – in particular when one business is a trading business and the other is not. Companies that own too many non-trading assets, like rental property, can lose important tax reliefs, including Business Asset Disposal Relief (previously known as Entrepreneurs Relief), Holdover Relief and Business Property Relief.

For example, someone who owns a software company and a property rental business may wish to keep them in separate companies so that the trading business (the software company) is not 'contaminated' by the non-trading business (the property rental business).

Using separate companies has drawbacks too. For example, if you initially expect losses from a new trading activity, those losses can usually be set off against the profits from an existing activity, if both businesses are in the same company. This is generally not possible if the businesses are in separate companies (unless you form a group).

With the increase in corporation tax some people may also be asking whether they can benefit from more than one company each enjoying up to £50,000 of profit taxed at just 19%.

The answer is generally no if the companies are controlled by the same people.

Associated Company Rules

To prevent people artificially spreading their business activities across multiple companies, the £50,000 lower limit and £250,000 upper limit will be divided up if there are any 'associated companies'.

A company will be associated with another company if:

- One company controls the other company
- Both are under the control of the same person or persons

For example, if you own all of the shares in two companies these companies will be associated. Each company will start paying corporation tax at 26.5% when its profits exceed £25,000 (i.e. £50,000/2). Each company will pay 25% tax on all of its profits if its profits are greater than £125,000 (£250,000/2).

If there are three associated companies, each company will start paying corporation tax at 26.5% when its profits exceed £16,667 (£50,000/3)... and so on.

Example
Let's assume the new higher rates of corporation tax are in operation. Jamie owns Company 1 which has annual profits of £100,000. He then decides to start a second business and is trying to decide whether to house it in Company 1 or set up Company 2. Let's say the new business makes a profit of £30,000. If he keeps it in Company 1 the additional profit will be taxed at 26.5% producing a total tax bill of £30,700.

If Jamie decides to house the new business in Company 2, the two companies will be associated if we assume he controls them both. The companies will pay corporation tax as follows:

Company 1: £25,000 x 19% + £75,000 x 26.5% = £24,625
Company 2: £25,000 x 19% + £5,000 x 26.5% = £6,075
Combined tax bill: £30,700

The total corporation tax bill will be the same whether Jamie uses one company or two. Jamie will still benefit from having £50,000 of profits taxed at 19% (£25,000 in each company).

If Company 2 has profits of less than £25,000, Jamie will effectively be penalised for running two companies. For example, if Company 2 breaks even (i.e. has a profit of exactly £0) he will pay £1,875 more tax with two companies. This is because Company 1 will have just £25,000 instead of £50,000 taxed at 19%.

For further details on the associated company rules, including situations where company shareholdings owned by your spouse, another close family member, or a business partner, may have to be counted when applying these rules, see the Taxcafe guide *'The Company Tax Changes'*.

Corporation Tax Quarterly Instalments

The associated company rules will also be relevant in deciding whether a company has to pay corporation tax in quarterly instalments. Instalments are generally payable by companies whose profits exceed £1.5 million but this amount will be divided up if there are any associated companies. Whereas small companies currently only have to pay corporation tax nine months after the end of their accounting period, companies subject to instalments have to start paying tax half way through the year.

Trading Companies vs Investment Companies

In tax jargon a 'trading' company is one involved in, for want of a better word, 'regular' business activities, e.g. a company that sells goods online, a catering company or a firm of garden landscapers.

Common types of *non-trading* company include those that hold substantial investments in property or financial securities or earn substantial royalty income.

Corporation Tax

Companies engaged mainly in non-trading activities have paid corporation tax at the same 19% rate as most other companies.

However, the increase in corporation tax will see some of these companies having to pay corporation tax at the main rate of 25% on all of their profits.

This is because a company classed as a close investment holding company (CIC) cannot benefit from the small profits rate. It will be forced to pay corporation tax at the main rate on all of its profits.

For example, a company that is set up to hold stock market investments may currently be paying 19% tax but when the new corporation tax rates come into effect it will pay 25%, even if it only makes a small amount of profit. (Having said that, companies do not pay corporation tax on dividend income: but they do on capital gains or other forms of investment income)

Companies that mainly derive their profits from renting property to unconnected third parties (i.e. not to family members, etc) are excluded from the CIC provisions. Hence, the vast majority of property investment companies will be allowed to enjoy the small profits rate where appropriate.

Capital Gains Tax

If a company has too many non-trading activities (including most property investment and property letting) it may lose its trading status for capital gains tax purposes.

This will result in the loss of two important CGT reliefs:

- Business Asset Disposal Relief (Entrepreneurs Relief)
- Holdover Relief

Business Asset Disposal Relief allows you to pay CGT at just 10% (instead of 20%) when you sell your company or wind it up.

Holdover Relief allows you to give shares in the business to your children, common-law unmarried partner, or other individuals and postpone CGT. (You don't need Holdover Relief to transfer shares to your spouse because such transfers are always exempt.)

Clearly, if the company's only business is property investment or property letting (or any other form of investment activity) then it will not be classed as a trading company and the relevant CGT reliefs will not be available. However, it's worth noting that qualifying furnished holiday letting businesses are treated as trading for CGT purposes (see the Taxcafe guide 'Using a Property Company to Save Tax' for details).

Where a company has both trading and non-trading activities, it will only lose its trading status for CGT purposes if its non-trading activities are 'substantial'. HMRC generally accepts the non-trading activities are not substantial where neither non-trading income nor non-trading assets exceed 20% of the totals for the company as a whole. However, this test is only a yardstick and is not conclusive. In a recent tax case, it was held that non-trading activities would only be regarded as substantial where they were of material or real importance in the context of the company's activities as a whole.

Nonetheless, to avoid any argument over the issue, it is wise to keep both non-trading income and non-trading assets below 20% in order to safely preserve the company's trading status wherever possible.

Inheritance Tax

Shares in trading companies generally qualify for business property relief which means they can be passed on free from inheritance tax. However, if the company holds investments (including rental property) this could result in the loss of business property relief.

The qualification criteria are more generous than for CGT purposes and a company generally only loses its trading status for inheritance tax purposes if it is 'wholly or mainly' involved in investment related activities. This time, however, furnished holiday letting is very rarely accepted as a trading activity.

For more information see the Taxcafe guide *'How to Save Inheritance Tax'*.

Chapter 2

How Directors Are Taxed: Employment Income

When HMRC and tax professionals talk about 'employment income', they are referring to salaries and bonuses.

Salaries and bonuses are subject to income tax and national insurance. They are also generally a tax deductible expense for the company.

Income Tax

For the 2022/23 tax year, starting on 6th April 2022, most individuals pay income tax as follows on their salaries:

• 0%	on the first	£12,570	Personal allowance
• 20%	on the next	£37,700	Basic-rate band
• 40%	above	£50,270	Higher-rate threshold

If you earn more than £50,270 you are a higher-rate taxpayer; if you earn less you are a basic-rate taxpayer.

The number £50,270 is important to remember because it will be mentioned repeatedly in the chapters that follow.

Transferable Personal Allowance

It is possible to transfer 10% of your personal allowance to your spouse or civil partner (£1,260 during the current tax year).

Only basic-rate taxpayers can benefit from this tax break, so the potential tax saving is £252 (£1,260 x 20%).

Unmarried couples are excluded – this was the rather feeble attempt by David Cameron (remember him?) to use the tax system to reward marriage.

Married couples can generally only benefit from this tax break if:

- One person earns less than £12,570 (not including savings interest of up to £6,000 or dividends of up to £2,000 this year) and is therefore wasting some of their personal allowance,
- The other person earns less than £50,270 (£43,662 in Scotland), and
- Both individuals were born after 5th April 1935.

You have to register to use it at: www.gov.uk/marriageallowance

Potential winners are married couples where one person does not work (e.g. full-time parents) or only has a part-time job.

Example
During the current tax year Bill earns a salary of £30,000 and his wife Daphne earns £6,000 working part time. Daphne has £6,570 of unused personal allowance. She can transfer £1,260 of this to Bill which means Bill no longer has to pay tax on £1,260 of his income. This will save him £252 in tax (£1,260 x 20%).

Income over £100,000

When your taxable income exceeds £100,000 your income tax personal allowance is gradually withdrawn. For every additional £1 you earn, 50p of your personal allowance is taken away.

What this means is that, when your income reaches £125,140, your personal allowance will have completely disappeared. It also means that those who earn salary income between £100,000 and £125,140 face a marginal income tax rate of 60%.

Example
Caroline, a company director, has received salary income of £100,000 so far during the current tax year. If she receives an extra £100 of salary she will pay an extra £40 of income tax. She will also lose £50 of her income tax personal allowance, so £50 of previously tax-free salary will be taxed at 40%, adding £20 to her tax bill. All in all, she pays £60 tax on her extra £100 of salary, so her marginal income tax rate is 60%.

Income above £150,000

Once your taxable income exceeds £150,000, you pay 45% income tax on any extra employment income. This is known as the additional rate of tax. The threshold is to be reduced to £125,140 next year (2023/24), aligning it with the point where your personal allowance is completely withdrawn. Throughout this guide, when considering current year planning, we will be concerned with the current £150,000 threshold. But when we look at saving tax by deferring income into later years, the future threshold of £125,140 will be critical.

National Insurance

National insurance has been changed three times this year. All the rates went up by 1.25% at the start of the tax year. Then a few months later the threshold where national insurance becomes payable was increased. Finally, the 1.25% national insurance increase was scrapped with effect from 6th November 2022.

National insurance for directors is assessed on an annual basis. The annualised rates for 2022/23 are as follows:

- 0%   on the first   £11,908   Primary threshold
- 12.73% on the next   £38,362
- 2.73%   above   £50,270   Upper earnings limit

Next year (2023/24) the national insurance threshold will be £12,570, aligning it with the income tax personal allowance. The rates will be reduced from 12.73% to 12% and 2.73% to 2%.

Combined Tax Rates

The combined marginal rates of income tax and national insurance applying to salaries in 2022/23 are as follows:

Income up to £11,908	0%
Income from £11,908 to £12,570	12.73%
Income from £12,570 to £50,270	32.73%
Income from £50,270 to £100,000	42.73%
Income from £100,000 to £125,140	62.73%
Income from £125,140 to £150,000	42.73%
Income over £150,000	47.73%

Employer's National Insurance

Most employees don't lose sleep over their employer's national insurance bill. However, for company owners this extra tax is an important consideration.

For salaries that exceed the 'secondary threshold' the rate is 15.05% until 5th November 2022 and 13.8% from 6th November 2022 onwards. The secondary threshold is £9,100 this year.

For directors who are subject to the annual earnings period rules employer's national insurance will typically be payable on their salaries at a blended rate of 14.53% on amounts over £9,100.

Employer's national insurance is a tax deductible expense. So if a company pays £100 of national insurance, this will reduce its taxable profits by £100, currently saving the company £19 in corporation tax (at 19%). Thus the net overall cost is actually £81.

There is no employer's national insurance on salaries paid to under 21s and apprentices under 25 provided they are not higher-rate taxpayers (i.e. they must earn less than £50,270). Note, the exemption is not lost if the employee earns more than £50,270. Employer's national insurance is only payable on the excess salary.

There is also a national insurance holiday for employers taking on military veterans. The holiday is for the employee's first year of civilian employment. The exemption applies to salary up to the higher-rate threshold.

£5,000 Employment Allowance

Most businesses qualify for the employment allowance which was increased from £4,000 to £5,000 in April 2022.

The allowance is only given to employers whose national insurance bill was less than £100,000 in the previous tax year. Fortunately, therefore, most small businesses are unaffected and can enjoy this tax break.

The reason for covering the employment allowance in this guide is because it may affect some company owners' own salary choice. For example, two company owners who have no other employees can pay themselves a salary of £26,306 each this year without having to pay any employer's national insurance.

But is it a good idea to take this much salary to avoid wasting the £5,000 employment allowance? We'll answer this question in Chapter 8. In this section we'll take a brief look at some of the employment allowance rules.

One Man Band Companies

Unfortunately the employment allowance is not available to 'one man band' companies where there is just one director who is the only employee.

According to HMRC guidance, the employment allowance also cannot be claimed if there are other employees BUT the director's salary is the only one on which employer's national insurance is payable. This is to prevent directors of one-man band companies employing friends or family and paying them a token amount in order to claim the employment allowance for their own salaries.

At least one of the additional employees must be paid more than the secondary threshold. For example, a company that employs a seasonal worker who earns above the secondary threshold in a week (£175 for 2022/23) will be eligible for the employment allowance for the whole tax year.

The second employee can be another director (e.g. your spouse/partner) provided both directors' salaries exceed the *annual* secondary threshold (£9,100 for 2022/23 or pro rata if the directorship begins after the tax year has started).

If circumstances change during the tax year and the director becomes the only employee paid above the secondary threshold, the employment allowance can still be claimed for that tax year.

If a company with just one director who earns less than the national insurance threshold employs just one other person (not a director), the company can claim the employment allowance if the employee earns more than the national insurance secondary threshold.

It should be pointed out that several expert commentators, including the Institute of Chartered Accountants, believe HMRC has not interpreted the law correctly and that it should be possible to claim the employment allowance even if the second employee receives a small salary on which no employer's national insurance is payable.

However, to play it safe it would be advisable to pay any second employee a salary slightly higher than the secondary threshold.

Other Employment Allowance Rules

The employment allowance can only be used against class 1 national insurance and not against class 1A national insurance. Class 1A is due on most taxable benefits in kind provided to employees, e.g. company cars.

If your company belongs to a group of companies, only one can claim the allowance. If your business runs multiple PAYE schemes, the allowance can only be claimed against one scheme.

The allowance is claimed as part of the payroll process. The full £5,000 can be claimed in month one of the tax year if your employer's class 1 national insurance exceeds £5,000 per month.

You can start claiming the allowance after the tax year has started and make a catch-up claim which can also be offset against your other PAYE costs.

If you claim the allowance at the end of the tax year and your remaining PAYE costs are not sufficient to use the entire allowance, the unclaimed balance can be carried forward to the next tax year.

Naturally, the amount claimed can never exceed the amount of employer's national insurance which would otherwise arise in the tax year.

Connected Companies

A company cannot claim the employment allowance if a 'connected company' already claims it.

Companies are connected if one company has control of the other company or both companies are controlled by the same person.

A person is generally considered to have control of a company if they hold more than 50% of the company's share capital or voting power or if they are entitled to more than 50% of the company's distributable income or assets if the company is wound up.

For example, if you own all the shares in two companies you will only be entitled to one employment allowance, even if the two companies are completely separate businesses with, for example, separate premises and staff.

If the company that claims the employment allowance has employer's class 1 national insurance of less than £5,000, the balance cannot be claimed by the other company.

Where there is 'substantial commercial interdependence' between two or more companies (see Chapter 1) the holdings of close relatives and other 'associates' are added together to determine whether the companies are controlled by the same person or group of persons.

For example, if you own all the shares in company X and your spouse owns all the shares in company Y, your spouse's holding in company Y is attributed to you and you are treated as controlling company X and Y, as is your spouse.

However, the two companies will only be treated as connected companies if there is substantial commercial interdependence between them (see the Taxcafe guide *'The Company Tax Changes'* for details of what this means and how this rule is applied in practice).

If the two companies are completely unrelated then two employment allowances can be claimed. If there is substantial commercial interdependence between the companies then only one allowance can be claimed.

Case Study – Total Tax Payable on Salary

Jane earns a salary of £60,000. Her income tax for 2022/23 can be calculated as follows:

- 0%   on the first   £12,570   = £0
- 20% on the next   £37,700   = £7,540
- 40% on the final   £9,730   = £3,892

Total income tax bill: £11,432

Her national insurance for 2022/23 can be calculated as follows:

- 0% on the first   £11,908   = £0
- 12.73% on the next £38,362   = £4,883
- 2.73% on the final   £9,730   = £266

Jane's national insurance bill: £5,149.

Her company claims the £5,000 employment allowance but this is used up paying salaries to other employees. Her company's national insurance bill on her salary is therefore:

- 0%   on the first £9,100   = £0
- 14.53%   on the next £50,900 = £7,396

The company's national insurance bill is £7,396. The company will enjoy corporation tax relief of *at least* 19% so its national insurance bill, net of corporation tax relief, will be £5,991 at most and possibly a bit lower (see Chapter 1).

The total tax paid by Jane and her company is as follows:

Income tax	£11,432
Employee's national insurance	£5,149
Employer's national insurance	£5,991
Total taxes	£22,572

When you include employer's national insurance, it's startling how much tax is paid on Jane's income. Her £60,000 salary is not low by any standards but you wouldn't describe her as a high income earner either. Nevertheless an amount equivalent to 38% of her salary is paid in direct taxes on her *whole* income.

TABLE 2
Total Tax Payable on Salary 2022/23

Salary	Income Tax	Employee NI	Employer NI	Total	%
10,000	0	0	106	106	1
20,000	1,486	1,030	1,283	3,799	19
30,000	3,486	2,303	2,460	8,249	27
40,000	5,486	3,576	3,637	12,699	32
50,000	7,486	4,849	4,814	17,149	34
60,000	11,432	5,149	5,991	22,572	38
70,000	15,432	5,422	7,168	28,022	40
80,000	19,432	5,695	8,344	33,472	42
90,000	23,432	5,968	9,521	38,921	43
100,000	27,432	6,241	10,698	44,371	44
110,000	33,432	6,514	11,875	51,821	47
120,000	39,432	6,787	13,052	59,271	49
130,000	44,460	7,060	14,229	65,749	51
140,000	48,460	7,333	15,406	71,199	51
150,000	52,460	7,606	16,583	76,649	51
160,000	56,960	7,879	17,760	82,599	52
170,000	61,460	8,152	18,937	88,549	52
180,000	65,960	8,425	20,114	94,499	52
190,000	70,460	8,698	21,291	100,449	53
200,000	74,960	8,971	22,468	106,399	53
225,000	86,210	9,654	25,410	121,274	54
250,000	97,460	10,336	28,352	136,148	54
275,000	108,710	11,019	31,295	151,023	55
300,000	119,960	11,701	34,237	165,898	55
350,000	142,460	13,066	40,122	195,648	56
400,000	164,960	14,431	46,006	225,397	56
450,000	187,460	15,796	51,891	255,147	57
500,000	209,960	17,161	57,775	284,897	57
600,000	254,960	19,891	69,545	344,396	57
700,000	299,960	22,621	81,314	403,895	58
800,000	344,960	25,351	93,083	463,395	58
900,000	389,960	28,081	104,853	522,894	58
1,000,000	434,960	30,811	116,622	582,393	58

Table 2 shows the total tax on a range of salaries. We assume that the employer's national insurance attracts 19% corporation tax relief and does not benefit from the employment allowance.

Once again, it's startling how much tax is paid on salaries, especially when you look at the overall tax rate (the last column).

Future Tax Changes

Many key tax thresholds and allowances have been frozen for seven years, until 5th April 2028, including the:

- Personal allowance   £12,570
- Income tax higher rate threshold   £50,270

If your income goes up with inflation you will end up paying tax at a higher rate which means you will be worse off after tax.

The latest victim of this stealth taxation strategy (or 'fiscal drag' as some commentators call it) is the employer's secondary national insurance threshold, which is to be frozen at its current level of £9,100 until 2027/28.

The proposed cut in the basic rate of income tax from 20% to 19% has been postponed indefinitely (current Government forecasts show the 20% rate continuing until at least 2027/28).

The proposed abolition of the additional tax rate (currently 45%) has not only been abandoned but, as stated above, the threshold at which the rate begins to apply will be reduced to £125,140 from 2023/24.

The Health and Social Care Levy, planned for introduction in April 2023, has now been scrapped. The levy was basically a new form of national insurance that would have been payable by everyone over the age of 16. Thanks to its abolition, those over state pension age will continue to pay no national insurance on their earnings.

Scottish Income Tax

The Scottish Parliament can set income tax rates and thresholds for most types of income including salaries, self-employment income, rental income and pensions.

It does NOT have the power to tax interest and dividend income (including small company dividends). These types of income continue to be taxed using UK rates and thresholds.

The Scottish Parliament also does not have the power to set the personal allowance. National insurance and most other taxes, including corporation tax, capital gains tax and inheritance tax, remain the preserve of the UK Government.

Scottish Income Tax 2022/23

The following income tax rates apply:

£0 - £12,570	0%	Personal allowance (PA)
£12,570 - £14,732	19%	Starter rate
£14,732 - £25,688	20%	Basic rate
£25,688 - £43,662	21%	Intermediate rate
£43,662 - £100,000	41%	Higher rate
£100,000 - £125,140	61.5%	PA withdrawal
£125,140 - £150,000	41%	Higher rate
£150,000 +	46%	Top rate

Coupled with national insurance (set by the UK Government), the combined tax rates on salary income are as follows:

£0 to £11,908	0%
£11,908 to £12,570	12.73%
£12,570 to £14,732	31.73%
£14,732 to £25,688	32.73%
£25,688 to £43,662	33.73%
£43,662 to £50,270	53.73%
£50,270 to £100,000	43.73%
£100,000 to £125,140	64.23%
£125,140 to £150,000	43.73%
Over £150,000	48.73%

Table 3 compares Scottish income tax with the rest of the UK. 'Income' does not include dividends or interest.

Table 3
Income Tax: Scotland vs Rest of UK
2022/23

Income	Scotland	Rest of UK	Difference
£20,000	£1,464	£1,486	-£22
£30,000	£3,508	£3,486	£22
£40,000	£5,608	£5,486	£122
£50,000	£8,975	£7,486	£1,489
£60,000	£13,075	£11,432	£1,643
£70,000	£17,175	£15,432	£1,743
£80,000	£21,275	£19,432	£1,843
£100,000	£29,475	£27,432	£2,043
£125,000	£44,850	£42,432	£2,418
£150,000	£55,129	£52,460	£2,669
£175,000	£66,629	£63,710	£2,919
£200,000	£78,129	£74,960	£3,169

Many Scottish taxpayers will pay more tax than those in the rest of the UK thanks to the extra 1% tax paid at many income levels and the lower higher-rate threshold (£43,662 compared with £50,270 in the rest of the UK).

For example, someone earning £50,000 in Scotland will pay £1,489 more tax than someone living elsewhere in the UK; someone earning £100,000 will pay £2,043 more tax.

Note, however, that Scottish taxpayers who earn less than £27,850 will pay less tax than those living elsewhere in the UK.

To date income tax increases in Scotland have been relatively timid because the Scottish Government has been worried about chasing away high earners. However, we strongly suspect that the 46% top rate will be increased again at some point in the future.

Who is a Scottish Taxpayer?

Someone is a Scottish taxpayer if their sole or main place of residence is in Scotland. For example, someone who rents a flat in London where they work during the week will probably be treated as a Scottish taxpayer if their spouse/partner and children live in the family home in Edinburgh and most of their friends and other social links are also in Edinburgh.

In some cases it may be difficult to establish where the main residence is located.

Where no close connection to Scotland can be identified (for example, because it is not possible to establish the person's main place of residence), Scottish taxpayer status will be determined through day counting.

You will be a Scottish taxpayer if you spend more days during the tax year in Scotland than you spend in England, Wales, or Northern Ireland (taking each country separately).

Scottish Company Owners

Scottish company owners who pay themselves a small tax-efficient salary (see Chapter 8) and take the rest of their income as dividends are completely immune from Scottish income tax. They pay exactly the same amount of tax as company owners living in the rest of the UK.

This is because the Scottish Parliament cannot change the income tax personal allowance or national insurance thresholds and cannot tax dividend income.

This assumes that the company owner does not have any other income subject to Scottish income tax, for example rental income.

Being subject to Scottish income tax is not necessarily a bad thing. It's only when Scottish company owners have salary income and other income subject to Scottish tax of more than £27,850 that they will pay more tax than those living elsewhere in the UK.

Welsh Income Tax

Since April 2019 the National Assembly for Wales has been able to vary the income tax rates payable by Welsh taxpayers.

However, this year Welsh taxpayers will pay exactly the same income tax as those in England and Northern Ireland.

According to Rebecca Evans, Minister for Finance and Local Government, "this reflects our Programme for Government commitment not to raise Welsh rates of income tax for as long as the economic impact of the pandemic lasts."

We wonder if she'll come to regret making such a generous commitment! (And also when she will consider the impact of the pandemic to be over)

As in Scotland, the Welsh powers are limited with the UK Government retaining responsibility for the income tax personal allowance and the taxation of savings and dividend income. The UK Government also retains control of most other taxes such as national insurance, VAT, corporation tax, capital gains tax and inheritance tax.

In fact, the Welsh powers are even more limited, as they can only vary income tax rates, not income tax thresholds.

Chapter 3

How Directors Are Taxed: Dividend Income

Dividends are subject to income tax but not national insurance. Also, the income tax rates on dividends are lower than the income tax rates on salaries because dividends are paid out of a company's *after-tax* profits: the money has already been taxed in the company's hands, whereas salaries are a tax deductible expense.

The first £2,000 of dividend income you receive in 2022/23 is, however, tax free thanks to the 'dividend nil rate band', also known as the 'dividend allowance'. We will use both terms in this guide, depending on the context, but they mean the same thing (and you only get one each tax year).

The dividend allowance is to be cut to £1,000 in 2023/24 and then to just £500 in 2024/25. Naturally, this reduction impacts on planning revolving around deferring income to future years and we will see this in later chapters. However, when we look at planning in the current, 2022/23, tax year, we will continue to refer to the £2,000 allowance that applies.

On 6th April 2022 the income tax rates on dividend income increased by 1.25%. They will **not** be reduced from 2023/24 onwards (former Chancellor Kwasi Kwarteng promised to cut them). For those receiving dividends in excess of the dividend allowance, the following tax rates apply:

	Old rates	Current rates
Basic-rate taxpayers	7.5%	8.75%
Higher-rate taxpayers	32.5%	33.75%
Additional-rate taxpayers	38.1%	39.35%

Overall Tax Rates on Dividend Income

Because income paid out as dividends is taxed twice (first in the hands of the company and second in the hands of the shareholder) it's easy to lose sight of how much tax is being paid overall.

As a company owner you are likely to be equally concerned about your company's tax bill as your own, so it's worth showing the overall combined tax rates on dividend income.

For a company that has paid 19% corporation tax, the total tax rates on dividend income are now as follows:

Total Tax Rate (rounded)
Basic-rate taxpayers   26%
Higher-rate taxpayers   46%
Additional-rate taxpayers   51%

For example, a company with £100 of profit will pay £19 corporation tax, leaving £81 to pay out as dividends. Ignoring the £2,000 dividend allowance, a higher-rate taxpayer will pay £27 tax on this income (£81 x 33.75%), so the total tax bill on the £100 profit is £46, which is 46%.

The above tax rates are higher than the regular income tax rates that apply to most types of income (20% for basic-rate taxpayers, 40% for higher-rate taxpayers and 45% for additional-rate taxpayers).

This is because the Government has been levelling the playing field between company owners (who often don't pay any national insurance) and self-employed business owners and regular employees, who pay national insurance on most of their earnings.

From a tax planning perspective, once a company owner has used up the £2,000 dividend allowance they are usually better off paying themselves income that is taxed at the 'regular' income tax rates in preference to dividends, wherever possible.

Examples include rental income and interest income. Salary also fits the bill whenever there is no national insurance cost (or in a few rare cases where the cost is only 2.73%: see Chapter 20).

After the Corporation Tax Increase

When corporation tax increases (see Chapter 1) the combined tax rates on dividend income will also naturally increase for many company owners. For example, where a company has profits greater than £250,000 and pays 25% tax on all of its profits, the total tax rates on dividend income will be:

	Total Tax Rate
Basic-rate taxpayers	31.56%
Higher-rate taxpayers	50.31%
Additional-rate taxpayers	54.51%

The corporation tax increase will thus make it even more attractive for company owners to pay themselves other types of income that are taxed at the 'regular' 20%, 40% and 45% income tax rates in preference to dividends.

Company owners whose companies have profits of £50,000 or less will continue to face the total tax rates listed at the start of this section.

For companies with profits of between £50,000 and £250,000, the combined tax rates on dividend income will vary according to the amount of profit the company makes. For example, a company with profits of £100,000 will face a total corporation tax bill of £22,750 (see Table 1), leaving £77,250 to pay out as dividends. If higher-rate tax at 33.75% is payable on all of this income the total tax bill on the £100,000 profit will be £48,822, which is 48.8%.

Table 4 contains the total tax rates that will apply at different profit levels and different income tax rates. (Note in all of these calculations we ignore the dividend allowance.)

Some of these tax rates are unrealistically low if we assume that all of the company's profits are paid out in a single year to a single director.

For example, if a company has pre-tax profits of £200,000, it would be impossible for its after-tax profits of £150,750 to be paid out to just one director in one tax year with just 8.75% basic-rate income tax payable (resulting in a total tax rate of just 31.22%).

However, this tax rate could be payable if dividends are paid to several directors who are all basic-rate taxpayers, or if the profits are paid out over a number of years.

TABLE 4
Total Tax Rates on Dividend Income
after the Corporation Tax Increase

Profits	Tax Rate @ 8.75%	Tax Rate @ 33.75%	Tax Rate @ 39.35%
£50,000	26.09	46.34	50.87
£60,000	27.23	47.17	51.63
£70,000	28.04	47.76	52.17
£80,000	28.65	48.20	52.58
£90,000	29.13	48.55	52.90
£100,000	29.51	48.82	53.15
£110,000	29.82	49.05	53.35
£120,000	30.08	49.24	53.53
£130,000	30.30	49.40	53.67
£140,000	30.49	49.53	53.80
£150,000	30.65	49.65	53.91
£160,000	30.79	49.75	54.00
£170,000	30.92	49.84	54.08
£180,000	31.03	49.93	54.16
£190,000	31.13	50.00	54.23
£200,000	31.22	50.06	54.29
£210,000	31.30	50.12	54.34
£220,000	31.38	50.18	54.39
£230,000	31.44	50.23	54.43
£240,000	31.51	50.27	54.47
£250,000	31.56	50.31	54.51

Similarly, some of the total tax rates are unrealistically high if the director does not have income from other sources. For example, if a company has pre-tax profits of just £50,000 this would never result in additional rate tax at 39.35% being payable if the director has no other sources of income. If, however, the director does have a significant amount of income from other sources, it is possible the total tax rate on some or all of their dividend income will be 50.87%.

Marginal Tax Rates

The total tax rates listed in Table 4 are calculated using the total corporation tax and income tax payable if all of the company's after-tax profits are paid out as dividends.

However, for companies with profits between £50,000 and £250,000 these are not the ones we would typically use to make tax planning decisions. For these purposes we would use the company's *marginal tax rate*.

Remember companies with profits between £50,000 and £250,000 will pay 19% on the first £50,000 and 26.5% on the rest. 26.5% is the company's marginal tax rate. Its total (average) tax rate will be lower because some of its profits will be taxed at 19%.

For companies with profits of £50,000 or less the total tax rate and the marginal tax rate will be the same: 19%. Similarly, for companies with profits of more than £250,000 the total tax rate and the marginal tax rate will also be the same: 25%. (However, if the company spends enough money to take its profits below £250,000, it will start to have a marginal tax rate of 26.5%)

Marginal Tax Rate Planning and Dividends

Take a company owner who is a higher-rate taxpayer and anticipates that, as things stand, their company will make a profit of £60,000. Let's say the company already pays them rent to use an office property they own personally and they want to know whether they'll be better off paying themselves an additional £1,000 of rent, or taking the money as a dividend.

If they pay themselves rent this will be a tax deductible expense for the company, so the whole £1,000 will be paid out and after paying 40% income tax they will be left with £600.

Alternatively the company will pay 26.5% corporation tax on this final £1,000 of profit, leaving £735 to pay out as dividend income. After paying income tax at 33.75% they will be left with £487.

The total tax payable on the additional dividend income is £513 which is 51.3%. Clearly in this case additional rental income is more attractive.

Note, 51.3% is higher than the 47.17% rate in Table 4 for a company with profits of £60,000. That total tax rate is calculated using the company's total corporation tax rate. Most of its profits are taxed at just 19%, so the total tax rate in the table is lower.

The rate we've used in this example, however, is the company's 26.5% marginal tax rate, the rate which applies to the final £1,000 of profit we are looking at.

In summary, the total tax rates listed in Table 4 give you some idea of the total amount of corporation tax and income tax that will be payable if all of a company's after-tax profits are paid out as dividends. But when it comes to choosing between a dividend and some other type of income, the marginal tax rate is more relevant.

For company owners whose companies have profits of between £50,000 and £250,000 the combined marginal tax rate (corporation tax and income tax) on dividend income will be as follows after the corporation tax increase is in full effect:

	Combined Marginal Tax Rate
Basic-rate taxpayers	32.93%
Higher-rate taxpayers	51.31%
Additional-rate taxpayers	55.42%

The £2,000 Dividend Nil Rate Band

Company owners do not enjoy an additional standalone amount of £2,000 tax free in 2022/23. Instead, the dividend nil rate band typically uses up some of your basic-rate band.

If you have a £55,000 dividend and no other income, the first £12,570 will be tax free thanks to your personal allowance and the next £2,000 will be tax free thanks to the dividend nil rate band. Only £35,700 of your remaining income will be taxed at 8.75% because the £2,000 dividend nil rate band uses up part of your £37,700 basic-rate band. The final £4,730 will be taxed at 33.75%.

The dividend nil rate band only uses up your basic-rate band if, like many company owners, you have dividend income subject to basic-rate tax. As we shall see later, it works differently if you have a lot of other income and all your dividends are subject to higher-rate tax.

Dividend Taxation – Examples

Let's take a look at some sample dividend tax calculations for the current 2022/23 tax year. To keep things simple we'll assume the company owners take a small salary of £11,908 and the rest of their income as dividends. There may be £408 of employer's national insurance payable by the company on this salary. See Chapter 8 for a discussion as to why this amount of salary may nevertheless be the most tax efficient.

We'll also assume the company owners have no other taxable income. The examples apply equally to Scottish company owners.

Example – Basic-Rate Taxpayer
Stuart is a company owner with a salary of £11,908 and cash dividend of £20,000. His total income is thus £31,908.

His salary is tax-free because it is covered by his personal allowance. The first £662 of his dividend income is tax free, being covered by the remainder of his personal allowance (£12,570 - £11,908).

The next £2,000 of his dividend income is also tax-free thanks to the dividend allowance. The final £17,338 of his dividend income is taxed at 8.75%, producing a total tax bill of £1,517.

Example – Higher-Rate Taxpayer
Robert is a company owner with a salary of £11,908 and dividend of £50,000. His total income is thus £61,908.

His salary is tax-free as it is covered by his personal allowance, as is the first £662 of his dividend.

The next £2,000 of his dividend is also tax-free thanks to the dividend allowance. The dividend allowance uses up £2,000 of his £37,700 basic-rate band so just £35,700 of his dividend income is taxed at 8.75%, producing a tax bill of £3,124. The final £11,638 of his dividend income takes him over the higher-rate threshold and is taxed at 33.75%, producing a tax bill of £3,928.

Robert's total tax bill is £7,052.

Example – Personal Allowance Withdrawal

Alpesh is a company owner with a salary of £11,908 and dividend of £100,000. His total taxable income is thus £111,908. His personal allowance is reduced from £12,570 to £6,616. Thus £5,292 of his salary is taxed at 20% (£11,908 - £6,616), producing a tax bill of £1,058.

The first £2,000 of his dividend income is tax free, being covered by the dividend allowance. The next £30,408 of his dividend income is covered by his remaining basic-rate band (£37,700 - £5,292 - £2,000) and taxed at 8.75%, producing a tax bill of £2,661.

The remaining £67,592 of his dividend income is taxed at 33.75%, producing a tax bill of £22,812.

His total tax bill is therefore £26,531.

Example – Additional-Rate Taxpayer

Maeve is a company owner with a salary of £11,908 and dividend of £200,000. Her total income is thus £211,908. Because her income exceeds £150,000 she is an additional-rate taxpayer.

The first £2,000 of her dividend income is tax free but her income tax personal allowance is completely withdrawn. This means she will pay 20% income tax on her salary – £2,382 – and her remaining basic-rate band will be reduced to just £23,792 (£37,700 - £11,908 salary - £2,000 dividend allowance). She will thus pay 8.75% tax on £23,792 of her dividend income (£2,082).

The next £112,300 of her dividend (£150,000 less £37,700) is subject to higher-rate tax at 33.75%, resulting in additional tax of £37,901. The remaining £61,908 of dividend income takes her over the £150,000 threshold and is taxed at 39.35%, resulting in additional tax of £24,361.

Maeve's total tax bill is £66,725.

Taxpayers with Lots of Non-Dividend Income

It's important to explain how the dividend nil rate band operates when you have lots of non-dividend income, for example a big salary or a significant amount of rental income.

The dividend nil rate band only forms part of your basic-rate band if you have dividend income that falls into the basic-rate band. It works differently if your basic-rate band is completely used up by other income, e.g. salary or rental income.

The way to think about it is like this: dividends are always treated as the top slice of your income and taxed at your highest marginal rate. In 2022/23, the dividend nil rate band exempts the bottom £2,000 of that income from tax. So if you have dividend income taxed at both 8.75% and 33.75%, the dividend allowance will exempt some of the income taxed at 8.75%.

But if ALL your dividend income is taxed at 33.75% (because you have lots of other income, e.g. rental income) the dividend nil rate band will be part of your higher-rate band and you'll pay 0% tax instead of 33.75% tax on £2,000 of your dividend income.

Example
In 2022/23 Julia has a £60,000 salary and £30,000 dividend. Her salary uses up her personal allowance and basic-rate band, taking her over the higher-rate threshold. The first £2,000 of her dividend is tax free; £28,000 is taxed at the 33.75% higher rate.

The dividend allowance does not form part of her basic-rate band as none of her dividend income falls into the basic-rate band.

Example
In 2022/23 Leon has a £130,000 salary and £50,000 dividend. With this much income his personal allowance is completely withdrawn.

The first £2,000 of his dividend income is covered by the dividend allowance, leaving £18,000 taxed at the 33.75% higher rate. Along with his salary this takes Leon up to the £150,000 additional-rate threshold. The final £30,000 of his dividend is taxed at 39.35%.

Leon has dividend income taxed at both the higher rate and additional rate. The dividend allowance reduces the amount of his dividend income taxed at the 33.75% higher rate.

Example

In 2022/23 Martin has a £100,000 salary, £50,000 of rental income and £50,000 dividend. With this much income his personal allowance is completely withdrawn.

His salary and rental income take him up to the £150,000 additional-rate threshold. The first £2,000 of his dividend income is covered by the dividend allowance leaving £48,000 taxed at the 39.35% additional rate.

All of Martin's dividend income is taxable at the additional rate. The dividend allowance therefore reduces the amount of his dividend income taxed at the additional rate.

Taxpayers with Other Dividend Income

Each individual gets one dividend allowance to cover all their dividend income each tax year. Hence, if you also have dividend income from other sources, you will not be able to use the full dividend allowance against dividends you take out of your company. For example, if you have £250 of dividend income from stock market investments in 2022/23, there is only £1,750 of your dividend allowance remaining to exempt dividends from your company.

Scottish Taxpayers

The Scottish Government can tax most types of income but not dividends or interest. It also cannot change the personal allowance or national insurance. This means:

- Scottish company owners pay exactly the same amount of tax on their dividend income as company owners living in the rest of the UK.

- Scottish company owners who also pay themselves a small tax-efficient salary (no higher than the £12,570 personal allowance) are completely immune from Scottish income tax, assuming they do not have any other income subject to Scottish tax.

- Scottish company owners whose salary income, rental income and other income (except interest and dividends) exceeds £12,570 will pay Scottish income tax.

  However, if this income is less than £27,850 they will pay less tax on this income than people living elsewhere in the UK. If this income exceeds £27,850 they will pay more tax.

  They will pay the same amount of tax on their dividend income as company owners living in the rest of the UK.

(See Chapter 16 for more information for high income earners.)

Example
Alan is a company owner living in Scotland. He has salary and rental income of £30,000 and dividend income of £25,000.

He is subject to Scottish income tax on his salary and rental income. As we saw in Table 3 in Chapter 2, this means he will pay £22 more tax on this income than someone living elsewhere in the UK; but what about his dividend income?

Although the higher-rate threshold is £43,662 in Scotland, it is the UK higher-rate threshold (£50,270) that applies to his dividend income.

The first £2,000 is tax free thanks to the dividend allowance. This leaves him with £18,270 of basic-rate band (£50,270 - £30,000 - £2,000). This income will be taxed at 8.75%.

The remaining £4,730 of his dividend income takes him over the £50,270 higher-rate threshold and will be taxed at 33.75%.

Will Dividend Tax Rates be Changed Again?

The tax rates for dividend income were increased by 1.25% on 6th April 2022. This increase was designed to match the increase in national insurance rates (because many company owners take most of their income as dividends and do not pay much national insurance). Unfortunately, dividend tax rates were not cut when the national insurance increase was later scrapped.

Thankfully, despite rumours that we might see a further increase in dividend tax rates next year, the Chancellor confined himself to the reduction in the dividend allowance discussed above.

Nonetheless, it must be remembered that the increase in corporation tax from April 2023 will result in an increase in the total combined tax rates on dividend income.

All in all, the tax payable on dividend income has been increased significantly in recent years. Beyond the reductions in the dividend allowance, we don't expect any further increases in the short term, but you can't rule anything out!

Dividend Tax Terminology

Note that the 0% tax rate applying to the dividend nil rate band is known officially as the 'dividend nil rate'. The 8.75% rate is known as the 'ordinary rate', the 33.75% rate is known as the 'upper rate' and the 39.35% rate as the 'additional rate'.

We do not use these terms much in this guide, preferring the terms basic rate, higher rate and additional rate.

Chapter 4

Making the Most of Your Personal Allowance

In all of the examples so far the taxpayer's personal allowance has been deducted from their salary rather than their dividends. This isn't mandatory – tax legislation states that your personal allowance can be used in the way that reduces your tax bill most.

Allocating some of your personal allowance from your salary to your dividend income is usually not worth doing but in a limited number of cases will produce further tax savings:

Example
In 2022/23 Antonia has salary income of £48,270 and dividend income of £50,000. If all of her personal allowance is allocated to her salary, her income tax will be calculated as follows:

Salary		**Tax**
Personal allowance	£12,570	£0
Taxed at 20%	£35,700	£7,140

Dividend		
Dividend allowance	£2,000	£0
Taxed at 33.75%	£48,000	£16,200
Total tax		£23,340

If instead Antonia allocates £2,000 of her personal allowance to her dividend income, her tax bill will be calculated as follows:

Salary		**Tax**
Personal allowance	£10,570	£0
Taxed at 20%	£37,700	£7,540

Dividend		
Personal allowance	£2,000	£0
Dividend allowance	£2,000	£0
Taxed at 33.75%	£46,000	£15,525
Total tax		£23,065

By reallocating her personal allowance, Antonia's tax bill falls by £275.

Why? Because she now pays 20% tax on £2,000 more salary BUT pays 33.75% tax on £2,000 less dividend income.

Does this means everyone should allocate some of their personal allowance to their dividend income? No because there is something else that usually increases your tax bill, although not in Antonia's case.

If you have £2,000 more salary taxed at 20% this means £2,000 more of your basic-rate band will be used up by your salary. This means £2,000 more of your dividend income will be pushed over the higher-rate threshold and taxed at 33.75% instead of 8.75%, adding a further £500 to your tax bill.

The reason Antonia's tax bill does not increase is thanks to the precise salary we gave her, close to the higher-rate threshold. In her case it doesn't matter if £2,000 of her dividend income is pushed over the higher-rate threshold because this is the dividend income that is always tax free thanks to her dividend allowance.

In Chapter 20 we will examine how a far greater number of taxpayers with <u>interest income</u> could benefit from having their personal allowance reallocated.

Chapter 5

Don't Forget about Payments on Account

Payments on account are made twice a year and allow HMRC to collect some of the tax you owe early. Common victims include sole traders and landlords, i.e. those whose income tax is not collected at source. Payments on account are not extra tax but they do affect your cashflow.

Most salary earners do not have to make payments on account because their tax is collected almost immediately through PAYE.

However, many company owners have to make payments on account as dividend income is not taxed at source and tax has to be paid through the self-assessment system.

How Payments on Account Are Calculated

If you paid yourself a dividend during the previous tax year, which started on 6th April 2021 and ended on 5th April 2022, the income tax is normally payable by 31st January 2023: almost 10 months after the tax year has ended.

For example, let's say a company owner paid themselves a salary of £12,570 and dividend of £22,000 and had no other taxable income. To keep the example simple let's also assume they have never had to make any payments on account in the past.

No income tax was payable on their salary because it was fully covered by their personal allowance and the first £2,000 of their dividend income is tax free thanks to the dividend allowance.

The remaining £20,000 of their dividend income for 2021/22 is taxed at 7.5%, producing a total income tax bill of £1,500 which has to be paid by 31st January 2023.

2022/23 Tax Year

Now let's move forward to the 2022/23 tax year which started on 6th April 2022 and ends on 5th April 2023.

We will assume our company owner pays themselves a tax-free salary of £12,570 and a dividend of £24,000. Their income tax bill will be £1,925 (the first £2,000 of dividend income is tax free, the rest is taxed at 8.75%). However, this time they cannot wait until 31st January 2024 to pay the tax.

On 31st January 2023, when they pay their 2021/22 tax bill, they will also have to make a £750 payment on account for 2022/23. They must also make another payment on account of the same amount on 31st July 2023. Thus their total tax payments will be as follows:

- 31st January 2023   £1,500 + £750 = £2,250
- 31st July 2023   £750

Each payment on account is normally half the previous year's (2021/22) self assessment tax.

In January 2024 they will have to make a final tax payment for 2022/23 but will be able to deduct the two payments on account.

In this example the company owner will have an additional £425 to pay in respect of 2022/23 (£1,925 - £1,500 payments on account) because their payments on account will not fully cover their tax bill.

Furthermore, they will usually also be paying their first payment on account for 2023/24 at the same time, so the total amount payable by 31st January 2024 would generally be £1,387.50 (£425 + £1,925/2).

Where the final self assessment tax liability for the year turns out to be less than the payments on account, the excess payment can either be refunded or set against the first payment on account for the following year. This might happen, for example, if a company owner takes a much smaller dividend in 2022/23 than they took in 2021/22.

Postponing Tax

Making payments on account is still much better than paying tax through the PAYE system. Take a look at our company owner's tax payments for 2022/23.

The first payment is due around *10 months* after the start of the tax year (January 2023), the second payment is due around *16 months* after the start of the tax year (July 2023) and the third payment is due around *22 months* after the tax year has started (January 2024).

This means that if you pay yourself a dividend at the start of the tax year, you will have free use of the taxman's money for well over a year.

That money could be invested in a cash ISA or an offset mortgage or some other low-risk investment. The returns are likely to be better than those available from your company's bank account.

Who Has to Make Payments on Account?

Payments on account are all about the tax you paid in the *previous tax year*.

You only have to make payments on account if your self-assessment tax (i.e. ignoring tax deducted at source) for the previous tax year was more than £1,000.

For example, if during the current 2022/23 tax year you pay yourself a salary of £12,570 and a dividend of £12,000 your total income tax bill will be £875 and you will not have to make any payments on account in January and July 2024.

Of course, if you have income from other sources (e.g. rental income from property) this will have to be factored into the equation too.

You do not have to make payments on account, however, if more than 80% of your total tax from the previous year was covered by tax deducted at source.

How to Reduce Payments on Account

Where your self-assessment liability for the current year can reasonably be expected to be less than that for the previous year, you can apply to reduce your payments on account to the appropriate level (i.e. half of the anticipated liability for the current year).

For example, if you take a much smaller dividend in 2022/23 than you took in 2021/22, you can apply to reduce your payments on account due on 31st January and 31st July 2023. You can do this when you submit your 2021/22 tax return.

You have to be careful when doing this, however. If you claim a reduction in your payments on account and then find you have more tax to pay than you expected, you will have to pay interest on the underpayment. There could also potentially be a penalty if there is a significant underpayment and you had no reasonable grounds for having reduced your payments on account by so much.

Chapter 6

Salary versus Dividends: The Basics

Unlike self-employed business owners (sole traders and partnerships), company owners are in the fortunate position of wearing two caps.

On the one hand, you can reward your work as a director; on the other hand, you can reward your entrepreneurship as a shareholder.

As a company director and shareholder you can split your income into salary and dividends and this can generate income tax and national insurance savings.

For example, while national insurance is payable on salaries, it is not payable on shareholder dividends.

By structuring distributions from your company carefully and taking the 'optimum' amount of salary and dividends, you could end up with a significantly higher after-tax income than a regular salaried employee who earns a higher income before tax.

However, while saving income tax will be an important consideration, other factors are important too.

Salaries & Dividends: What's the Difference?

The major differences between a salary and dividend are:

Salaries Are Tax Deductible

Salaries usually qualify for corporation tax relief, dividends do not. If the company pays you a salary, its taxable profits will be reduced and it will pay less corporation tax.

Dividends are paid out of a company's after-tax profits, so paying a dividend does not reduce the *company's* tax bill.

This is an important point to remember because most company owners are concerned about both their own and their company's tax bill.

For example, if a company has a taxable profit of £10,000 it will pay £1,900 corporation tax (19%), leaving only £8,100 to distribute as dividends. This corporation tax must be added to any income tax paid by the shareholder on their dividend income when calculating the total tax suffered.

Dividends Require Profits

Only companies that have made profits can pay dividends. Profits are usually calculated when the company's annual accounts are drawn up (often many months after the end of the company's accounting period).

So dividends will usually be paid out of profits made in a previous accounting period. It is, however, possible to pay dividends out of profits made during the current year, for example if accurate management accounts are drawn up to determine the level of the company's distributable profits (see Chapter 35).

Salaries can be paid even if the company is making losses.

Income Tax and National Insurance

Salaries and dividends are subject to different rates of income tax.

Salaries are generally subject to national insurance, dividends are not. Both the director and the company may be subject to national insurance.

Tax Payment Dates

The income tax and national insurance payable on salaries is collected almost immediately via PAYE. The income tax on dividends is collected via self assessment: generally at a later date.

Earnings

Salaries are classed as 'earnings' which is important if you want to make significant pension contributions personally. Dividends are not classed as earnings.

Chapter 7

Company Owners Can Control Their Income Tax Bills

In Chapter 6 we mentioned that a company owner can often decide whether any distribution of the company's money is classified as salary or dividend.

Another advantage of being a company owner is that you have complete control over *how much* income you withdraw in total. This gives you significant control over your income tax bill.

Unlike sole traders, who pay tax each year on ALL the profits of the business, company owners only pay tax on the income they decide to pay themselves.

This allows company owners to reduce their income tax bills by adopting the following strategies:

- 'Smooth income'
- 'Roller-coaster income'

Smooth Income

With smooth income, the company owner withdraws roughly the same amount of money each year, even though the company's profits may fluctuate considerably.

Smooth income allows the company owner to stay below the key income tax thresholds that could result in a higher tax bill:

- £50,000   Child benefit tax charge
- £50,270   Higher-rate tax
- £100,000   Personal allowance withdrawal
- £150,000   Additional rate tax (£125,140 from next year)

We will return to how you can plan your salary and dividend withdrawals around these key income tax thresholds in the chapters that follow.

The higher-rate threshold generally increases each year with inflation but has now been frozen until 5th April 2028. The other thresholds have *never* been increased. This means more taxpayers have been dragged into a higher tax bracket, even though their income has not increased in real terms.

The £100,000 threshold was introduced in April 2010. If it had gone up with inflation you would only start losing your personal allowance with an income of around £155,000 today.

The child benefit tax charge was introduced in 2013. If the £50,000 threshold where it kicks in had gone up with inflation, you would only start paying the extra tax with an income of around £70,000 today.

By freezing these thresholds the Government has decided to deploy 'fiscal drag' to raise taxes. Fiscal drag occurs when an increase in your income, which is purely down to inflation, pushes up your tax rate. At Taxcafe we call fiscal drag the Silent Killer.

Less silent, and more deadly is the Government's decision to reduce the additional rate tax threshold to £125,140 from 2023/24. The original £150,000 threshold was introduced in 2010. If it had gone up with inflation, you would only start paying 45% tax with an income of £235,000 today. Yet, instead, from next year, this threshold will be just over half what it should have been by now.

Roller-coaster Income

With 'roller-coaster income', the company owners take a bigger or smaller salary or dividend than would normally be required to fund their lifestyles. Roller-coaster income could save you tax in the following circumstances:

Income Tax Rates Are Going Up Or Down

If the Government announces that income tax rates will *rise* during a future tax year, you may wish to pay yourself more income now and less income later on. And if your tax rate will *fall* during a future tax year, you may wish to pay yourself less income now and more income later on.

Note, the fact that corporation tax is increasing from April 2023 is NOT a reason to take bigger dividends now and smaller dividends after the increase. Dividends do not alter a company's corporation tax bill because they are paid out of profits that have already been taxed.

You Want to Save Capital Gains Tax

It may also make sense for company owners to pay themselves less income during tax years in which they sell assets subject to capital gains tax such as rental properties.

Why? This may allow some of your basic-rate band (£37,700 this year) to be freed up, which means some of your capital gains will be taxed at 10% or 18% instead of 20% or 28% (see Chapter 38).

Living Abroad

If you intend to move abroad and become non-resident in the future, you could consider withdrawing less income from your company while you are UK resident and more income after you become non-resident.

Providing you move to a country with favourable income tax rates, this strategy could potentially save you significant amounts of UK income tax (but see Chapter 39 for potential dangers).

Pension Income

When you reach age 55 you may decide to start withdrawing money from any private pension scheme you belong to, for example a self-invested personal pension (SIPP). Any amount you withdraw over and above your 25% tax-free lump sum will be subject to income tax.

Fortunately, with a drawdown arrangement you can vary the amount of income you withdraw from your pension scheme every year and there are no limits placed on the amount of income you can withdraw.

Coupled with the fact you can vary the amount of income you withdraw from your company, this could allow you to minimise your income tax bill by staying below any of the income tax thresholds listed earlier.

Part 2

Tax-free Salaries
& Dividends

Chapter 8

Tax-free Salaries

After reading the preceding chapters you should have a good understanding of how salaries and dividends are taxed.

The next question is: What is the most tax-efficient mix of salary and dividends for directors who want to extract money from their companies?

In this chapter we will attempt to calculate the 'optimal' amount of salary you should withdraw from your company this year.

The answer depends on various factors including whether your company's £5,000 national insurance employment allowance is used up paying salaries to other employees.

All amounts are for the current 2022/23 tax year which ends on 5th April 2023. The answer changes every year, so it's important to stay up to date.

Assumption: No Other Taxable Income

We will assume for now that the company owner has no taxable income from other sources (just his or her company salary and dividends). This keeps the number crunching as simple as possible.

It's not a totally unrealistic assumption either. Although most company owners will have at least some other taxable income, for example bank account interest or stock market dividends, many will have no more than a few hundred pounds.

For those company owners who do have significant amounts of other taxable income, for example rental profits from a portfolio of properties, more information is provided in Part 4.

Why a Small Salary Is Tax Efficient

The first point to make is that most company owners should pay themselves a small salary. They should not take all of their income as dividends.

The first few thousand pounds of either salary or dividend income you receive are tax free thanks to your income tax personal allowance. However, a dividend is not as tax efficient for the *company*. This is because dividends are paid out of the company's *after-tax* profits, once corporation tax has been paid. So every dividend has a corporation tax bill attached.

(As a company owner you should be equally concerned about your company's tax position as your own personal tax position.)

A salary, on the other hand, is a tax deductible expense for the company.

In summary, a small salary is usually more tax efficient than a dividend. It's potentially tax free in the hands of the company owner and provides a corporation tax saving for the company.

What if You Don't Need the Money?

Because a small salary is so tax efficient most company owners should take one, even if they don't need the income. The money can always be left inside the company until a decision is made to withdraw it.

The general rule is that remuneration cannot be deducted from a company's current taxable profits unless it is 'paid' within nine months of the company's year end. However, HMRC will generally accept that remuneration is paid when it is credited to the director's loan account. So if you don't need the cash, there's nothing to stop you running your salary through the monthly payroll as normal and crediting the amounts to your director's loan account.

The fact that small salaries are so tax efficient is also why company owners should consider paying salaries to their spouses or partners and children, including their minor children wherever possible (see Part 5).

How Much Salary?
Companies with Employees
(i.e. with no spare employment allowance)

We'll start off with owners of companies whose £5,000 employment allowance (see Chapter 2) is used up paying salaries to other employees, i.e. there is no spare employment allowance for the directors' own salaries.

This section also applies to 'one man band' companies with just one director who is the only employee and other companies that are not entitled to the employment allowance (see Chapter 2).

So how much salary should a company owner in this position take? There are three relevant thresholds for the 2022/23 tax year:

- Employer's national insurance   £9,100
- Employee's national insurance   £11,908
- Income tax   £12,570

For 2022/23 the 'optimal' salary for many directors of companies with no spare employment allowance is £11,908.

The word 'optimal' is in inverted commas because every company and company owner is different. Clearly, a salary of £11,908 will not be optimal for every single company owner in the land. There are many factors that may influence a salary decision.

At first glance a salary of £9,100 looks better because there isn't any national insurance payable at all. By contrast, a salary of £11,908 will result in an employer's national insurance bill:

$$£11,908 - £9,100 = £2,808 \times 14.53\% = £408$$

However, the extra salary and employer's national insurance will attract corporation tax relief. We'll assume for now this is at 19%:

Corporation tax relief on extra salary: £2,808 x 19% = £534
Corporation tax relief on employer's NI: £408   x 19% = £78

The extra corporation tax relief (£612) outweighs the national insurance cost (£408) by £204.

Extra tax on dividends

That's not the end of the story. To get their hands on this additional £204 in the company's bank account, the director will have to pay additional income tax. If the director is a basic-rate taxpayer additional income tax of roughly £18 will be payable, assuming the money is taken as a dividend taxed at 8.75%. If the director is a higher-rate taxpayer additional income tax of roughly £69 will be payable (£204 x 33.75%).

The net effect is that basic-rate taxpayers will typically be £186 better off by taking a salary of £11,908 instead of £9,100 and higher-rate taxpayers will typically be £135 better off.

When a Salary of £9,100 May Be Preferable

Some company owners may still prefer to take a salary of £9,100 to avoid the hassle or having to make any national insurance payments. This would include one-man band companies that don't have any employees but don't enjoy the benefit of the £5,000 employment allowance for the director's own salary.

Most other company owners have nothing to lose by paying themselves a salary of £11,908. If the company has other employees and is making monthly national insurance payments anyway, there is no extra effort involved adding a national insurance payment on behalf of the directors.

Salary of £12,570?

Why not take a salary of £12,570 instead of £11,908 to use up your personal allowance (i.e. an additional £662)? To answer this we have to examine the tax position of the company and the director:

The Company

Employer's national insurance (£662 x 14.53%)	£96
Corporation tax relief on extra salary (£662 x 19%)	£126
Corporation tax relief on employer's NI (£96 x 19%)	£18

The corporation tax relief outweighs the employer's national insurance cost by £48.

The Director

That's not the end of the story. To get his hands on this additional £48 sitting in the company's bank account the director will have to pay additional income tax (£4 as a basic-rate taxpayer and £16 as a higher-rate taxpayer).

The director will also have to pay employee's national insurance of £84 on the additional salary (£662 x 12.73%).

Thus basic-rate taxpayers will typically be £40 worse off taking a salary of £12,570 instead of £11,908 (£48 - £4 - £84 = -£40). Higher-rate taxpayers will typically be £52 worse off.

Having to pay *both* employee's and employer's national insurance on any salary payment will usually make it less tax efficient.

Summary

Clearly the extra tax cost is not significant, so whether you take a salary of £11,908 or £12,570 won't make a huge amount of difference.

Some owners of one-man band companies may still prefer to take a salary of £9,100 to avoid having to make any national insurance payments at all.

Although the tax savings are fairly trivial, this juggling act gets to the heart of the salary/dividend question: as a company owner you have to compare the tax cost to you *personally* with the tax cost and tax relief enjoyed by your *company*.

In many of the examples throughout this guide we will assume that directors whose companies have no spare employment allowance (for example, where it is used up paying salaries to other employees) take a salary of £11,908 during the 2022/23 tax year.

Also, remember that for now we are assuming that the company owner has no taxable income from other sources. We will take a closer look at company owners with other income in Part 4.

How Much Salary?
Companies with No Employees
(i.e. with spare employment allowance)

In this section we'll take a look at companies that do NOT use up their £5,000 employment allowance paying salaries to other employees, i.e. there is spare employment allowance for the directors' own salaries.

This group includes companies with no employees other than the directors and companies with just a couple of low-paid employees (please see Chapter 2 for more information about which companies qualify for the employment allowance).

Directors of these companies may be able to pay themselves higher salaries without having to worry about *employer's* national insurance. The question is, should they?

Salary of £11,908 versus £9,100

A salary of £9,100 will not attract any employer's or employee's national insurance and will also be free from income tax, assuming it is covered by the director's income tax personal allowance.

But if there is spare employment allowance, a salary of £11,908 will not attract any national insurance or income tax either, so it makes sense to take a salary of £11,908 instead of £9,100. This will produce a saving of several hundred pounds in most cases.

Salary of £12,570?

If the company owner takes a salary of £12,570 instead of £11,908 no national insurance will be paid by the company itself but the extra salary will result in a national insurance bill of £84 for the director personally (£662 x 12.73%). That's the bad news.

The good news is that, by increasing the director's salary from £11,908 to £12,570, £126 of extra corporation tax relief is obtained for the company (again we'll assume for now that this is at 19%).

To get his hands on the additional £126 that ends up in the company's bank account the director will pay extra income tax.

Assuming the extra money is taken as a dividend this will currently be £11 as a basic-rate taxpayer and £43 as a higher-rate taxpayer.

The net effect of all this is that basic-rate taxpayers will typically save £31 by taking a salary of £12,570 instead of £11,908 and higher-rate taxpayers will typically be worse off by £1!

In summary, for company owners with spare national insurance employment allowance, taking a salary of £12,570 instead of £11,908 can produce a very small additional saving if you're a basic-rate taxpayer and will leave you in pretty much the same position overall if you're a higher-rate taxpayer.

Salary Greater than £12,570?

A company with no employees and two directors (for example a husband and wife) can pay the directors a salary of £26,306 each this year with no employer's national insurance liability.

But is it worth paying salaries of more than £12,570 to avoid wasting the £5,000 employment allowance? In most cases the answer is typically no.

For example, if a salary of £26,306 is taken instead of £12,570, with the company's remaining profits paid out as dividends, the director will typically end up worse off by £912 if they are a basic-rate taxpayer and worse off by £1,565 if they are a higher-rate taxpayer.

Is a Lower Salary Preferable?

Although a salary of £12,570 may be 'optimal' for some company owners with spare employment allowance, a lower salary may be preferable in some cases.

For example, if the company doesn't have any other employees, the directors may prefer to pay themselves a salary of £11,908 each to avoid the hassle of having to make any payments of employee's national insurance (for example, to avoid late payment penalties).

Although a salary of £11,908 may be tax free, it still has to be reported to HMRC as part of the normal payroll process (although it may be possible to make a single annual payroll submission in some circumstances).

It's also worth remembering that there may be a limited number of directors' salaries of £12,570 that can be paid before the company's national insurance employment allowance is used up.

Higher Salaries

Although the salaries discussed in this chapter are 'optimal' from a strict comparison of tax rates and thresholds, there may be other tax and non-tax reasons why you may wish to pay yourself a higher salary (see Part 7).

Companies with Higher Corporation Tax Relief

So far we've assumed that the director does not have any income from other sources. We will revisit this assumption in Part 4.

We've also assumed that any savings made by the company are paid out to the director as additional dividends. For many small companies this will generally by the case sooner or later, even if not in the same accounting period, so this is a fair assumption for the sake of our analysis in this part of the guide (although we will look at other scenarios later).

But the assumption we should now address is that, up to now, we've assumed the company enjoys 19% corporation tax relief on its salary and national insurance payments. However, many companies will in fact enjoy more corporation tax relief during the current 2022/23 tax year.

Take a company with profits of between £50,000 and £250,000 and a January to December accounting period. In Chapter 1 we showed that such a company will enjoy 19% tax relief on salaries paid between April and December 2022 and 24.65% tax relief on salaries paid between January and March 2023 – a total of 20.41% tax relief if salaries are paid monthly.

The higher the corporation tax relief, the more attractive a higher salary becomes. However, in most cases this will not change the optimal salary decision for 2022/23.

For owners of companies that do NOT have any spare employment allowance a salary of £11,908 will still be more tax efficient than a salary of £9,100. However, taking a salary of £12,570 will not produce any additional tax savings in most cases.

For owners of companies that DO have spare employment allowance, a salary of £11,908 will still be more tax efficient than a salary of £9,100.

Furthermore, where the company has spare employment allowance, a salary of £12,570 may sometimes be more tax efficient than a salary of £11,908. As we saw above, this is already the case for basic rate taxpayer directors where the company's marginal corporation tax rate is just 19%. This salary level will also be more tax efficient for higher rate taxpayer directors where the company enjoys corporation tax relief of 19.35% or more. Many companies will enjoy more than 19.35% tax relief this year. However, the additional saving for a higher rate taxpayer director is very small (just a few pounds in many cases).

A salary higher than £12,570 will not produce any additional savings in most cases.

Conclusion

Assuming the director does not have any taxable income from other sources:

- A salary of £11,908 will in many cases be 'optimal' in 2022/23 where the company does not have any spare national insurance employment allowance.

- A salary of £12,570 will be 'optimal' in many cases when the company does have spare national insurance employment allowance, in particular when the company enjoys corporation tax relief of 19.35% or more on the salary payments (see Appendices A and B for effective rates of corporation tax relief on salaries paid in 2022/23).

Chapter 9

Older & Younger Directors

Younger Directors

You can be a company director as long as you are 16 or older. When you turn 16 you also become subject to *employee's* national insurance.

However, if you are under 21 there is no *employer's* national insurance payable on your salary, as long as it does not exceed the higher-rate threshold (currently £50,270). Employer's national insurance is only payable on the portion that exceeds £50,270.

For young directors, a salary of £12,570 is often more tax efficient than a salary of £11,908 (for the same reason it is often more tax efficient when the company has spare employment allowance: see previous chapter).

Older Directors

If a company director is over state pension age there is no *employee's* national insurance payable on their salary.

Employer's national insurance is still payable, however.

For these older directors a salary of £12,570 is generally more tax efficient than a salary of £11,908 or £9,100, even if there is some employer's national insurance payable. This is assuming that the director does not have any taxable income from other sources.

However, as we shall see in Part 4, if you have income from other sources (which would include your state pension) you should take this other income into account when deciding how much salary to pay yourself.

Where the director is in receipt of a state pension and their company salary is subject to employer's national insurance, a salary of £9,100 will often be more tax efficient than a salary of £11,908 or £12,570.

National Insurance Free Salaries

A company director can receive a fairly large salary with no national insurance payable at all if:

- The director is over state pension age, and
- The company has spare employment allowance

It may be possible for a director in these circumstances to receive a salary of around £43,500 with no national insurance liability at all (for example, when there is just one other low-paid, part-time employee who earns a little bit more than the secondary national insurance threshold).

Where there are two directors over state pension age, and no other employees, it will be possible for the directors to receive salaries of £26,306 each with no national insurance liability at all.

In some cases an overall saving of over £1,000 can be achieved by taking a larger national insurance free salary in preference to a smaller salary and dividends.

The only tax payable on the salary will be income tax, usually at just 20% (once the director's personal allowance has been exhausted), compared with the much higher combined tax rate on dividend income (income tax and corporation tax – see Chapter 3).

Fortunately for older directors the 1.25% Health and Social Care Levy (due to be introduced from 6th April 2023) has been scrapped. Unlike national insurance, it would have been payable by individuals over state pension age, but we can forget about it now. (Correction: we should probably say 'we can forget about it **for now**'.)

Chapter 10

Salaries: Pension Benefits

Apart from being tax efficient a salary confers two extra benefits on the director/shareholder:

- State pension entitlement
- Ability to make private pension contributions

State Pension Entitlement

To protect your state pension entitlement you should pay yourself a salary that is greater than the national insurance 'lower earnings limit'.

For 2022/23, the lower earnings limit is £123 per week which requires a total annual salary of at least £6,396.

If you want to protect your state pension entitlement, a salary of at least £6,396 should be paid in 2022/23 in preference to taking dividends or any other types of income.

Private Pension Contributions

Everyone under the age of 75 can make a pension contribution of £3,600 per year. The actual cash contribution would be £2,880, with the taxman adding £720 to bring the total gross contribution to £3,600.

If you want to make bigger pension contributions the contributions you make *personally* (as opposed to contributions made by your company) must not exceed your 'relevant UK earnings'. Salaries count as earnings but dividends, rental income and interest income do not.

For a company director taking the 'optimal' tax-free salary of £11,908, the maximum pension contribution he or she can make is £11,908.

This is the maximum *gross* contribution. The director would personally invest £9,526 (£11,908 x 80%) and the taxman will top this up with £2,382 of basic-rate tax relief for a gross contribution of £11,908.

Similarly, a director taking a salary of £12,570 can make a maximum pension contribution of £12,570. The director would personally invest £10,056 (£12,570 x 80%) and the taxman will top this up with £2,514 of basic-rate tax relief for a gross contribution of £12,570.

Company owners can also get their companies to make pension contributions, instead of making them personally. And as we shall see in Chapter 28, company pension contributions are more tax efficient than contributions made personally in many circumstances.

Chapter 11

Tax-free Dividends

If a company owner needs more income this year than the small 'optimal' salary, as most probably do, the most tax-efficient solution is generally to take a dividend rather than a bigger salary.

In this chapter we'll take a look at how much tax-free dividend income you can take and then in the next chapter we'll look at how much dividend income you can take taxed at just 8.75%.

We know from Chapter 3 that dividends attract no national insurance and are free from income tax if they're covered by the director's personal allowance or their dividend allowance.

Companies with Employees
(i.e. with no spare employment allowance)

A director/shareholder who takes a tax-free* salary of £11,908 and has no other income can take a tax-free dividend of £2,662 in 2022/23.

The first £662 will be covered by their remaining personal allowance and the final £2,000 will be tax free thanks to the dividend allowance.

Combined with the tax-free salary, this gives the director/shareholder the maximum total tax-free income for 2022/23 – £14,570:

- £11,908   Tax-free salary
- £2,662   Tax-free dividend

* By 'tax free' we mean in the hands of the director. As we saw in Chapter 8, there is £408 of employer's national insurance payable by the company on this level of salary.

The £14,570 maximum is the maximum tax-free income comprised of salary and dividends alone: further tax-free income of other kinds is sometimes possible, as we shall see later.

The Corporation Tax Bill

Although a dividend of £2,662 can be paid with no tax consequences for the director/shareholder, the payment is not completely tax free.

Dividends are paid out of a company's after-tax profits. So for a company that pays 19% corporation tax, a dividend of £2,662 will have a corporation tax bill of £624:

Pre-tax profits	£3,286
Less: corporation tax @ 19%	£624
After-tax profits/dividend	£2,662

So while dividends are tax efficient they are NOT tax free. This is an important point to remember, especially if you want to grow your business rather than extract income from it.

If, for example, a company incurs £3,286 of tax deductible expenditure before the end of its accounting period, its corporation tax bill will be reduced by £624. This will leave less after-tax profit to distribute as dividends but such a strategy may appeal to some business owners who would prefer to re-invest profits and minimise all taxes, including corporation tax.

The fact that dividends come with a corporation tax bill is why company owners should consider other profit extraction strategies, for example paying interest or making company pension contributions (Chapters 25 and 27). Some payments like these can be both tax free in the hands of the director and provide corporation tax relief. This is the best case scenario when it comes to extracting money from your company.

Having said this, most company owners need to extract additional cash from their companies every year to cover their living costs. This means some tax will usually always be payable, either by the company or the director personally. The key is to minimise it.

Companies with No Employees
(i.e. with spare employment allowance)

Company owners with no other income who decide to take a salary of £12,570 (because the company has spare employment allowance or because the director simply wants a larger salary) can take a tax-free dividend of £2,000 in 2022/23.

Combined with an after-tax salary of £12,486 (£12,570 less £84 employee's national insurance), this gives the director/shareholder a total income of £14,486 in 2022/23:

- £12,486   After-tax salary
- £2,000   Tax-free dividend

Doubling the Tax-Free Income
(Companies owned by couples)

Many companies are started and run by married or unmarried couples.

For couples in business together, the salaries and tax-free dividends outlined above can be doubled up.

In other words, where salaries of £11,908 are taken:

Tax-free salaries	£23,816
Tax-free dividends	£5,324
Total tax-free income	£29,140

Where salaries of £12,570 are taken (£12,486 after employee NI):

Salaries	£24,972
Tax-free dividends	£4,000
Total income	£28,972

Spouses/Partners Brought into the Business

Of course, not all companies are started or managed by couples. In some cases the business may have been started before the couple met. In other cases, one member of the couple may not want to become actively involved in the business, for example if they have their own career or do not work at all. In these cases the questions from a tax planning perspective are:

- Can a spouse/partner be employed in the business?
- Can company shares be transferred to a spouse/partner?
- How much tax will the above two strategies save?

We'll return to these important tax planning issues in Chapter 21.

Use it or Lose It!

A company owner may decide to not withdraw the maximum tax-free dividend for several reasons. However, it really is a case of use it or lose it: if you don't take the maximum tax-free dividend this year, you cannot take a bigger tax-free amount next year. Furthermore, with the dividend allowance reducing to just £1,000 next year, it is even more important to make the most of the £2,000 allowance available this year.

Company Directors' Tax Returns

Note that, even if you don't have any income tax to pay on your salary and dividends, you may still have to complete a tax return. All company directors have this duty where they either have any taxable income (or benefits in kind), or have been issued with a notice to file a tax return.

In fact, HMRC seem to be under the impression that all company directors must file a tax return, even if they have no taxable income. In practice, it's probably easier to file a tax return than to get into an argument with them over this point.

The Next Step: Taxable Dividends

The tax-free salaries and dividends listed above will not provide enough income for the vast majority of company owners, even if the amounts are doubled up where the company is owned by a couple. Those that require more income will have to pay income tax on any additional dividends withdrawn, as we shall now see.

Part 3

How to Extract More Income Tax Efficiently

Chapter 12

The Next Step:
Dividends Taxed at Just 8.75%

So far we've shown that a company owner who has no other income and takes a tax-free salary of £11,908 can also take a tax-free dividend of £2,662 for a total tax-free income of £14,570.

A company owner who takes a salary of £12,570 can take a tax-free dividend of £2,000 for a total income of £14,486 (net of employee's national insurance).

These amounts can be doubled up where the company is owned by a couple.

Of course, most company owners will require more income and the most tax-efficient route is normally to take a bigger dividend.

Any additional dividend income you take will be taxed, however as long as you keep your total income below the £50,270 higher-rate threshold you will pay just 8.75% income tax. If you take any more dividend income the tax rate jumps to 33.75%!

Salary of £11,908

If you've taken a salary of £11,908 and tax-free dividend of £2,662 the maximum amount of additional dividend income you can take taxed at just 8.75% is £35,700. The income tax payable on this additional dividend income will be £3,124.

In summary, you can take a salary of £11,908 and a total dividend of £38,362 for a total pre-tax income of £50,270. After paying £3,124 tax you'll be left with an after-tax income of £47,146.

These amounts can be doubled up if the company is owned by a couple, leaving them with a total after-tax income of £94,292 and a total income tax bill of £6,248.

Salary vs Dividends

Even though the additional dividend income is taxed, it is still much more tax efficient than taking a bigger salary.

To end up with the same after-tax income of £47,146, a director/shareholder would require an additional salary payment of £51,107, on top of the £11,908 already paid and the maximum tax-free dividend of £2,000.

Overall, the director would end up with the same amount of after-tax income but the company would end up with £11,050 less cash (because it has to make such a large salary payment to cover all the extra tax, especially national insurance).

The table below illustrates this effect in two companies: one paying a small salary and dividends, the other paying a big salary plus a £2,000 tax-free dividend.

In each case the director ends up with £47,146. The company paying the big salary ends up with £11,050 less cash.

	Small Salary £	Big Salary £
Company's tax		
Company profit	100,000	100,000
Less: Salary	11,908	63,015
Less: Employer's NI	408	7,834
Net Profit	87,684	29,151
Less: Corporation tax @ 19%*	16,660	5,539
After-tax profit	71,024	23,612
Less: Dividend	38,362	2,000
Company cash	32,662	21,612
Director's tax		
Total income	50,270	65,015
Income tax	3,124	12,638**
National insurance	0	5,231
After-tax income	47,146	47,146

*   Corporation tax would be higher for some companies this year
** Higher for Scottish taxpayers

Salary of £12,570

If you've taken a salary of £12,570 and tax-free dividend of £2,000 the maximum amount of additional dividend income you can take taxed at just 8.75% is £35,700. The income tax payable on this additional dividend income will be £3,124.

In summary, you can take a salary of £12,570 and a dividend of £37,700 for a total pre-tax income of £50,270. After paying £84 national insurance on your salary and £3,124 income tax on your dividend income you'll be left with an after-tax income of £47,062.

These amounts can be doubled up if the company is owned by a couple, leaving them with a total after-tax income of £94,124 and a total tax and national insurance bill of £6,416.

Company Owners with Bigger Salaries

Of course not all company owners take a salary of £11,908 or £12,570. Some take a bigger salary because it suits them to do so, even if this is not the most tax efficient or 'optimal' thing to do.

For example, a company owner who takes a salary of £30,000 can still take a tax-free dividend of £2,000 plus additional dividend income of up to £18,270 taxed at 8.75% (£50,270 - £30,000 - £2,000).

A company owner who takes a salary of £50,000 can still take a tax-free dividend of £2,000. However, because their total taxable income exceeds the higher-rate threshold any additional dividend income will be subject to tax at the higher rate of 33.75%.

Chapter 13

Making the Most of the 8.75% Tax Rate

So far we have shown that a company owner who takes a salary of £11,908 can receive dividend income of £2,662 tax free and a further £35,700 taxed at 8.75%.

A company owner who takes a salary of £12,570 can receive dividend income of £2,000 tax free and a further £35,700 taxed at 8.75%.

Company owners who extract more money from their companies will go over the £50,270 higher-rate threshold and start paying income tax at 33.75% on their dividends, which is a big leap!

(Remember, at this point, to keep things simple, we are assuming the company owner does not have income from other sources.)

An important tax planning question is whether you should pay yourself as much dividend income as you can taxed at 8.75%, even if you don't need the money immediately?

It's impossible to provide a definitive answer because every company owner is different. However, we will attempt to outline the main benefits and drawbacks in this chapter.

One of the main reasons why you may NOT want to pay yourself the maximum amount taxed at 8.75% this year is if you expect to be able to withdraw the same money tax free next year or in another tax year.

We've shown that a couple who take salaries of £11,908 each can also pay themselves tax-free dividends of £2,662 each – a total tax-free income of £29,140 in 2022/23.

Although some company owners may be able to survive on the tax-free amounts, most will not and will have to withdraw at least some dividend income each year taxed at 8.75%. Arguably you then have fairly little to lose by withdrawing the maximum amount you can have taxed at 8.75% this year (£35,700).

The main drawback is you will end up paying income tax earlier than may be necessary. In other words, the extra money you pay in income tax will earn interest in the taxman's bank account instead of your company's bank account.

Most company bank accounts pay paltry amounts of interest at present so the potential loss is very small. Anything you lose can probably be more than made up by investing the extra dividend income in a cash ISA (the rates are typically far higher than for company bank accounts).

So what are the benefits of paying tax early? By paying yourself the maximum dividend taxed at 8.75% you stand to protect against:

- Further dividend tax increases
- Business risk
- Becoming a higher-rate taxpayer

In previous editions of this guide we warned that dividend tax rates could be increased. This has now happened. The rates were all increased by 1.25% on 6th April 2022 and the dividend allowance is to be reduced from 6th April 2023. It is possible that dividend tax rates could be increased again and there were rumours circulating to this effect prior to the Autumn Statement on 17th November 2022. Since those rumours proved unfounded, we feel further increases are unlikely in the short term, although they certainly cannot be ruled out.

If you are concerned that dividend tax rates could be increased again, it may be better to withdraw as much income as you can taxed at 8.75% in case the rate is increased to, say, 10%.

Of course it's also possible that dividend tax rates could be reduced at some point, but this seems highly improbable for the foreseeable future in light of recent Government announcements.

Some company owners may wish to remove cash from their companies to protect against business risk (arguably your money is at greater risk in the company's bank account than your own).

It may also be worth paying yourself the maximum dividend taxed at 8.75% if you think you may become a higher-rate taxpayer in the future. In other words, it may be better to *definitely* pay 8.75% tax this year rather than *possibly* 33.75% in a future tax year.

Avoiding 33.75% Tax

Why would you expect to become a higher-rate taxpayer in the future? Perhaps you expect the profits of your business to grow significantly or you expect to receive more income from other sources, for example an inheritance.

It's likely many basic-rate taxpayers will become higher-rate taxpayers, even if their income simply increases because of inflation. This is because the higher-rate threshold has been fixed at £50,270 for seven years (until 5th April 2028).

Although you might never become a higher-rate taxpayer, you arguably have very little to lose by paying yourself the maximum dividend taxed at 8.75%. If you do become a higher-rate taxpayer you will save 25% (by paying 8.75% tax this year rather than 33.75% in the future). If you don't become a higher-rate taxpayer you will probably lose nothing because you will pay 8.75% tax this year instead of 8.75% in the future.

Reasons to Pay Smaller Dividends

A company owner may decide to not withdraw the maximum dividend taxed at 8.75% for several reasons:

- The company hasn't made enough profit
- The company needs the cash to grow
- The company owner doesn't need the money
- The company is forced to restrict its dividends
- The company owner has taxable capital gains

The Company Hasn't Made Enough Profit

The company doesn't need to have made any profit to pay *salaries* and tax-efficient salaries should be paid wherever possible because they are also a tax deductible expense and reduce the company's corporation tax bill (even if this is only at a later date if the company is currently not making profits). For example, a salary of £11,908 will reduce a company's tax bill by *at least* £2,263.

Dividends, on the other hand, can only be declared if the company has sufficient distributable profits. It is not necessary for the company to actually make a profit in the year the dividend is paid, as long as there are sufficient accumulated profits (after tax) from previous years. (See Chapter 35 for more information on this issue.)

The Company Needs the Cash to Grow

Even if the company has made sufficient profits, the directors may wish to keep the cash in the company to grow the business.

In these circumstances it may be possible for a dividend to be declared but not paid out. The dividend can simply be credited to the director's loan account and withdrawn at a later date when it is more convenient.

This may be more tax efficient than reducing dividends during one year and then declaring bigger dividends taxed at 33.75% in another year.

Note that the director will generally be subject to income tax on any dividend that has been declared but not paid out. In practice, this means it may be necessary to pay out a small portion of the dividend to help the director pay their tax bill.

The Company Owner Doesn't Need the Money

A company owner may decide to take a smaller dividend if they have other resources such as inherited money or proceeds from selling another business or from selling other assets like property and shares. The company owner may also have a spouse/partner who earns enough income to support the family.

In these circumstances the company owner may believe it is sensible to limit the amount taken as dividends to avoid paying tax at 8.75%. In reality, however, the company owner may simply be storing up an income tax problem for the future. If accumulated profits are eventually paid out as a large dividend, an income tax charge of 33.75% or 39.35% could be payable on a significant portion of any dividend declared.

If income is withdrawn on a more regular annual basis, even if not required immediately, income tax can be restricted to 8.75%.

There is one important exception. If the company owner has taxable income from other sources, it may be prudent to take a smaller dividend. So far we have been assuming the company owner has no other taxable income. If there is other taxable income that uses up some or all of the director's basic-rate band, it may be necessary to restrict dividends to avoid paying income tax at 33.75%. (There is more about directors with other income in Part 4.)

The Company is Forced to Restrict its Dividends

Lenders may place restrictions on dividend payments to protect their interests (i.e. to stop cash leaking out of the company that should be going to them). In these circumstances it may be difficult for the company owners to structure their dividend payments to mitigate tax.

The Company Owner Has Taxable Capital Gains

If you have taxable capital gains you may want to reduce the amount of income you withdraw from your company to free up some of your basic-rate band. This may allow you to pay less capital gains tax: see Chapter 38.

Alternatives to Dividends

Although paying tax at 8.75% is a lot better than paying tax at 33.75%, it's important to remember that dividends are paid out of income that has already been subjected to corporation tax.

Thus, if you are a basic-rate taxpayer, the true effective tax rate on your dividend income is currently at least 26%, not 8.75% (see Chapter 3).

This means dividends are less tax efficient than certain other types of income that you may be able to extract from your company. And they are becoming even less attractive with the increase in corporation tax (see Chapter 1).

Take rental income for example. If your company pays you rent of £10,000, the amount will be a fully deductible expense (providing the rent is no more than a reasonable market rate for the company's occupation of a property you own personally). If you are a basic-rate taxpayer you will pay 20% tax on the amount received, leaving you with £8,000.

On the other hand, if your company does not pay you rent it will have extra profits of £10,000 on which it will pay at least 19% corporation tax, leaving £8,100 at most to distribute as dividends. After paying 8.75% tax you will be left with £7,391 at most.

Clearly, rental income is a fair bit more tax efficient than dividend income in this situation (see Chapter 24 for more information).

We also suspect some directors will be getting their companies to make bigger pension contributions following the increase in dividend tax rates. If your company contributes £10,000 to your pension it can claim corporation tax relief. Ignoring investment growth, when you retire you will be able to withdraw 25% tax free and the rest could be taxed at just 20% if you are a basic-rate taxpayer.

After tax you'll be left with £8,500, compared with £7,391 from a dividend (see Chapter 27 for more on pension contributions).

It's worth bearing all this in mind before you pay yourself any dividends, as these may effectively limit your ability to make other tax efficient payments. We'll take a closer look at this potential conflict in Chapter 35.

Furthermore, paying dividends may also limit the financial resources available to the company to make other tax efficient payments, e.g. rent or pension contributions.

Chapter 14

Making the Most of the 33.75% Tax Rate

Summary So Far

So far we have shown that a company owner who takes a tax-free salary of £11,908 can extract a tax-free dividend of £2,662 and a dividend of £35,700 taxed at 8.75%, leaving them with an after-tax income of £47,146.

A company owner who takes a salary of £12,570 (£12,486 after national insurance) can extract a tax-free dividend of £2,000 and a dividend of £35,700 taxed at 8.75%, leaving them with an after-tax income of £47,062.

In both scenarios the company owner ends up with a taxable income of £50,270 and is on the cusp of being a higher-rate taxpayer.

These amounts can be doubled in the case of companies owned and run by couples.

If you generally do not require more income, you may be able to adopt an 'income smoothing' strategy – taking the maximum tax-free salary and dividend plus the maximum dividend taxed at 8.75% every year where possible, regardless of whether the company has made bigger than normal profits or lower than normal profits.

Taking Bigger Dividends

If you want more income the optimal strategy is usually to take additional dividends rather than salary, in order to avoid the national insurance payable on employment income. However, now that you have reached the £50,270 higher-rate threshold you will pay a whopping 33.75% income tax on any additional dividend income you take.

You also have to watch out for two further tax stings:

- Child benefit tax charge – Income over £50,000
- Personal allowance withdrawal – Income over £100,000

In this chapter we will assume that neither the company owner, nor any other member of their household, is claiming any child benefit. We will return to child benefit in the next chapter.

If no child benefit is being claimed, the next threshold to watch out for is £100,000, where your personal allowance starts to be withdrawn. The personal allowance currently saves higher-rate taxpayers up to £5,028 in income tax, so many company owners will want to keep their income below £100,000 to avoid losing it.

Maximum Income

With total income of £50,270 the director can take additional dividend income of up to £49,730 taxed at 33.75% before the £100,000 threshold is reached.

A director who takes a salary of £11,908 and the rest of their income as dividends will be left with total after-tax income of £80,092:

£11,908 salary + £88,092 dividend - £19,908 tax = £80,092

A director who takes a salary of £12,570 (£12,486 after national insurance) will be left with a total after-tax income of £80,008:

£12,486 salary + £87,430 dividend - £19,908 tax = £80,008

If the company is owned and managed by a couple, the above amounts can potentially be doubled up.

Don't Forget the Corporation Tax Bill!

It's tempting to think that company owners who pay themselves any of the above amounts are paying relatively little tax. After all, a total of £100,000 is being extracted from the company with a total income tax bill of just £19,908. The effective income tax rate is just 19.9%!

However, it's important to remember that dividends are always paid out of a company's *after-tax* profits.

To pay a dividend of £88,092 the company will have had to make taxable profits of at least £108,756, resulting in a corporation tax bill of at least £20,664 (at 19%). Coupled with an income tax bill of £19,908, the total tax bill attached to the dividend is £40,572.

Alternatives to Dividends

In Chapter 3 we pointed out that, as a higher-rate taxpayer, the total tax rate on your dividend income is at least 46%. With the tax rate at this level, some small company owners may decide to not pay themselves any dividend income which takes them over the higher-rate threshold. They may simply roll up cash inside their companies, possibly until the business is sold or wound up.

At this point it may be possible to pay just 10% capital gains tax on the funds extracted if the company owner qualifies for Business Asset Disposal Relief. We'll explore this issue more in Chapter 30.

Other company owners may decide to pay themselves less dividend income and focus on other techniques to extract money from their companies, such as pension contributions.

For example, if your company contributes £10,000 to your pension the payment will be a tax deductible expense for the company. Ignoring investment growth, when you retire you can withdraw 25% tax free and the rest will possibly be taxed at just 20% if you are basic-rate taxpayer, as most retirees are. After tax you'll be left with £8,500. This compares with at most £5,366 if instead a dividend is taken equal to what is left of that pre-tax profit of £10,000 (after corporation tax) and then taxed again in your hands at 33.75%. (See Chapter 27 for more information.)

With the corporation tax rate going up the total tax rate on dividend income is rising too. For many company owners who are higher-rate taxpayers the combined marginal tax rate on dividend income will rise to roughly 51% (see Chapter 3). This will make it even more attractive to extract other types of income from your company (for example rental income and interest income) or focus on other profit extraction techniques such as pension contributions.

If the total tax rate on your dividend income will rise further does this mean you should pay yourself bigger dividends now, before the increase is in full effect? No because dividends do not affect the amount of corporation tax your company pays: dividends are paid out of the company's *after-tax* profits.

The amount of dividend income you take is mostly an *income tax* planning decision, based on your personal tax position.

What the corporation tax increase does mean for tax planning is that company owners should consider postponing certain types of discretionary spending, where possible, in order to enjoy corporation tax relief at 25% or 26.5% in the future, instead of 19% or slightly higher at present.

In most cases it is not possible to postpone paying yourself things like rent (if your company uses a property you own) or interest (if your company owes you money). For tax purposes these types of expense are generally allocated to the period they relate to. It may, however, be possible to postpone making pension contributions and various other expenses.

Postponing and Bringing Forward Dividends

In last year's edition we pointed out that company owners who regularly extract dividends taxed at the higher rate (then 32.5%) should consider paying themselves additional dividend income taxed at 32.5%, unless they could extract money from their companies in a more tax efficient way.

Why? With the public finances in such a poor state it seemed unlikely the higher-rate threshold would be increased significantly or that the 32.5% higher rate would be reduced. As things transpired, the higher rate was increased to 33.75% on 6th April 2022. Thus anyone who paid themselves additional dividend income last year will have saved a little bit of tax.

Should higher-rate taxpayers pay themselves additional dividend income this year? You're probably less likely to save tax now that dividend tax rates have already been increased.

However, you may have very little to lose by paying yourself additional dividend income, unless the higher-rate threshold is increased significantly or dividend tax rates are reduced in a future tax year. Neither of these is likely in the foreseeable future since the current Government plan is to freeze the higher rate tax threshold at £50,270 until 2027/28 and we don't expect them to be reducing dividend tax rates during that period either.

One group who should certainly consider paying themselves as much dividend income as they can taxed at 33.75% are company owners whose taxable income is anywhere close to £100,000. This is because, once your income rises above £100,000, your marginal income tax rate will typically rise from 33.75% to an effective rate of 56% (see Chapter 16).

For example, if you expect your taxable income to be, say, £85,000 this year it may be better to pay yourself an additional £15,000 this year instead of in a future tax year when your income may have already risen to around £100,000.

The £100,000 threshold has not been increased since it was introduced in 2010 and we don't expect it to be increased any time soon. As a result more and more taxpayers will probably have their personal allowances withdrawn in the years ahead.

Sample Tax Bills

For company owners who want to withdraw more than £50,270 *this year*, Table 5 contains some sample income tax bills. It's assumed that a tax-free salary of £11,908 or £12,570 is taken, with the remaining income taken as dividends. The table goes up to £100,000 – beyond that your personal allowance is withdrawn.

The numbers are fairly easy to calculate. The first £12,570 is tax free thanks to your personal allowance and the next £2,000 of dividend income is also tax free thanks to the dividend allowance. The next £35,700 of dividend income is taxed at 8.75%, resulting in tax of £3,124. At this point the company owner has income of £50,270 and is on the higher-rate threshold. Any additional dividends will be taxed at 33.75%.

Someone who extracts £75,000 will pay £3,124 on the first £50,270 and £8,346 on the final £24,730 (£24,730 x 33.75%), resulting in a total tax bill of £11,470.

TABLE 5
Income between £50,270 and £100,000

Income £	Income Tax £	After-tax Income £
50,270	3,124	47,146
55,000	4,720	50,280
60,000	6,408	53,592
65,000	8,095	56,905
70,000	9,783	60,217
75,000	11,470	63,530
80,000	13,158	66,842
85,000	14,845	70,155
90,000	16,533	73,467
95,000	18,220	76,780
100,000	19,908	80,092

Notes:
1. Salary of £11,908 or £12,570 taken with rest of income as dividends
2. Where salary is £12,570 national insurance of £84 must also be included
3. For income over £50,270 the extra tax is simply 33.75% of the excess
4. Table may contain rounding errors

In all cases the amounts listed in Table 5 can be doubled for companies owned and run by couples. For example, a couple can withdraw £150,000 (£75,000 each) with a total income tax bill of £22,940 (£11,470 each).

Income Smoothing

If your company makes bigger than normal profits during one accounting period you may be tempted to pay yourself a bigger dividend, even if this results in income tax being payable at a higher rate. Paying a bigger than normal dividend is perfectly acceptable from a tax planning perspective IF you expect the company's profits to remain at a higher level, or continue to grow, AND expect to extract those profits as dividends each year. If, however, you expect the company's profits to fall back, it may be wiser to 'smooth' your income and withdraw any bumper profits gradually, paying tax at no more than 8.75%.

Chapter 15

How to Protect Your Child Benefit

If you wish to withdraw more than £50,270 income from your company *and* you are the highest earner in a household that receives child benefit, you will be subject to two tax stings:

- 33.75% tax on your dividend income, and
- The High Income Child Benefit Charge

To avoid *both* you have to keep your salary and dividends below £50,000.

Child benefit is gradually withdrawn when any member of your household has over £50,000 income. This is done by imposing a child benefit charge on the highest earner in the household. Once the highest earner's income reaches £60,000, all of the child benefit is effectively taken away in higher tax charges.

The £50,000 threshold does not increase with inflation and, in fact, has never been increased since the child benefit charge was introduced in 2013. This means more and more households have been drawn into its net.

Why the £50,000 threshold was not increased to align it with the £50,270 higher-rate threshold is anyone's guess.

The child benefit charge has important implications for company owners who want to determine how much income to withdraw from their companies during the current and future tax years.

Child Benefit: How Much is it Worth?

Child benefit is a valuable *tax-free* handout from the Government. Those who qualify will receive the following payment in 2022/23:

- £1,133.60 for the first child
- £751.40 for each subsequent child

Depending on the number of children, a family can expect to receive the following total child benefit payment:

Children	Total Child Benefit
1	£1,134
2	£1,885
3	£2,636
4	£3,388

Plus £751 for each additional child

How Long Do Child Benefit Payments Continue?

Child benefit generally continues to be paid until your children are 16 years old. The payments will continue until age 20, however, if the child is enrolled in full-time 'non-advanced' education, including:

- GCSEs
- A levels
- Scottish Highers
- NVQ/SVQ level 1, 2 or 3
- BTEC National Diploma, National Certificate, 1st Diploma

So if your child is 16, 17, 18 or 19 and enrolled in one of the above courses, child benefit will continue to be paid. Once the child is 20 years old all child benefit payments will cease.

The following courses do NOT qualify:

- Degrees
- Diploma of Higher Education
- NVQ level 4 or above
- HNCs or HNDs
- Teacher training

In other words, if your children are 16, 17, 18 or 19 and enrolled in any of these courses, you will not receive any child benefit.

Total Value of Child Benefit

Child benefit payments continue for between 16 and 20 years. Based on current child benefit rates, the total amount you can expect to receive over the total period your child qualifies is:

- £18,144 to £22,680 tax free for the first child
- At least £12,016 tax free for each additional child

These are very much 'back of the envelope' figures because they ignore the potential danger that child benefit may not hold its real value if it doesn't increase with inflation (as has happened in recent years).

Furthermore, the amount received for second and subsequent children will vary from family to family. When your first child ceases to qualify your second child will step into their shoes and receive the higher payment. In other words, when you stop receiving £1,134 for your first child, the payment for your second child will increase from £751 to £1,134.

Thus families will receive different overall amounts depending on the age difference between their children and where they study.

The above overall figures nevertheless illustrate how valuable child benefit is over many years and why it's worth protecting.

How the Child Benefit Charge is Calculated

For every £100 of income over £50,000 an income tax charge equivalent to 1% of the child benefit is levied on the highest earner in the household.

For example, if the highest earner in the household has income of £52,500, the tax charge will be equivalent to 25% of the child benefit claimed.

If the highest earner in the household has income of £55,000, the tax charge will be equivalent to 50% of the child benefit.

And if the highest earner has income of £60,000 or more the tax charge will be equivalent to 100% of the child benefit.

Income between £50,270 & £60,000: 1970s Style Tax Rates

Once your income goes above £50,270 you will have to pay the child benefit charge _and_ 33.75% tax on your dividend income.

For the highest earner in the household the child benefit charge creates the following marginal tax rates on dividend income in the £50,270-£60,000 tax bracket:

Children	Marginal Tax Rate on Dividends
1	45%
2	53%
3	60%
4	68%

Example

David, a company owner, has taken a salary and dividends totalling £50,000 so far in 2022/23. He is the highest earner in a household claiming child benefit for two children.

David decides to withdraw additional dividend income of £10,000. His total income will be £60,000 so he will face the maximum child benefit charge. The tax payable on the additional dividend is £5,193, calculated as follows:

£270 dividend x 8.75%	*£24*
£9,730 dividend x 33.75%	*£3,284*
£1,885 child benefit x 100%	*£1,885*
Total additional tax	*£5,193*

Before he decided to take the additional £10,000 dividend he was paying just 8.75% income tax on his dividend income. The overall tax rate on the additional £10,000 dividend is 52%.

Clearly David should think twice about withdrawing the additional income, especially if he does not need the money urgently.

Income between £60,000 and £100,000

If you have more than £60,000 of income you will already be paying the maximum child benefit charge. Income between £60,000 and £100,000 does not incur any further charge. Hence, dividends falling into the income bracket between £60,000 and £100,000 are simply taxed at 33.75%.

Once your income rises above £100,000, you face a fresh tax sting: withdrawal of the income tax personal allowance.

How to Avoid the Child Benefit Charge

Clearly taxpayers have an incentive to escape the much higher tax rates that apply to dividends when the child benefit charge is payable. Company owners may find it easier than other taxpayers to escape the child benefit charge because they can alter the amount of dividend income they pay themselves each year.

Some company owners will be able to *mostly* avoid the charge and the 33.75% tax rate applying to dividend income by paying themselves no more than £50,270 this year. But it's probably worth paying yourself no more than £50,000 because that final £270 will be taxed at 27% if you have two children, compared with the 8.75% rate that generally applies to basic-rate taxpayers.

Other company owners, including those who usually withdraw more than £60,000 each year, may be able to avoid the charge in some tax years but not others, or partly reduce the charge.

Company owners can also spread their income among family members: for example, by gifting shares in the company to their spouse (see Chapter 21).

For the current and future tax years, the following dividend strategies could be considered:

Smooth Income

If the income you withdraw is currently somewhere *below* £50,000 and you expect your income to continue growing above £50,000, you should consider extracting approximately £50,000 for several tax years, where possible.

This may mean that you pay yourself more income than you need to begin with and less income than you need later on, but by doing so you may be able to avoid the child benefit charge (and the 33.75% tax rate that kicks in after £50,270) for several years.

In other words, it's better to pay 8.75% tax now rather than, say, 53% in the future.

For example, if you withdrew £40,000 from your company last year you should consider withdrawing £50,000 this year even if this is more money than you need. The extra income will be taxed at just 8.75%.

Roller-Coaster Income

If you plan to withdraw *more than* £60,000 from 2022/23 onwards, you could consider taking big dividends during some tax years and smaller ones in other tax years.

For example, instead of withdrawing a total income of £75,000 every year, consider taking £100,000 every second year, if possible, and £50,000 in the intervening years. This will allow you to avoid the child benefit charge every second year.

Similarly, a company owner who normally takes around £60,000 every year could consider taking £70,000 in year 1 and £50,000 in year 2, where possible.

Better still, such a company owner could even consider taking £80,000 in year 1 and £50,000 in each of years 2 and 3, where circumstances allow. The more years you can keep your income to the £50,000 threshold, the more times you can avoid the child benefit charge.

Austerity

If your taxable income is normally over £50,000, you could consider keeping your income below £50,000 for several years to avoid the child benefit charge.

For example, let's say you have three children and your taxable income is normally around £60,000. If for the next three years you can afford to withdraw just £50,000, you may be able to protect over £7,908 of child benefit.

Other Issues

When paying yourself dividends that are smaller than normal or bigger than normal there may be lots of other issues to consider.

For example, you can only declare bigger dividends if the company has sufficient distributable profits.

If you postpone taking some of your dividends until a future tax year, you may leave yourself exposed to any future increase in tax on company owners. Remember tax rules are constantly changing.

If you take a smaller than normal dividend this may have other financial repercussions, for example it may affect the size of mortgage you are able to get.

Chapter 16

Income over £100,000

Summary So Far

So far we have shown that a director/shareholder of a company that has no spare employment allowance can extract a tax-free salary of £11,908 and a dividend of £88,092 (with £2,662 tax free, £35,700 taxed at 8.75% and £49,730 taxed at 33.75%). Total pre-tax income: £100,000. Total after-tax income: £80,092.

If the company has spare employment allowance, a salary of £12,570 can be taken with a total national insurance cost of £84. On top of this, a dividend of £87,430 can be taken (with £2,000 tax free, £35,700 taxed at 8.75% and £49,730 taxed at 33.75%). Total pre-tax income: £100,000. Total after-tax income: £80,008.

The above amounts can be doubled up if the company is also owned and run by your spouse/partner.

The child benefit charge is payable if the highest earner in the household has income of more than £50,000 (see Chapter 15).

Income between £100,000 and £125,140

Many company owners will be satisfied with a net after tax income of around £80,000.

For those who wish to extract more cash, a dividend is often the best option. However, now you face an additional tax sting: withdrawal of your £12,570 income tax personal allowance.

Once your taxable income rises above £100,000, your personal allowance is gradually withdrawn. It is withdrawn at the rate of £1 for every £2 of additional income.

In other words, if you have income of £101,000 your personal allowance will be reduced by £500. Once your gross income reaches £125,140 you will have no personal allowance left at all.

Company owners with income in the £100,000-£125,140 bracket could end up paying income tax at an effective rate of over 50% on any additional dividends they withdraw.

Example

Annabel, a company owner, has already taken a salary of £11,908 and dividend of £88,092. Total income: £100,000. She decides to pays herself additional dividend income of £25,140. On the additional dividend she will pay 33.75% income tax: £8,485. She will also lose all of her personal allowance which means her salary of £11,908 will now be taxed at 20%. Additional tax: £2,382.

In addition, £662 of dividend income, previously covered by her personal allowance, will be taxed at 33.75%. Additional tax: £223. Finally, her salary uses up £11,908 of her basic-rate band which means £11,908 of dividends will be taxed at 33.75% instead of 8.75%. Additional tax: £2,977.

The total additional income tax is £14,067 which is equivalent to 56% of the £25,140 dividend.

To be precise, Annabel suffers effective tax rates of 50.625% on the first £1,324 of her additional dividend and 56.25% on the remaining £23,816 (i.e. twice the amount of her salary). This averages out at around 56%.

Don't Forget the Corporation Tax Bill!

As always, it's important to remember that dividends are paid out of a company's *after-tax* profits.

To pay an additional dividend of £25,140 the company will have had to make profits of at least £31,037, resulting in corporation tax of at least £5,897. Coupled with an income tax bill of £14,067, the total tax bill on the £31,037 of profit is £19,964, i.e. 64%!

Income between £125,140 and £150,000

These extortionate tax rates do not apply to all dividend income over £100,000 – only income between £100,000 and £125,140.

Once your income exceeds £125,140 your personal allowance will have disappeared altogether. In the current, 2022/23 tax year, additional dividends will be taxed at the regular rate applying to higher-rate taxpayers: 33.75%.

After that, the next threshold you have to watch out for is £150,000, where the additional rate of tax currently kicks in (see Chapter 17).

From 2023/24, however, additional rate tax will apply to income over £125,140. Hence, in future tax years, once you have lost your personal allowance, any further dividends will be taxed at 39.35%.

The reduction in the additional rate tax threshold next year means that, if you are able to do so, and you are already planning to take at least £125,140 out of your company this year, it could make sense to top it up to £150,000.

For each £1,000 of income falling into the £125,140 to £150,000 bracket that you take this year instead of in a later year, you will save at least £56.

But that modest saving is dwarfed by the potential savings available if taking more income this year means you can reduce your income in a later year to less than £125,140, as we shall see a little later in this chapter.

How to Avoid 56% Tax

Unlike regular salaried employees or owners of unincorporated businesses (sole traders and partnerships), company owners can avoid this extortionate tax rate by simply not paying themselves salary and dividends in excess of £100,000 per year.

Thus a company owner taking a salary of £11,908 could extract dividends not exceeding £88,092; a company owner taking a salary of £12,570 could extract dividends not exceeding £87,430.

A company owner whose income may fluctuate from year to year, in line with the company's profits, may want to consider smoothing income to avoid the £100,000 threshold. In other words, if possible try not to pay yourself a salary and dividend of £80,000 in year 1 and £120,000 in year 2. It may be better to pay yourself £100,000 during both tax years, to preserve all of your income tax personal allowance in year 2.

Bigger Companies

Owners of companies earning substantial profits face a dilemma. While they may choose to extract no more than £100,000 per year, ultimately they may end up with a lot of surplus cash inside their companies.

For example, if you are the only shareholder in a company that is making an after-tax profit of £200,000 per year, you may not wish to extract just £100,000 per year indefinitely, especially if the surplus cash is not needed to help grow the business.

Company owners who wish to pay themselves more than £100,000 per year may be able to occasionally keep their personal allowances by using the 'roller-coaster' strategy: paying bigger dividends in some tax years and smaller dividends in other years.

Remember, once your income exceeds £125,140, your personal allowance will have disappeared altogether and there is currently no additional penalty for taking further dividend income, providing you keep your total income below £150,000.

From next year, 2023/24, income over £125,140 will be subject to additional rate tax. But this only increases the tax rate on dividend income to 39.35%, still far better than the punitive effective rates of up to 56.25% applying to income between £100,000 and £125,140.

What this all adds up to is the fact that 2022/23 is an ideal year to start your roller-coaster strategy: if you're going to take income of much more than £100,000 this year, it may make sense to take £150,000 in order to benefit from the current additional rate tax threshold while you can.

For example, let's say you had been planning to withdraw a salary of £11,908 and dividend of £113,092 this year, and then a salary of £12,570 and dividend of £112,430 next year (total income £125,000 in each year). With this level of income almost all your personal allowance will be withdrawn in both years.

If instead you pay yourself a total of £150,000 this year, but only £100,000 next year, this will allow you to keep all your personal allowance in 2023/24. Potential net tax saving across the two years: £5,594.

The reduction in the additional rate tax threshold from 2023/24 onwards will reduce this saving in future but, at the rates we currently expect to see, a bi-annual saving of £4,201 will still be possible using the same strategy.

For more potential savings based on the roller-coaster strategy, see Chapter 17.

Salary vs Dividends

If you intend to pay yourself one of the small salaries discussed in Chapter 8 (£11,908 or £12,570) and extract the rest of the company's profits as dividends, it *may* be possible to achieve a small additional saving by paying yourself an even smaller salary, if you expect to have taxable income of more than £100,000.

The potential tax savings depend on a number of factors, including how much profit the company makes, its marginal corporation tax rate, and whether the company has spare national insurance employment allowance.

For example, we saw in Chapter 8 that, where a company does not have any employment allowance available, the optimal salary for most company owners is typically £11,908. Where the company owner's taxable income exceeds £100,000, a small tax saving can sometimes be achieved by taking a smaller salary, such as £9,100, which is the employer's national insurance threshold.

The potential tax saving is not very impressive – around a couple of hundred pounds at best, which is a very small saving for someone with so much income. Nevertheless this may suit some company owners, for example owners of one man band companies that aren't entitled to the employment allowance and don't want the hassle of making any national insurance payments.

Theoretically, slightly greater savings might sometimes be achieved with even smaller salaries. However, when it comes to reducing your salary to achieve additional tax savings the permutations are too many to provide any simple guidelines here. Any analysis would have to be performed on a case by case basis.

When You Should Not Reduce Your Salary

There are also various tax and non-tax reasons why you may not want to reduce your salary too far. In other words, what may be 'mathematically optimal' does not always make for sound tax planning.

Pensions are a case in point. Anyone who personally wants to make a gross pension contribution of more than £3,600 requires earnings. Salaries count as earnings, dividends do not.

Furthermore, in order to protect your state pension entitlement, you should always make sure you receive a salary that exceeds the national insurance 'lower earnings limit'. For 2022/23, the lower earnings limit is £123 per week which requires a total annual salary of at least £6,396.

Scottish Company Owners

In previous chapters we have stated that company owners in Scotland who take a small salary and the rest of their income as dividends are completely immune from Scottish income tax.

However, those with income over £100,000 will have their personal allowances gradually taken away, which means their salaries will become subject to Scottish income tax. Their dividends will continue to be taxed using UK rates and thresholds.

As it happens this is not necessarily a bad thing. As long as your salary and other income subject to Scottish tax (e.g. rental income) do not exceed £15,280 this year, you will pay a bit less tax than company owners living elsewhere in the UK, even if you lose your personal allowance.

In this way the SNP Government has unwittingly handed a tax cut to company owners who have big dividends but only small salaries!

Chapter 17

Income over £150,000

Once your income for 2022/23 rises above £150,000, you become an 'additional rate' taxpayer. Most people are familiar with the 45% tax rate that applies to most types of income above this threshold.

However, if you are a company owner it's likely it will be your dividends that take you over the £150,000 threshold (dividends are always treated as the top slice of income: see Chapter 18).

Once your dividend income rises above £150,000, the income tax rate rises from 33.75% to 39.35%.

In future years, the additional rate tax threshold will be reduced to £125,140, aligning it with the point at which an individual's personal allowance is completely withdrawn. It will then be dividend income over this level which is taxed at the rate of 39.35%.

Hence, as far as this guide is concerned, when looking at planning focussed purely on the current, 2022/23 tax year, the additional rate tax threshold we need to use is £150,000, but when looking at future years it is £125,140.

Don't Forget the Corporation Tax Bill

Although 39.35% is lower than the 45% rate most people associate with high income levels, we mustn't forget that dividends are paid out of profits that have already been taxed.

For example, a company paying 25% tax after the corporation tax rate increase is in full force will pay £250 tax on every £1,000 of profit. That leaves £750 to distribute as a dividend. If the director/shareholder then pays 39.35% income tax on the £750 distribution, the additional tax comes to £295. The total tax paid by the director and the company is £545 which is 54.5%!

Will the Additional Rate Ever Be Abolished?

Hopes that the additional rate might be abolished were briefly given credence when former Chancellor Kwasi Kwarteng announced that very proposal in his now infamous September 2022 'Mini Budget'. However, the backlash was so great the proposal was scrapped within days. We now doubt the political will to abolish the additional rate will exist again for quite some time. In short, we think the additional rate is here to stay for the foreseeable future.

In Scotland the top rate is 46% and we think it might be increased further in the future. It also seems likely that the threshold at which it starts to be charged (currently £150,000) will be reduced in future, in line with the position in the rest of the UK.

However, the key thing to remember is that the Scottish Parliament can NOT tax dividend income, so most Scottish company owners will not be affected by any changes to Scotland's top rate of tax.

Avoiding the 39.35% Tax Rate

The simplest way to avoid paying 39.35% tax on your dividends in 2022/23 is to keep your taxable income below £150,000 (e.g. by extracting higher than normal profits over more than one tax year).

In principle, this is fairly simple for company owners to do because, unlike most other taxpayers, they can control their personal incomes to a large extent. However, following this simple strategy will now be much more difficult as it will be necessary to keep income below £125,140 in future years. And, as we saw in Chapter 16, if you're going to keep it below £125,140, it makes sense to keep it below £100,000: at least in most years, anyway.

But owners of more profitable companies (who don't want to roll up profits inside the company indefinitely) should remember that going over the additional-rate threshold is not as painful as going over other key thresholds.

When your income rises above £50,270 the dividend tax rate goes from 8.75% to 33.75% and you start paying an extra £250 tax on every additional £1,000 of dividend income you receive. When your income rises above £100,000, you start to lose your personal allowance and you may end up paying up to £225 extra on every additional £1,000 of dividend income.

But when your income rises above £150,000 in 2022/23, the dividend tax rate goes from 33.75% to 39.35% and you pay just £56 more tax on every additional £1,000 of dividend income.

That's a relatively small price to pay. But, from next year onwards, when the additional rate threshold is just £125,140, allowing your income to go over that threshold will mean you could pay up to £169 **LESS** on every additional £1,000 of dividend income.

In short, compared with the other key income tax thresholds, the additional rate tax threshold is really nothing to fear.

When Paying 39.35% Is a Good Idea

In many cases, it is better to pay the 39.35% tax rate during one tax year in order to protect your income tax personal allowance during another tax year. This is because losing your income tax personal allowance is generally more costly than paying the additional rate.

Example
Sam owns a successful chain of gyms. In 2022/23, he decides to take a salary of £11,908 and a dividend of £138,092. His total taxable income is £150,000, so he avoids paying the 39.35% additional rate of tax this year. He has been withdrawing £150,000 for several years now.

With this much income he does, however, lose all of his income tax personal allowance every year. His total income tax bill for 2022/23 will be £42,365.

In 2023/24, Sam takes a salary of £12,570 and a dividend of £137,430, giving him an income tax bill of £43,919. Hence, over two years, his total tax bill will be £86,284.

Sam could instead consider withdrawing £200,000 in 2022/23 and £100,000 in 2023/24: the same total income but split differently. If he does this, his income tax bills will be £62,040 and £19,995 respectively: a total tax bill of £82,035.

Sam saves £4,249 by following this strategy. In 2022/23 he has to pay income tax of 39.35% on an extra £50,000 of dividend income: £19,675. However, in 2023/24 his taxable income falls by £50,000 to £100,000 so his income tax personal allowance is fully retained. He would have paid 56.25% tax on the first £25,140 of that income (see Chapter 16) and 39.35% on the final £24,860: a total of £23,924. The difference is £4,249 (£23,924 - £19,675).

Sam could repeat this strategy, withdrawing income of £100,000 every second year in order to protect his personal allowance. The bi-annual saving of £4,249 amounts to around 4% of Sam's annual after tax income, so it's well worthwhile and shows how company owners can use 'roller-coaster income' (see Chapter 7) to lower their tax bills.

If both Sam and the company meet the necessary conditions, even more might be saved by varying income over a longer cycle. For example, if Sam withdraws income of £250,000 in tax year 1, and £100,000 in each of tax years 2 and 3, he would save £8,498 over the three years compared with taking income of £150,000 in each year (assuming the expected income tax rates for 2023/24 continue to apply).

The savings produced by the roller-coaster strategy have been increased by the Government's decision to reduce the additional rate tax threshold to £125,140 next year. Before the increase, taking income of only £100,000 in one year and £200,000 in the next meant sacrificing £24,860 of dividends taxed at 33.75% for additional dividends taxed at 39.35%. It was worth it to save the director's personal allowance, but the overall saving was less than £2,800.

From next year, there will be no such sacrifice and each year's personal allowance that can be saved at the cost of additional dividends taxed at 39.35% will produce an overall net saving of up to £4,249 (at 2023/24 rates).

Note that the saving produced by the roller-coaster strategy will be a little different if the director would otherwise have taken a lower salary when they knew they were going to lose their personal allowance. Trying to analyse that would lead us into some rather tortuous, circular arguments, so it's not really worth going into in detail but, suffice to say, even at a salary of £9,100, the saving generated by each personal allowance preserved is still at least £3,858: however you choose to look at it.

Salary versus Dividends

In Chapter 8 we saw that, if the company does not have spare national insurance employment allowance, the 'optimal' salary for many company directors this year is £11,908. Company owners who are additional-rate taxpayers may be able to save themselves a couple of hundred pounds by paying themselves a salary of £9,100 instead.

If the company does have spare national insurance employment allowance, and the director is an additional-rate taxpayer, the optimal salary in most cases is £11,908. However, the additional tax saving is minuscule in most cases (less than £10!).

In both cases the tax savings are extremely modest for someone with this much income and it doesn't make much difference whether the director takes a salary of £9,100, £11,908 or £12,570.

In fact, the director won't be much worse off if they pay themselves no salary at all. However, there are other reasons why taking a salary is desirable. For example, a salary of at least £6,396 this year is essential to preserve your state pension entitlement.

Larger Salaries

Some company owners may desire the convenience of a larger salary, even if this is not strictly speaking 'optimal'. That's up to them, but it's worth understanding the additional tax cost arising. In many cases, it may be more than they realise.

For example, if the owner of a company making profits of £250,000 takes a salary of £30,000 instead of £9,100 and extracts the company's remaining profits as dividends, he or she will be worse off by around three to four thousand pounds (the precise tax cost depends on the company's corporation tax rate this year).

If the owner of a company with profits of £500,000 takes a salary of £50,000 instead of £9,100 he or she will be worse off by around five to six thousand pounds.

Although these extra tax costs may seem relatively small in *percentage* terms (compared with the company's profits), they still represent a significant additional burden. And it's worth bearing in mind that to make up for each thousand pounds of extra tax suffered, these additional rate taxpayers will need to make more than **two thousand pounds** of extra pre-tax profit in their company. So, what's easier, changing the level of salary you take so you can pay £6,000 less tax, or finding a way to make an extra £12,000 profit?

Interestingly, despite all of the above, **very** large salaries may become preferable to dividends in some cases next year (2023/24): but that's for our next edition.

Using a Company versus Self-Employment

Most company owners probably realise that if they take all of their income as salary they could end up paying significantly more tax than a self-employed person (sole trader or partner) with the same income. This is because of the additional employer's national insurance payable on most salary income.

It's interesting to note that, even if a company owner structures their pay in the most tax efficient manner, taking most or all of their income as dividends, they could still end up paying significantly more tax than a self-employed person. This situation will typically arise when the company owner withdraws most or all of the company's profits and is a high income earner.

Table 6 compares the total after-tax income of a company owner with that of a self-employed business owner at different profit levels in future tax years. In each case the business owners have at least £150,000 of pre-tax income and are additional-rate taxpayers (remember, the additional rate tax threshold will be reduced to £125,140 from 2023/24 onwards).

For the company owner, it is assumed that a salary of £9,100 is taken and all of the remaining after-tax profits are extracted as dividends. (This is not necessarily the 'optimal' salary but note that a salary of at least £6,396 is necessary at present to protect state pension entitlement.)

The 'Extra Income' column is the additional income enjoyed by the *self-employed* person. For example, when profits are £500,000 a self-employed person will enjoy £31,960 more after-tax income than a company owner.

TABLE 6
After-tax Income Compared
Company Owner vs Self Employed

Profits	Company Owner	Self-Employed	Extra Income
£150,000	£87,532	£90,730	£3,198
£200,000	£108,345	£117,230	£8,885
£250,000	£130,634	£143,730	£13,096
£300,000	£153,295	£170,230	£16,935
£400,000	£198,783	£223,230	£24,447
£500,000	£244,270	£276,230	£31,960
£600,000	£289,758	£329,230	£39,472
£700,000	£335,245	£382,230	£46,985
£800,000	£380,733	£435,230	£54,497
£900,000	£426,220	£488,230	£62,010
£1,000,000	£471,708	£541,230	£69,522

Notes:
1. Company owner withdraws all the profits of the business
2. Company owner takes £9,100 salary and remaining income as dividends
3. Company owner tax = corporation tax (at the new rates) + income tax
4. Self-employed tax includes income tax and national insurance
5. NI primary threshold = £12,570
6. Self-employed tax bills are higher in Scotland
7. For the purposes of this table, we have used a dividend allowance of £500: the amount applying from 2024/25 onwards.

This doesn't necessarily mean that owners of companies with significant profits would be better off self-employed. If profits are kept inside the company to help it grow, the only tax payable will be corporation tax. Clearly paying just corporation tax (25% in future) is a lot better than the 47% tax that will be paid by self-employed people who are additional-rate taxpayers from 2023/24 onwards (48% in Scotland).

It is in these circumstances – when profits are reinvested – that companies are most powerful as tax shelters. For example, where a company has profits of £500,000 and only half the after-tax profits are paid out as dividends, the total tax bill will be around £40,000 less than the tax paid by a self-employed person.

Impact of the Threshold Reduction

The reduction in the additional rate tax threshold from £150,000 to £125,140 from 2023/24 onwards will affect company owners and the self-employed alike. Company owners with small salaries plus enough dividend income to take their total income over £150,000 will be £1,392 worse off as a result of this change.

Most company owners will also see modest tax increases of £88 in 2023/24 and £131 each year thereafter as a result of the reductions in the dividend allowance.

The self-employed are also suffering, but not quite as much. Those with profits of £150,000 or more will pay an extra £1,243 in income tax due to the reduction in the additional rate tax threshold. Most self-employed INDIs also face an extra £16 in class 2 national insurance next year.

Taken together, these changes mean the amount of extra income enjoyed by self-employed taxpayers compared with company owners who take a small salary and extract all their company's remaining after tax profits as dividends will increase by £264. (Note, this increase is already reflected in the table above.)

None of these changes are significant for business owners with this level of income, but it's worth noting that the gap is continuing to widen further.

What remains more important, however, is the point discussed above: companies can produce sizeable tax savings when a significant proportion of the profits are reinvested within the company each year.

Alternative Profit Extraction Strategies

Company owners faced with paying additional rate tax on their dividend income may wish to consider alternative profit extraction strategies, including:

- Gifting shares in the business to family members, including family members who are higher-rate taxpayers (see Part 5).
- Making personal or company pension contributions (see Chapters 27 and 28).

- Keeping cash inside the company until the business is sold or wound up (see Chapter 30). At this point it may be possible to pay just 10% capital gains tax on the extracted funds.

Pension Contributions

Company owners who pay themselves small salaries can only make small pension contributions *personally* – your pension contributions cannot exceed your earnings (dividends don't count as earnings).

For example, if you pay yourself a salary of £9,100 in 2022/23 you can only make a pension contribution of £9,100 personally (£7,280 contributed by you, with a further £1,820 added to your pension by the taxman).

Company owners who wish to make bigger pension contributions can either pay themselves higher salaries or get their companies to make the contributions on their behalf.

A higher salary usually comes with a punitive national insurance bill, so company pension contributions are often the preferred route.

Company pension contributions enjoy corporation tax relief, providing they are not excessive (see Chapter 28).

The Pension Taper

High income earners face another restriction. The annual allowance – the maximum amount that can be invested in a pension each year – can be reduced from £40,000 to just £4,000.

Fortunately, following changes made in 2020, this pension taper now only kicks in at much higher income levels than previously. As a result, many high earning company owners can benefit from much higher pension contributions than before.

The first thing you have to calculate is your 'threshold income'. If your threshold income is £200,000 or less you are completely exempt from tapering and can make pension contributions just like anyone else.

Your threshold income is, broadly speaking, your total taxable income. This includes your salary, dividends, rental profits, interest income and any other taxable income you receive.

From this you deduct any pension contributions you have made *personally* (you deduct the gross contributions).

You can also deduct other reliefs listed in Section 24 of the Income Tax Act 2007. These include things like trade loss relief.

Employer pension contributions are ignored when calculating threshold income. But you must add back any salary sacrificed in exchange for employer pension contributions.

The threshold used to be £110,000 but was increased to £200,000 with effect from 6th April 2020.

Example 1
Dirk takes a salary of £9,100 and a dividend of £190,900 out of his company. He has no other income so his total taxable income is £200,000. His company makes a pension contribution on his behalf but we ignore that when calculating his threshold income. He doesn't make any pension contributions personally so his threshold income is exactly £200,000. Dirk is unaffected by the tapered annual allowance. This means his annual allowance for the current tax year is £40,000.

Example 2
Beric is a company owner who pays himself salary and dividend income totalling £200,000. He also has taxable rental profits of £40,000, so his total taxable income is £240,000.

His company makes a pension contribution of £35,000 on his behalf but we ignore this when calculating his threshold income. He doesn't make any pension contributions personally.

Beric's threshold income is therefore £240,000. Because this exceeds £200,000, he is potentially affected by the tapered annual allowance.

If your threshold income exceeds £200,000 the next thing you have to calculate is your 'adjusted income'.

Broadly speaking, your adjusted income is your total taxable income *plus* any pension contributions made by your company (your employer).

You also add back any contributions to an occupational pension scheme under a net pay arrangement (where your contributions are deducted from your salary before calculating PAYE).

You can also deduct the reliefs listed in Section 24 of the Income Tax Act 2007.

Your £40,000 pension annual allowance will only be reduced if your adjusted income exceeds £240,000 (previously £150,000).

Your annual allowance is reduced by £1 for every £2 your adjusted income exceeds £240,000. For example, an individual with adjusted income of £270,000 will have their annual allowance reduced by £15,000 (£30,000/2), giving them an annual allowance of £25,000.

The annual allowance cannot fall below £4,000 – this is the minimum contribution that those affected by the taper can make.

Pension contributions that exceed the tapered annual allowance face the annual allowance charge. The excess contributions will be added to your income and taxed. If the charge exceeds £2,000 it may be possible to have it paid out of your pension savings. This may only be possible if total contributions to the scheme in question exceed the £40,000 annual allowance.

Example 2 continued
As we saw earlier, Beric has total taxable income of £240,000 and his company makes a contribution of £35,000 on his behalf.

Beric's adjusted income is £275,000 (£240,000 + £35,000)

His annual allowance is cut by (£275,000 - £240,000)/2 = £17,500

His annual allowance is therefore £40,000 - £17,500 = £22,500

He faces an annual allowance charge on £35,000 - £22,500 = £12,500

Calculating the Tapered Annual Allowance in Practice

Beric can avoid the charge by getting his company to make a smaller pension contribution (no more than £26,667). Alternatively, he may be able to extract less income from his company (no more than £175,000) to ensure his total taxable income reduces to £215,000 and he is able to benefit from a tapered annual allowance of £35,000. Company owners may find it easier than others to control their taxable income to reduce their threshold income and adjusted income. However, if they do this they may have to be wary of triggering a special tax anti-avoidance rule (see below).

Company owners will find it fairly easy to calculate their adjusted and threshold income when it comes to salaries and dividends. Problems may arise when the company owner has other income that is less predictable, for example rental income from properties. Company owners who are also landlords may not know precisely how much taxable income they have earned (and thus their tapered annual allowance) until *after* the tax year has ended. By then it will be too late to make pension contributions.

Those who wish to benefit from pension contributions and think they may be affected by the tapered annual allowance may need to estimate their taxable income just *before* the end of the tax year.

The Tapered Annual Allowance and Carry Forward

All is not lost if your pension contributions exceed your tapered annual allowance for the year. Those affected by the tapered annual allowance can still carry forward any unused annual allowance from the three previous tax years. For example, if your annual allowance this year is reduced from £40,000 to £30,000 and you make a £20,000 pension contribution, you will have £10,000 left to carry forward to next year (£30,000 - £20,000).

Carry forward could act as a lifeline for those whose pension contributions accidentally exceed the tapered annual allowance in any given year. Beric in the above example will avoid the annual allowance charge if he has at least £12,500 of unused annual allowance from the three previous tax years.

Example
Mario is a company owner with taxable income of £200,000. He gets his company to make a £60,000 pension contribution (utilising £20,000 of unused annual allowance carried forward from previous years).

His adjusted income is £260,000 but his threshold income is £200,000, so his annual allowance for the current year is not reduced.

If your threshold income does not exceed £200,000 you cannot be subject to the tapered annual allowance, even if your adjusted income is greater than £240,000.

Anti-Avoidance Rule

There is an anti-avoidance rule to prevent anyone entering into an arrangement which involves reducing their adjusted or threshold income and increasing their income in a different tax year.

The anti-avoidance provisions apply when it is reasonable to assume that the main purpose, or one of the main purposes of the arrangement, is to reduce the impact of the tapered annual allowance. If the anti-avoidance provisions apply, then the relevant arrangement will be ignored for the purposes of calculating the tapered annual allowance.

It is unclear how this anti-avoidance rule could be applied to company owners who vary their income from year to year.

Enjoying 51% Tax Relief

Thanks to the changes made in 2020, many additional rate taxpayers are unaffected by the tapered annual allowance and can once again make fairly big pension contributions with full tax relief.

Any company owner with taxable income of no more than £200,000 can get their company to make a pension contribution of up to £40,000 every year with full tax relief. Other high earning company owners can make the following maximum pension contributions:

Taxable Income	Maximum Contribution*
£215,000	£35,000
£230,000	£30,000
£245,000	£25,000
£260,000	£20,000
£275,000	£15,000
£290,000	£10,000
£305,000	£5,000
£308,000+	£4,000

* Ignores potential carry forward from previous tax years

Additional-rate taxpayers currently face a combined marginal tax rate of at least 51% on their dividend income (corporation tax and income tax). So a company owner with £1,000 of pre-tax profit will be left with at most £490 after tax.

By contrast, with a pension contribution the whole £1,000 can be paid into the director's pension fund. Income tax will be payable when they eventually take the money out but the effective tax rate could be between 15% and 30%, leaving them with between £700 and £850 after tax. (See Chapter 27 for an explanation of how these tax rates are calculated.)

Thus the director can choose between £490 today and £700 to £850 in the future. It's easy to see why pensions are such powerful tax shelters!

Part 4

Company Owners with Income from Other Sources

Chapter 18

Keeping Income Below the Key Thresholds

Introduction

In Chapter 7 we explained why company owners, when deciding how much income to withdraw from their companies, need to be aware of the following income tax thresholds and brackets:

- Over £50,270   Higher rate tax
- £50,000-£60,000   Child benefit tax charge
- £100,000-£125,140   Personal allowance withdrawal
- Over £150,000*   Additional rate of tax

* £125,140 from 2023/24 onwards

Basic-rate taxpayers generally pay no more than 8.75% income tax on their dividends. Once your income exceeds £50,270 you become a higher-rate taxpayer and start paying 33.75% tax. However, dividend income that falls into the final three tax brackets is taxed at much higher rates:

- £50,270-£60,000   45% to 68%, or even more
- £100,000-£125,140   56% in some cases
- Over £150,000   39.35%

(Note: the £50,270-£60,000 bracket only applies to households in receipt of child benefit. The child benefit charge actually kicks in at £50,000, where basic-rate tax is still payable. For example, dividend income in the tiny £50,000-£50,270 bracket is taxed at 27.6% if you have two children. What unnecessary complication!)

When trying to avoid these extortionate tax rates, you must remember to include any other taxable income you receive. If you have taxable income from other sources it may force your company income, in particular your dividend income, into a higher tax bracket. To avoid a potential tax sting you may wish to reduce the amount of income you withdraw from your company or take other steps to reduce your tax bill.

The Order in which Income is Taxed

Income is taxed in the following order:

- Non-savings income:
  - Employment income
  - Self-employment income
  - Rental income
  - Pension income
- Savings income
- Dividend income

Pension income includes the UK state pension. Some readers may find it odd that pension income is not classed as savings income but, for income tax purposes, pension income is taxed at normal, 'non-savings' rates (subject to the exemption for the 25% tax-free lump sum). See Chapter 27 for further details.

More importantly for the purposes of this guide though, dividends are always treated as the top slice of income.

Let's say you expect to earn £10,000 of rental income during the current tax year but, so far, have not withdrawn any income from your company. As things stand, all of your rental income will be tax free, being covered by your income tax personal allowance.

Let's say you now decide to withdraw a salary of £12,570 and a dividend of £37,700 from your company (the maximum amount you can withdraw tax free or taxed at just 8.75%, in the absence of any other income). The decision to take a salary means you now have £22,570 of non-savings income and your income tax bill will increase by £2,000:

£22,570 - £12,570 personal allowance = £10,000 x 20% = £2,000

And what about your dividends which are supposedly taxed at no more than 8.75%?

Thanks to your rental income, £10,000 of your dividend income will now be pushed into the higher-rate tax bracket and taxed at 33.75% instead of 8.75%, resulting in additional tax of £2,500.

In summary, having £10,000 of rental income increases the company owner's tax bill by £4,500!

Income from Other Sources

With the exception of self-employment and pension income, it may be possible to extract all the other types of income listed above from *your own company*: employment income, rental income, interest income, and dividend income.

We've already talked extensively about salaries (employment income) and dividends. If your company uses a property that you own personally (for example, an office or shop) it can also pay you rent; and if your company borrows money from you it can pay you interest.

In Chapters 24 and 25 we take a look at whether it is tax efficient to get your company to pay you rent or interest and how much.

In this part of the guide the focus is on company owners who have income from *other sources*: i.e. income that does not come from their own company. More specifically, the focus is on company owners who have income from other sources that is subject to *income tax*.

Some income (e.g. most interest income and stock market dividends) can be sheltered from income tax inside an ISA or pension scheme.

It is also possible to shelter assets from income tax inside another company. Many property investors do this. Corporation tax is still payable on any rental profits produced by the properties but the income tax position of the company owner will be unaffected, unless those profits are extracted.

Those company owners who do have a significant amount of taxable income from other sources, and cannot shelter it from income tax, may wish to reduce the amount of income they withdraw from their own companies, so as to avoid paying income tax at some of the extortionate rates listed at the beginning of this chapter.

Other Income – Control

One of the benefits of being a company owner is you can control how much income you withdraw from your business. This allows you to control your income tax bill from year to year.

Income from other sources is often less easy to control. For example, it may not be possible to shift it from one tax year into another tax year. You may be able to control the dividends declared by your own company but if you own a few shares in BP you can't force their directors to increase or lower the company's dividend!

Company owners who want to keep their taxable income just below any of the key income tax thresholds may therefore have to increase or decrease their *company income* – it may not always be possible to alter the amount of income you receive from other sources.

Table 7 shows the maximum dividend you can withdraw during 2022/23 if you have other taxable income (including your company salary) and want to avoid some of the key income tax thresholds.

For example, if you have other taxable income of £20,000 a dividend of no more than £30,270 will prevent your income going over £50,270 which means you will avoid paying 33.75% tax.

A dividend no higher than £30,000 will ensure that you avoid the child benefit tax charge, where relevant.

A dividend of up to £80,000 will ensure that your income does not exceed £100,000. A significant amount of your dividend income will be taxed at 33.75% and you may end up paying the maximum child benefit tax charge but you will not lose any of your personal allowance.

Note, Table 7 is equally relevant to Scottish taxpayers because it is the *UK* thresholds that apply to your dividend income.

For example, a Scottish taxpayer with £40,000 of salary and rental income can still receive a dividend of £10,270 without paying 33.75% tax because it is the UK higher-rate threshold that applies to dividend income.

TABLE 7
Avoiding the Tax Thresholds
Maximum Dividend 2022/23

Other Income		Threshold		
	£50,000	£50,270	£100,000	£150,000
£9,100	£40,900	£41,170	£90,900	£140,900
£11,908	£38,092	£38,362	£88,092	£138,092
£12,570	£37,430	£37,700	£87,430	£137,430
£15,000	£35,000	£35,270	£85,000	£135,000
£20,000	£30,000	£30,270	£80,000	£130,000
£25,000	£25,000	£25,270	£75,000	£125,000
£30,000	£20,000	£20,270	£70,000	£120,000
£35,000	£15,000	£15,270	£65,000	£115,000
£40,000	£10,000	£10,270	£60,000	£110,000

Remember, no matter how much other income you have, you can always receive at least £2,000 of tax-free dividend income in 2022/23 thanks to the dividend allowance.

For example, someone with other income of £50,000 can still receive a tax-free dividend of £2,000 without having to worry about paying 33.75% tax. However, do not forget that the dividend allowance is used up by all the dividend income you receive, not just dividends from your own company. Hence, if that other income from outside your company includes £400 of dividends, you can only take a tax-free dividend of £1,600 from your company this year.

Furthermore, in some cases, taking supposedly 'tax-free' dividend income will have other negative tax consequences.

For example, someone with other income of £50,000 who receives a £2,000 tax-free dividend will end up with total income of £52,000, which means they could end up losing some of their child benefit.

Someone with other income of £100,000 can also receive £2,000 of tax-free dividend income. However, this will bring their total income to £102,000, which means they will lose some of their personal allowance.

Other Income – Predictability

At the start of a new tax year you may not know with complete certainty how much taxable income you will receive from other sources during the year. This could be problematic if you wish to withdraw dividends from your company *at the beginning of the tax year*.

If you withdraw dividends from your company and your other income then turns out to be higher than anticipated, you may end up paying more income tax than you expected on your company dividends.

Some types of income are, however, more predictable than others. For example, interest income, stock market dividends and pension income are arguably more predictable than, say, the profits of a sole trader business (self-employment income).

Some types of income, if not completely predictable, are more likely to end up being *less than expected*, rather than higher than expected. For example, a rental property that normally generates rental income of £1,000 per month may lie empty for three months, thereby producing an annual income of £9,000 rather than £12,000.

If your income from other sources turns out to be less than expected, you may be able to get your company to pay you additional dividend income before the end of the tax year.

If your income from other sources turns out to be *higher than expected* you generally cannot reverse any dividends you have already taken out of your company, although it may be possible to do some emergency year-end tax planning (see Chapter 20).

Company owners who have unpredictable income from other sources may therefore wish to postpone paying dividends until closer to the end of the tax year, if they are concerned that their dividend income may fall into a heavily taxed bracket.

Chapter 19

Should I Pay Myself a Smaller Salary?

So far we have shown that if you have income from other sources (e.g. rental income) you may wish to reduce your company *dividends* to avoid various tax thresholds.

Another important question is, "Should I pay myself a smaller salary?"

If you intend to pay yourself one of the small salaries discussed in Chapter 8 (typically £11,908 or £12,570) and extract the rest of the company's profits as dividends, it may be possible to save a small amount of tax by reducing your company salary in some circumstances.

For example, in Chapter 8 it was shown that, where a company does have spare national insurance employment allowance, the optimal salary for some company owners is £12,570.

However, where the company owner has taxable income from other sources that uses up their personal allowance, it may be possible to achieve a small tax saving (less than a hundred pounds in most cases) by taking a salary equal to the £11,908 national insurance primary threshold instead.

Although the director's salary will be subject to income tax, there will be no national insurance payable by either the director personally or by the company.

In Chapter 8 it was also shown that, where a company has other employees and does not have any spare employment allowance, the optimal salary for many company owners is £11,908.

Where the company owner has taxable income from other sources a small tax saving of up to around a couple of hundred pounds can be obtained by taking a salary of £9,100 (the employer's national insurance threshold) instead of £11,908.

Again, although the director's salary will be subject to income tax, there will be no national insurance payable by either the director personally or by the company.

It generally doesn't pay to reduce your salary any further.

The reason why it's generally tax efficient to pay yourself a smaller salary is because, if you have other income that uses up your personal allowance, any salary you receive will effectively be subject to income tax. If there is also any national insurance payable, the total tax rate (income tax and national insurance) will often exceed the combined tax rate on dividend income (corporation tax and income tax).

So once you've exhausted your national insurance free salary, dividends are generally better.

Having said all this, there are reasons why you may not wish to reduce your salary or why it may not be practical to reduce your salary:

- To make bigger pension contributions personally (see Chapter 28).
- Because your income from other sources may not be known at the beginning of the year, when you may wish to start making monthly salary payments.
- Because the taxman may question any reduction in your salary (see Chapter 36).

Finally, remember it may be important to pay yourself a salary above the lower earnings limit (£6,396 in 2022/23) to protect your state pension entitlement (see Chapter 10): unless, of course, your other income already includes sufficient qualifying earnings from a different source (over £6,396 from a different employment, or over £6,725 in profits from self-employment or furnished holiday letting).

Chapter 20

The Different Types of Income

Let's take a closer look at the different types of income you may earn from sources outside your company and how they may affect the income you decide to withdraw from your company:

Employment Income

It is possible to have more than one source of employment income, for example:

- Salary from a second job with a separate employer, or
- Salary from a second company you own

If you have recently started out in business, it's possible you will have a second job (possibly a part-time job) to help pay the bills.

If you start a second company for a separate business venture there is, of course, nothing to stop you paying yourself a second salary.

For income tax purposes you are only entitled to one personal allowance (£12,570 at present). This generally means that you can only have one tax-free salary (unless, of course, the two salaries, when added together, total less than £12,570). Some or all of the second salary may be taxed at 20%.

National insurance is calculated differently. Directors who have more than one salary of £11,908 this year may not have to pay national insurance contributions personally. This is because the earnings from each job may be treated separately.

If the two businesses are 'in association' however, the salaries will be added together and national insurance may be payable. Employers are considered to be in association if:

- The businesses serve a common purpose, and
- There is significant sharing of things like premises, personnel, equipment or customers

Following the increase in dividend tax rates, a second salary may be more tax efficient than a dividend, providing there is no national insurance payable.

If you wish to pay yourself two salaries it may be necessary to obtain professional advice to satisfy yourself that the companies will not be treated by HMRC as being in association, with resulting national insurance liabilities.

Finally, there may be other tax and non-tax reasons why you wish to pay yourself a second salary or a bigger second salary.

Salary from Other Job Exceeds £50,270

Where a company owner earns a salary of more than £50,270 (the upper earnings limit) from a different employment, it may be possible to reduce the employee's national insurance rate on the salary they receive from their own company.

In other words, instead of paying 12% national insurance it may be possible to pay just 2% on all of the second salary the director receives from their own company (using next year's national insurance rates).

This is because there is a limit to the amount of salary income on which you have to pay 12% national insurance each year.

Applications can be made using form CA72A, available from HMRC's website.

Note, employer's national insurance may still be payable unless the company has spare employment allowance.

Where you are eligible to pay just 2% national insurance on the salary you take from your company (or 2.73% this year) AND there is spare employment allowance available, it will often be tax efficient to increase your company salary. In such cases, the optimal salary will often be the maximum amount covered by the available employment allowance (see Chapters 2 and 9 for further guidance).

Self-Employment Income

You may have self-employment income if you have another business that is not a company (i.e. you're a sole trader or belong to a partnership). Naturally, when we refer to self-employment income, we are actually talking about the taxable profits of your sole trader business, or your share of the taxable profits of a partnership.

Many entrepreneurs have multiple businesses and it's possible a second or third business will not be a company.

Companies can be wonderful tax shelters but unincorporated businesses have advantages of their own, including lower accountancy fees, more generous treatment of certain expenses, and more generous capital allowances for cars used in the business.

Self-employment income may be difficult to predict – especially close to the beginning of a new tax year – making it difficult to decide how much income to withdraw from the other company business.

Fortunately, as far as your self-employment business is concerned, it may be possible to do some emergency year-end tax planning to reduce your tax bill (for example, by making pension contributions or incurring other tax deductible expenditure).

Rental Income

When we use the term 'rental income' what we mean is taxable rental *profit*. You may receive rents of £10,000 per year but your taxable rental profit may only be £5,000, after deducting all the expenses property investors can claim.

Unlike interest income and stock market dividends, most rental income cannot be sheltered from income tax in an ISA, pension scheme or other tax shelter.

There are, however a couple of exceptions:

- Commercial property held in a pension scheme
- Residential or commercial property held in a company

Some business owners place their business premises inside a self-invested personal pension (SIPP) to avoid income tax and capital gains tax (see Chapter 29).

Others put their properties in a separate company. Corporation tax is payable on the rental income and capital gains but the company owner's own income tax bill will be unaffected, unless the property company's profits are extracted.

Apart from these two exceptions, most landlords own their properties *personally*, which means they are fully exposed to income tax on their rental profits. These rental profits may then need to be factored into the mix when deciding how much income you withdraw from your other business which is held inside a company.

For example, in 2022/23 if you take a salary of £11,908 and expect to have taxable rental profits of £20,000 you can take tax-free dividend income of £2,000 plus additional dividend income of £16,362 taxed at 8.75%. This takes you up to the £50,270 higher-rate threshold. Any additional dividend income you receive will be taxed at a rate of at least 33.75%.

If you take a salary of £11,908 and expect to have taxable rental profits of £50,000 you can still take tax-free dividend income of £2,000 this year (because everyone can benefit from the dividend allowance). However, you will pay at least 33.75% tax on any additional dividend income.

Mortgage Tax Relief Restrictions

Landlords who own residential property no longer enjoy full tax relief on their mortgage interest and other finance costs. Instead what they receive is a 'tax reduction' equal to the 20% basic rate of income tax.

These rules do not apply to commercial properties or furnished holiday lettings or to properties held inside companies.

The reduced tax relief on mortgage interest means many landlords have bigger taxable rental profits.

This in turn has pushed more of the dividend income they receive from their other company business over the higher-rate threshold where it is taxed at 33.75% instead of 8.75%.

Many company owners who are also landlords have seen their tax bills increase by an amount equivalent to 25% of their mortgage interest (compared with the position if their interest was fully deductible).

For example, a company owner with £20,000 of buy-to-let interest could be paying £5,000 more tax than before this tax change.

Tax Planning for Landlords

If you are a company owner and separately own mortgaged rental properties personally you will have to be careful about the amount of dividend income you pay yourself if you want to avoid going over the various tax thresholds.

Example
Jessie owns a small engineering company and some rental property. Because she earns rental income she decides to pay herself a salary of £9,100 in 2022/23 (Chapter 19 explains why this may be the optimal salary for someone with income from other sources).

Her rental property produces income of £20,000 net of all expenses except mortgage interest. Her mortgage interest is £7,500 so her true rental profit is £12,500.

However, her taxable rental profit is £20,000 and it is this number she must use when deciding how much dividend income to take.

With a salary of £9,100 and taxable rental profit of £20,000 Jessie can pay herself a dividend of up to £21,170 before she becomes a higher-rate taxpayer and has to pay 33.75% tax (£50,270 - £9,100 - £20,000).

Example
Cillian owns a software company and a portfolio of rental properties. Because he earns rental income he decides to pay himself a salary of £9,100 in 2022/23.

His rental property produces income of £50,000 (net of all expenses except interest). His mortgage interest is £15,000 so his true rental profit is £35,000. However, his taxable rental profit is £50,000.

With a salary of £9,100 and taxable rental profit of £50,000, Cillian is a higher-rate taxpayer and will pay 33.75% tax on his dividend income (except the first £2,000 which is always tax free this year).

Cillian can pay himself a dividend of up to £40,900 before he reaches the £100,000 tax threshold where his personal allowance will be gradually withdrawn. He will then pay tax at an effective rate of 53.75% on the next £25,140 of dividend income he receives (see Chapter 16 for an explanation of how the withdrawal of the personal allowance works).

For the rest of this guide, when we refer to 'rental income' received by an individual, unless expressly stated to the contrary, this means their taxable rental profits, after deducting all allowable expenses EXCEPT interest and finance costs relating to residential rental property.

In the case of non-residential property or qualifying furnished holiday lettings, 'rental income' simply means rental profits.

Rental losses

If you have rental losses brought forward from previous years you may not have to pay any income tax on the rental profit you make during the current tax year (providing the loss brought forward is big enough to completely offset the current year's profit).

If the rental profit you make during the current tax year is not taxable it does not need to be factored into the mix when deciding how much income you withdraw from your company.

However, because of the restrictions on relief for interest and finance costs discussed above, most residential landlords with rental losses brought forward have seen these effectively eroded away over the last few years and turned into what is officially termed 'unused residential property finance costs', better known as 'unrelieved interest'.

Where you have unrelieved interest brought forward rather than old-style rental losses, it will attract tax relief at the 20% basic rate, the same as your current interest costs, but it will not reduce your taxable rental profit, which will therefore still have to be factored into your decision-making when considering how much income to withdraw from your company.

Pension Income

If you have any pension income, this will usually need to be taken into account when deciding how much income to withdraw from your company. Most pension income is taxable, including:

- Your UK state pension, where applicable
- Occupational pensions
- Private pensions
- Income withdrawn under a drawdown arrangement
- Foreign pensions (subject to the terms of any applicable Double Tax Treaty)

However, there is one key exemption to be aware of, namely the 25% tax-free lump sum available from most private pension schemes.

Optimal Salaries for Pension Recipients (No Spare Employment Allowance)

Where there is no spare employment allowance, the optimal salary level for a company owner in receipt of £3,470 or more of pension income is generally £9,100 this year, regardless of whether or not they are over state pension age.

For smaller amounts of pension income, the optimal salary level depends on whether the director is over state pension age and what other sources of income they have. For those over state pension age, it will generally be the greater of:

a)   £9,100, or
b)   £12,570 LESS their total non-savings income for the year (remember, pension income is classed as non-savings income)

For those under state pension age, it will be the lower of £11,908 or the amount derived as above: i.e. the greater of (a) or (b).

Optimal Salaries for Pension Recipients (Spare Employment Allowance)

For those under state pension age, the optimal salary where there is spare employment allowance available will generally be the greater of:

a) £11,908, or
b) £12,570 LESS their total non-savings income for the year (remember, pension income is classed as non-savings income)

So, usually £11,908 in a nutshell, unless you have a really tiny pension!

Directors over state pension age in this situation will benefit from the national insurance free salaries we looked at in Chapter 9. These generally remain tax efficient where the director has other income from outside the company, although there are some exceptions where the director's total taxable income falls into the £100,000 to £125,140 bracket.

Dividends for Pension Recipients

Once a director in receipt of pension income has worked out their optimal salary, the next step is to decide how much dividend income they would like to take. As usual, any amount covered by the dividend allowance will be tax free. Beyond that, we are back into the usual tax planning territory where the director needs to keep an eye on the key income tax thresholds we've looked at previously.

Example
George and Gracie are the owner/directors, and only employees, of Like Old Times Ltd. In 2022/23, they each receive a state pension of £9,000 and each take a salary of £26,306 out of the company. They have no other income from outside the company.

If they each take dividends of £14,964 out of the company, £2,000 (each) will be tax free and the remaining £12,964 (each) will be taxed at 8.75%.

Any further dividends will be taxed at 33.75% and if they take any more than £64,694 each in total, they will start to lose their personal allowances, leading to further tax costs.

I've assumed in this example that George and Gracie each own 50% of the shares in their company.

Example

Bob is below state pension age, but enters a drawdown arrangement and takes £50,000 out of his pension scheme during 2022/23. However, only £16,000 of this is taxable as the remaining £34,000 represents his 25% tax free lump sum.

Bob also takes a salary of £9,100 out of his company, but has no other sources of income.

It's still worth Bob taking a dividend of £2,000 as this is tax free. He can also take up to a further £23,170 in dividends this year, which will only be taxed at 8.75% (£50,270 - £16,000 - £9,100 - £2,000 = £23,170).

If Bob had taken only his 25% tax free lump sum, it would have had no impact on his company income and he could then have taken an optimal salary of £11,908 plus dividends of up to £38,362 without suffering any tax at 33.75%.

Interest Income

Most personal interest income can be sheltered from tax inside an ISA or SIPP. Other tax-free investments include index-linked savings certificates (when they're available) and offset mortgages (instead of earning interest, your savings are used to reduce the interest on your mortgage). Even paying off personal debts is effectively a way to earn tax-free interest (you pay less interest on your debts and that reduction is not taxed: unless it counts as qualifying loan interest, which we will look at in Chapter 25).

Wealthier individuals, with large cash balances or holdings of corporate and government bonds may, however, have a significant amount of *taxable* interest income and there may also be times in life when less wealthy taxpayers have significant amounts of taxable interest income:

- You sell your home and have a large cash lump sum
- You lend money to a friend or family member
- You receive a big dividend and put the cash in the bank
- You lend money to your company (see Chapter 25)

This income may need to be factored into the equation when you decide how much income to withdraw from your company.

The £5,000 Starting Rate Band

When it comes to interest income, many company owners are in a fortunate position. They can receive up to £5,000 of interest *tax free* each year thanks to the 0% starting-rate band.

The starting rate is supposed to benefit those with low incomes. Hence the £5,000 starting rate band is reduced by any *non-savings* income you have in excess of the personal allowance, including:

- Employment income
- Self-employment income
- Pension income
- Rental income

Hence, if your non-savings income exceeds £17,570 in total (£12,570 + £5,000), none of your interest income will be covered by the starting rate band.

Of course, most regular salary earners and self-employed business owners will have more than £17,570 of non-savings income. Many *company owners* are in a different position, however. Note that the above list of non-savings income does NOT include dividends. Dividends are the top slice of income and do not use up the starting rate band.

Because company owners often pay themselves small salaries and take the rest of their income as dividends, they will often have little or no taxable non-savings income. As a result, many can earn at least £5,000 of tax-free interest.

Example
Mandy is a company owner with a salary of £12,570, dividend income of £32,700 and interest income of £5,000. Her salary is tax free* thanks to her personal allowance and she therefore has no taxable non-savings income that uses up her starting rate band (her dividend income does not count). Her interest income is fully covered by her £5,000 starting rate band and taxed at 0%.

* Free of income tax, to be more precise. It will generally suffer some national insurance, but that doesn't affect the starting rate band.

Many directors will thus pay 0% tax on their interest if they:

- Take a small salary from their company,
- Do not have another source of employment income,
- Do not have a sole trader or partnership business,
- Don't earn much, if any, rental income, and
- Do not receive much, if any, pension income.

It is important to point out that the 0% starting rate band is not given in addition to your basic-rate band (currently £37,700). Instead it is part of your basic-rate band.

If you qualify to use the starting rate band your basic-rate band will be reduced, possibly pushing some of your dividend income into a higher tax bracket.

The Personal Savings Allowance

The personal savings allowance (also known as the savings nil rate band) exempts the first £1,000 of your interest income from tax if you're a basic-rate taxpayer and the first £500 if you're a higher-rate taxpayer. Additional-rate taxpayers get nothing.

The personal savings allowance operates separately from, and in addition to, the starting rate band. This means some company owners can earn up to £6,000 of tax-free interest every year.

Income that falls within the savings nil rate band uses up some of the band that it falls into. For example, if you have £49,400 of salary and rental income, and £1,000 of interest income, you will have total income of £50,400.

As a higher-rate taxpayer you will therefore be entitled to a £500 personal savings allowance. Thus £500 of your interest income will be tax free and this will use up £500 of your basic-rate band, leaving £370 taxed at 20%. The final £130 will be taxed at 40%.

The personal savings allowance is helpful to company owners who cannot use the starting rate band because they have too much non-savings income such as rental income. Most can enjoy £1,000 or £500 of tax-free interest. It may also be useful for extracting interest from your own company (see Chapter 25).

Interest Income - Examples

The somewhat complex operation of the starting rate band and savings nil rate band is best explained with some examples. These examples are all based on the current, 2022/23 tax year.

Example
Samantha is a company owner with a salary of £12,570 and interest income of £5,000. She also has £10,000 of rental income.

Her salary is covered by her personal allowance but thanks to her rental income she has £10,000 of taxable non-savings income. Because her taxable non-savings income exceeds the £5,000 starting rate limit, none of her interest income is covered by the 0% starting rate.

However, because she is a basic-rate taxpayer (her total income is less than £50,270) she is entitled to a £1,000 personal savings allowance. So £1,000 of her interest income will be tax free, the remaining £4,000 will be taxed at 20%.

Example
Elaine is a company owner with a salary of £9,100, rental income of £7,500, interest income of £1,500 and dividends of £20,000 (total income £38,100).

There is no income tax on her salary and the first £3,470 of her rental income is covered by her remaining personal allowance. The final £4,030 of her rental income is taxed at 20% and uses up £4,030 of her £5,000 starting rate band. Thus £970 of her interest income is covered by her remaining starting rate band and is tax free.

As a basic-rate taxpayer she is also entitled to a £1,000 personal savings allowance, so the final £530 of her interest is also tax free.

The first £2,000 of her dividend income is covered by the dividend allowance; the remaining £18,000 is taxed at 8.75%.

Example
Ollie is a company owner with a salary of £12,570 and dividends of £37,700. He also has interest income of £5,500 (total income £55,770).

There is no income tax on his salary and £5,000 of his interest income is tax free thanks to the 0% starting rate band (dividends do not count as non-savings income and do not use up the starting rate band).

Because his total income is £55,770 he is a higher-rate taxpayer and is entitled to a £500 savings nil rate band, so the final £500 of his interest income will also be tax free.

Turning to his dividend income, Ollie has £32,200 of his basic-rate band remaining (£50,270 - £12,570 - £5,500). Of this £2,000 will be tax free thanks to the dividend allowance and £30,200 will be taxed at 8.75%. The final £5,500 of his dividend income is taxed at 33.75%.

Although all of Ollie's interest is tax free it uses up some of his basic-rate band, pushing £5,500 of his dividend income over the higher-rate threshold where it is taxed at 33.75%.

Example
Mark is a company owner with a salary and rental income totalling £50,000 (his non-savings income) and dividend income of £20,000. He also has interest income of £5,000. His total income is £75,000.

Because his taxable non-savings income exceeds the £5,000 starting rate limit, none of his interest is covered by the 0% starting rate. Furthermore, as a higher-rate taxpayer he is entitled to a £500 savings allowance. The final £4,500 of his interest income is taxed at 40%.

Turning to his dividend income, the first £2,000 will be tax free thanks to the dividend allowance and the final £18,000 is taxed at 33.75%.

Making the Most of Your Personal Allowance

In Chapter 4 we showed how a small number of company owners may be able to save some tax by allocating some of their personal allowance from their salary to their dividend income.

Those who also have interest income are more likely able to save tax by allocating some of their personal allowance from their interest income to their dividend income. This is because their interest income will still be tax free thanks to the 0% starting rate.

Example
In 2022/23 company owner Jameel has salary income of £9,100, interest income of £4,000 and dividend income of £50,000. If all of his personal allowance is allocated to his salary and interest his tax bill will be calculated as follows:

Salary		Income Tax
Personal allowance	£9,100	£0

Interest		
Personal allowance	£3,470	£0
Starting rate	£530	£0

Dividend		
Dividend allowance	£2,000	£0
Taxed at 8.75%	£35,170	£3,077
Taxed at 33.75%	£12,830	£4,330
Total tax		£7,407

This is not the optimal outcome. Jameel can reduce his tax bill by reallocating some of his personal allowance from his interest income to his dividend income. This is because his interest income will still be tax free thanks to the 0% starting rate.

Salary		Income Tax
Personal allowance	£9,100	£0

Interest		
Starting rate	£4,000	£0

Dividend		
Personal allowance	£3,470	£0
Dividend allowance	£2,000	£0
Taxed at 8.75%	£31,700	£2,774
Taxed at 33.75%	£12,830	£4,330
Total tax		£7,104

In this case Jameel saves £303 tax. This is because his salary does not use up his personal allowance so £3,470 of his dividend income can be tax free instead of taxed at 8.75%. His interest income remains tax free thanks to the 0% starting rate.

Note, good tax software should perform the optimal tax calculation automatically.

Scottish Company Owners with Interest Income

The Scottish Parliament can tax most types of income but not interest and dividends. So Scottish taxpayers will not pay more tax on their interest income than other taxpayers.

This year it's only when Scottish company owners have salary income and other income subject to Scottish tax of more than £27,850 that they will pay more tax than other UK taxpayers.

Thus in all of the above examples the company owners will pay the same tax on their interest and dividend income if they live in Scotland. Samantha and Elaine will, however, pay less tax on their rental income if they live in Scotland, whereas Mark will pay more tax on his salary and rental income.

Stock Market Dividends

The big difference between dividends from your own company and stock market companies is that stock market dividends can be completely sheltered from income tax in an ISA or SIPP.

In practice, many investors do in fact end up with a mixture of shares held inside and outside the tax protection of ISAs and SIPPs (for example, those who inherit a big share portfolio or want to invest more than the current £20,000 ISA allowance but do not want to put money in a pension).

These investors could consider:

- Holding high-income shares inside an ISA (to protect the dividends from income tax), and
- Holding growth shares that produce capital gains outside an ISA (because some capital gains will be tax free anyway thanks to the annual capital gains tax exemption: see Chapter 38)

This simplistic strategy will not always produce the biggest tax savings, however. If you bought Apple shares back in 2003 – before their 65,000% rise – you would be kicking yourself if you didn't stick them in an ISA!

Stock Market Dividends – How Big a Problem?

Unlike dividends from your own company, you cannot control the amount of income you receive from stock market companies. So if you have significant dividends from stock market companies, and the shares are not sheltered inside an ISA or SIPP, you may want to reduce the dividends you extract from your own company to avoid going over one of the key income tax thresholds.

However, our gut feeling is that stock market dividends do not cause a significant tax problem for most small investors. Even if you own, say, £100,000 worth of shares outside an ISA or SIPP you will probably receive no more than £5,000 per year in dividends, producing an income tax bill of £1,688 for a higher-rate taxpayer.

Remember, of course, that you only get one dividend allowance each tax year, so stock market dividends may use up some or all of this allowance: meaning you are able to take less tax-free dividends from your company; or perhaps none at all.

Short-term (Emergency) Tax Planning

If your total taxable income is higher than expected, there are some steps you can take to reduce it before the end of the tax year:

Pension Contributions

Everyone under age 75 can make a gross pension contribution of £3,600 per year. The taxpayer personally contributes £2,880 and the taxman tops up the pension plan with £720 of basic-rate tax relief. To make bigger pension contributions you require earnings: generally salary income or self-employment profits.

If you have a salary of £9,100 you can make a gross pension contribution of £9,100 (£7,280 from you, £1,820 from the taxman). Your basic-rate band will be increased by £9,100 so up to £9,100 of your dividends will escape higher-rate tax.

If you have a modest amount of self-employment income, you can generally make an additional gross pension contribution equivalent to the taxable profits of the business, thereby eliminating any tax problem caused by this type of income.

See Chapters 27 and 28 for more on pension contributions.

Tax Deductible Expenditure

Self-employed business owners (sole traders and partnerships) can also reduce their taxable income by incurring tax deductible expenditure before the end of the business's accounting period. Possibly the easiest way is to incur expenditure that qualifies for an immediate tax deduction thanks to the annual investment allowance. The allowance used to be £200,000 per year. However, this has been increased to £1 million to encourage investment and help the economy recover.

Property investors with higher than expected rental profits can spend money on property repairs before the end of the tax year: e.g. replacement kitchens and bathrooms.

Long-term Tax Planning

Company owners with significant amounts of income from other sources may be able to take the following steps to shift income from themselves to another entity or person:

Self-Employment Income

Consider putting the business into a second company (company 2) so that corporation tax is payable rather than income tax and national insurance.

Dividends can then be extracted from company 2, taking into account dividends withdrawn from company 1. This will allow you to control your income tax bill from year to year.

Of course, it's not always advantageous to incorporate a second business. Sole traders and partnerships enjoy certain tax benefits, including more generous tax treatment of various expenses (including home office, travel and car capital allowances).

Incorporation could also cost you a significant amount in professional fees.

Another possibility for sole traders may be to transfer their sole trade business into their existing company. This may sometimes cost less overall in corporation tax than having two companies; although there are also instances where it will make no difference, or may even cost more.

Furthermore, while it is possible for a single company to operate two distinctly separate businesses, there are significant commercial implications to this strategy which must be considered.

Rental Income

- Transferring properties to your spouse if he/she pays income tax at a lower rate.
- Holding commercial properties inside a pension scheme.
- Holding investment properties inside a company, so that corporation tax is payable instead of income tax and the extraction of rental profits (as dividends) can be controlled. See the Taxcafe guide *'Using a Property Company to Save Tax'* for a full discussion of the benefits and drawbacks of using a company to invest in property.
- Consider alternative investments (e.g. blue chip shares) that can be sheltered from tax in an ISA or pension scheme.

Interest Income

Some company owners can receive up to £6,000 of tax-free interest and most can receive at least £500 (except additional-rate taxpayers). Where tax is payable on your interest income, or you fear it will push some of your dividend income into a higher tax bracket, the following strategies can be adopted:

- Transfer savings into an ISA or SIPP.
- Use savings to pay off debt or take out an offset mortgage.
- Transfer cash to family members who pay tax at a lower rate (but not minor children).
- Invest in assets that produce capital growth rather than interest income.

Note that large cash transfers to anyone other than your spouse may have inheritance tax implications (although these can often be beneficial).

Stock Market Dividends

- Hold shares in an ISA or SIPP.
- Transfer holdings to a spouse and possibly other family members.

Transfers of shareholdings to anyone other than your spouse may have both capital gains tax and inheritance tax implications.

Part 5

Splitting Income with Your Family

Chapter 21

Splitting Income with Your Spouse or Partner

In Chapter 12 we saw that couples can double up the tax-free salary and dividend and the amount of dividend income taxed at just 8.75%.

That's all very well if the couple own and run the company together. But what if your spouse/partner isn't involved in the business, for example if the company was started before you met or if they have a separate career and receive salary income from another employer?

In situations like these it may be possible to save income tax by gifting shares in the company to your spouse/partner. It may even be possible to save tax by paying them a salary as well.

The amount of tax that can be saved depends on individual circumstances, for example how much profit the company makes and how much taxable income each person has already.

Tax savings are typically achieved where one spouse/partner is a higher-rate taxpayer (paying 33.75% tax on their dividend income) and the other spouse/partner has no income at all or is a basic-rate taxpayer.

However, it's not just these couples who can save tax. It's possible to pay income tax at more than 33.75% on dividend income that falls into any of the following tax brackets:

- £50,270-£60,000   Child benefit charge
- £100,000-£125,140   Personal allowance withdrawal
- Over £150,000*   Additional-rate tax

* £125,140 from 2023/24

If your income falls into one of these tax brackets you may be able to save tax by transferring income to your spouse/partner, even if they are a higher-rate taxpayer.

And because *every* taxpayer is entitled to a dividend allowance, it may be possible to save a little tax by shifting some dividend income to your spouse/partner, even if they're in the same tax bracket as you, or a higher tax bracket. Unfortunately, the potential tax savings are only modest and are set to reduce still further, as the current £2,000 dividend allowance is to be cut to £1,000 next year, and then to just £500 from 2024/25.

Before we look at some sample tax savings it is important to point out that there are also potential dangers when it comes to splitting dividend income with your spouse/partner. We will return to this important issue later in the chapter.

Capital Gains Tax (CGT)

If you wish to split your dividend income with your spouse/partner you generally have to transfer shares in the company to them.

In the case of married couples, a gift of shares would be exempt from CGT. CGT will, however, be payable if the spouse who receives the gift later disposes of the shares. The original base cost of the spouse who made the transfer will be used to perform the CGT calculation.

Gifts between unmarried couples are normally subject to CGT. However, the couple may be able to jointly elect to claim holdover relief.

Holdover relief allows a chargeable gain to be deferred (held over) when gifts of qualifying business assets are made. The person who receives the shares may eventually have to pay CGT on the original owner's held over gain, as well as their own, when the shares are sold.

To qualify for holdover relief the company must generally be a regular trading company, although companies running a qualifying furnished holiday letting business will also qualify.

Unmarried couples who want to split their income face a further potential danger (see below).

Giving the Business Away

To successfully split your dividend income with your spouse/partner it is essential that genuine beneficial ownership of shares in the company is handed over. This means your spouse/partner must be able to do what they like with any dividends and any proceeds from a sale of the business.

As we shall see shortly, it is also safer to transfer ordinary shares rather than shares that have fewer voting rights or other rights.

It is probably wise to have any dividends received by your spouse/partner paid into a separate bank account in their name, to show HMRC that you have not retained control of the money.

Dividends are generally payable in proportion to shareholdings. So if you normally take a dividend of £100,000 and want to transfer £40,000 of this income to your spouse/partner, you will generally have to transfer 40% of the business to them or, to be more precise, 40% of your shares in the company.

Because this sort of tax planning, if done correctly, involves effectively giving away ownership and control of part of your business, it is only suitable where there is a significant amount of trust between the parties involved.

How Much of the Business Should Be Transferred?

For many company owners, a 50:50 ownership split with their spouse or partner will prove optimal, but a smaller stake can be transferred if the founder wants to retain more control over the business.

Example
Steve owns 100% of Steve's Spices Ltd, a small trading company. Steve currently pays himself a salary of £15,000 and dividends of £80,000.

His total income is £95,000 which means he is close to the £100,000 threshold. If his income rises above this threshold he will start to lose his income tax personal allowance.

As things stand he will pay income tax of £18,008 on his dividend income in 2022/23 – see Chapter 3 for how dividends are taxed.

Steve's wife Lara does not own any shares in the company but she does receive rental income of £13,000 from a buy-to-let property. This means she can receive dividends of up to £37,270 this year before she becomes a higher-rate taxpayer (£50,270 – £13,000). Of this, £2,000 will be tax-free and the rest will be taxed at just 8.75%.

Steve therefore transfers 45% of the ordinary shares in the business to Lara. The company continues to pay total dividends of £80,000 but now Steve's dividend is £44,000 and Lara's is £36,000.

Lara's total taxable income is now £49,000 and the tax bill on her dividend income is £2,975. Steve's total taxable income is now £59,000 and the tax bill on his dividend income is £5,858.

The tax on the total dividend income has been reduced by £9,175.

Furthermore, Steve's income is now well below the £100,000 threshold which means he doesn't have to worry about losing his income tax personal allowance for now.

Additional tax savings may be achieved if the couple are currently receiving child benefit. As we know from Chapter 15, the child benefit charge is payable if, like Steve, the highest earner in the household has income of more than £50,000.

But if Steve transfers 50% of the business to Lara, instead of 45%, his total taxable income will fall to £55,000. Lara will pay 33.75% tax on most of the additional £4,000 of dividend income she receives. However, because Steve's income is now £55,000 instead of £59,000, the child benefit charge will be reduced by a further 40%, saving the couple an additional £754 in 2022/23 if they have two children: with similar savings in future years (see Chapter 15).

Potential Tax Savings

The potential tax savings from transferring dividend income to your spouse/partner will vary from case to case. The analysis set out below is based on the current, 2022/23 tax year. Savings will generally reduce slightly in future years, due to the reductions in the dividend allowance, but the impact will not be significant enough to prevent the planning being worthwhile.

Spouse/Partner Has No Income

If you are a basic-rate taxpayer (income under £50,270) and your spouse/partner is a 'house-spouse' with no taxable income, they can receive tax-free dividends of up to £14,570 this year (made up of the £12,570 personal allowance and £2,000 dividend allowance). The potential tax saving is £1,275 (£14,570 x 8.75%).

If you are a higher-rate taxpayer and your spouse/partner has no taxable income, they can receive less heavily taxed dividends of up to £50,270 this year. The first £14,570 will be tax free and the remainder will be taxed at 8.75%.

By contrast, you as a higher-rate taxpayer could be paying at least 33.75% tax on all of this income.

For example, let's say you gift enough shares in the company so that your spouse/partner receives dividend income of £40,000. Your spouse/partner will pay £2,225 tax (first £14,570 tax free, the remainder taxed at 8.75%).

If we assume you would have paid tax at 33.75% on all of this income, this would have amounted to £13,500, so the net tax saving in this example would be £11,275.

The tax saving may be even greater if you have income of more than £100,000 before the transfer. Reducing your income may allow you to claw back some or all of your personal allowance, which will produce an additional tax saving.

Spouse/Partner is Basic-Rate Taxpayer

Even if your spouse/partner works and has taxable income, it may be possible to save tax by gifting shares in the business to them. Again, the tax savings will vary from case to case.

Example
Rupert is a company owner who expects to have a taxable income of £70,000 this year, made up of a £60,000 dividend and £10,000 of salary and other income. He will pay 33.75% tax on £19,730 of his dividend income (£70,000 - £50,270 higher-rate threshold).

His wife, Wendy, receives taxable income of £30,000 from another source. Thus she has £20,270 of her basic-rate band left and can receive £20,270 of dividends that will be less heavily taxed in her hands.

If Rupert gifts one third of the shares to Wendy and the company normally pays dividends of £60,000, she'll receive £20,000. The first £2,000 will be tax free thanks to the dividend allowance and tax of £1,575 will be payable on the remaining £18,000 (at 8.75%). Rupert would've paid £6,750 tax on this income so the tax saving is £5,175.

Spouse/Partner is Higher-Rate Taxpayer

If you and your spouse/partner are both higher-rate taxpayers (income over £50,270) it may still be possible to save tax by gifting them shares in the company.

For starters your spouse/partner will have their own dividend allowance which means they can receive up to £2,000 of dividend income tax free in 2022/23, no matter how much other income they have.

If your income exceeds £100,000 some or all of your personal allowance will have been withdrawn and it may be possible to save more tax by transferring dividend income to your spouse/partner.

Example
Saul is a company owner who expects to have a taxable income of £130,000 this year, made up of £120,000 of dividend income and £10,000 of salary and other income. With this much income all of his personal allowance will be withdrawn.

His wife Kylie has income of £60,000 from another source. If Saul transfers 25% of the company to Kylie she will receive dividend income of £30,000. The first £2,000 will be tax free but she will pay 33.75% tax on the rest (£9,450).

Saul's income will fall from £130,000 to £100,000 which means he will recover all of his personal allowance and his tax bill will fall from £35,400 to £19,908.

All in all the couple will save £6,042 in tax by transferring the dividend income to Kylie, even though she is also a higher-rate taxpayer.

If you have income of more than £150,000 and are an *additional-rate* taxpayer this year, it may be possible to save tax by gifting shares to your spouse/partner who is a higher-rate taxpayer.

The first £2,000 of their dividend income will be tax free this year and they will pay 33.75% tax on the rest, compared with the 39.35% you would pay as an additional rate taxpayer.

The tax savings are not huge: You save £787 on the first £2,000 of dividend income transferred then just £56 on every additional £1,000 thereafter. And that initial £787 will drop to £394 next year then just £197 per year after that.

It's also important to be careful that the dividend income transferred to your spouse/partner does not push *their* total taxable income over the £100,000 threshold, so that they begin to lose their personal allowance. In most cases, this would wipe out the saving and turn it into an overall additional tax cost!

If their taxable income is already over £125,140, they are back to being a normal higher rate taxpayer for 2022/23 and transferring dividend income to them will produce that same £56 per £1,000 saving until they too become an additional rate taxpayer: BUT that's only this year. From next year, they will also be an additional rate taxpayer and the only saving you would achieve is by using their dividend allowance, which will only be £1,000 and will thus only save you £394 at most (reducing to just £197 in subsequent years).

Would you really want to give part of your business away to save £197 per year?

Spouse/Partner is Additional-Rate Taxpayer

There is a situation where it may actually be beneficial to transfer dividend income to your spouse/partner even if they are an additional rate taxpayer (income over £150,000 this year, income over £125,140 in future years).

This arises where your income falls into the £100,000 to £125,140 bracket and you are suffering income tax at effective rates of up to 56.25% on some of your dividend income.

Example Revisited

Let's go back to Saul and Kylie in our last example, but change just one thing: let's say Kylie's income from another source is £150,000 instead of £60,000.

Saul transfers 25% of the company to Kylie as before and she receives the same £30,000 of dividend income. The first £2,000 will be tax free this year, and she will pay 39.35% tax on the rest: £11,018.

Saul will recover his personal allowance and his tax bill will fall from £35,400 to £19,908, as before.

All in all the couple now save £4,474 in tax. It's not quite as good as we saw before, but it's not bad considering Kylie is an additional rate taxpayer.

Next year the same scenario will produce a slightly different result. Only the first £1,000 of Kylie's dividend income will be tax free. On the other hand, the top £4,860 of Saul's dividend income would already be taxed at 39.35% without the transfer. Overall, this year's saving of £4,474 will fall, but only to £4,353.

Transferable Tax Allowance for Married Couples

Married couples can transfer 10% of their personal allowances to each other (£1,260 during the current 2022/23 tax year). Only basic-rate taxpayers can benefit, so the potential tax saving is currently £252 (£1,260 x 20%).

Married couples can generally only benefit if one person earns less than £12,570 (i.e. is wasting some of their personal allowance). However, some company owners who earn more than this can achieve a small additional saving by using this tax break:

Example

David owns a small company. In 2022/23 he takes a salary of £11,908 and dividend of £25,000, i.e. he is a basic-rate taxpayer. His wife Michelle doesn't own any shares in the company. She's a teacher with a salary of £30,000, i.e. also a basic-rate taxpayer. If David elects to transfer £662 of his personal allowance to Michelle, this will reduce her income tax bill by £132 (£662 x 20%). David will pay 8.75% tax on an additional £662 of dividend income: £58. The overall net saving for the couple is £74.

160

This strategy won't work if David takes a salary of £12,570 instead. Although Michelle will save tax, David will pay the same amount of income tax on his own salary.

It also won't work if David takes a salary of £11,908 and dividend of more than £37,700 in 2022/23 – reducing his personal allowance will push some of his dividend income into the higher-rate bracket – higher-rate taxpayers cannot transfer their personal allowances.

Why the Tax Savings May Not Last

There are many reasons why any tax savings that may be achieved in one tax year by splitting income with your spouse/partner may not be achievable in full in future tax years, including:

- Changes to tax rates and thresholds
- Changes to personal circumstances

Changes to Tax Rates & Thresholds

We have already seen the impact that the forthcoming reductions in the dividend allowance will have on this area of planning. By 2024/25, the maximum annual saving provided by using a spouse/partner's dividend allowance will be just £281: and that's for a company owner with taxable income between £100,000 and £125,140. For a typical higher rate taxpayer, the maximum saving produced by the dividend allowance will fall to just £169 per year.

In short, any planning that relies on a saving produced by the spouse/partner's dividend allowance alone is not worthwhile. Hence, it is not generally worth transferring dividend income to a spouse/partner who is in the same tax bracket or a higher one.

Furthermore, the forthcoming reduction in the additional rate tax threshold means it will not usually be worth transferring income to any spouse/partner with income in excess of £125,140: although there is a key exception for company owners whose own income is between £100,000 and £125,140.

There may also be some exceptions for couples claiming child benefit and, of course, we are only talking about transfers being made in order to save *income tax* here.

It's also important to remember that, according to the latest Government proposals, the higher-rate threshold is to remain frozen at £50,270 until 5th April 2028. As a result more and more basic-rate taxpayers are likely to become higher-rate taxpayers.

This may make it less attractive for some higher-rate taxpayers to shift income to spouses/partners who are currently basic-rate taxpayers. If your spouse/partner's income simply increases with inflation, they will have less of their basic-rate band left to enjoy dividends taxed at just 8.75%.

Changes to Personal Circumstances

As discussed above, relying on the dividend allowance alone to save tax by shifting income to your spouse/partner is generally no longer viable. Beyond the dividend allowance, income tax savings can usually only be achieved if your spouse/partner has a lower tax rate than you.

It is possible that, over time, your tax rate will fall or your spouse/partner's tax rate will increase. This could eliminate or even reverse any initial income tax saving that is achieved.

Your tax rate could fall if the company's profits fall, resulting in lower dividends. Your spouse/partner's tax rate could rise if their income from other sources increases (for example, if another business they own produces bigger profits).

There are many different permutations. The key point is that couples should look further ahead than just one tax year when deciding what proportion of the company each should own.

HMRC's Attacks on Income Shifting

Income splitting arrangements like those described in this chapter have come under attack in the past. The taxman has tried to prevent dividends being paid to non-working spouses/partners, or spouses/partners who do just a small amount of work for the company.

In particular, the taxman's target has been small 'personal service companies' (IT consultants and the like) where most of the work is carried out by one person.

It all came to a head in the notorious 'Arctic Systems' case. HMRC tried to use the so-called settlements legislation to prevent Geoff Jones, a computer consultant, from splitting his dividend income with his wife.

The settlements legislation is designed to prevent income being shifted from one individual to another via a 'settlement', for example by transferring an asset or making some other 'arrangement'.

In the Arctic Systems case Mr Jones did most of the work in the company. Mrs Jones did a few hours admin each week. Because Mr Jones only paid himself a small salary despite all the work he did, more money was left to pay out as dividends to Mrs Jones. HMRC therefore decided that a settlement had taken place and tried to have Mrs Jones' dividend income taxed in her husband's hands.

HMRC originally won the case but the decision was overturned by the House of Lords.

The judges agreed with HMRC that a settlement had taken place **but** decided that the settlement provisions could not be applied because in this case the couple were protected by the exemption for gifts between spouses. This exemption applies where:

- There is an outright gift of property to a spouse, and
- The property is not wholly or mainly a right to income

On the first point, the judges ruled that, although Mrs Jones had subscribed for her share when the company was set up (i.e. it was not strictly speaking gifted to her by her husband), her share was essentially a gift because it contained an 'element of bounty': the share provided a benefit that Mr Jones would not have given to a complete stranger.

On the second point, the judges also ruled that a gift of *ordinary* shares is not wholly or mainly a right to income because ordinary shares have other rights: voting rights and the right to capital gains if the company is sold.

Thanks to the courage of Mr and Mrs Jones, who were prepared to fight HMRC all the way to the House of Lords, this exemption should safeguard most types of income splitting arrangements between married couples where ordinary shares are involved.

For this reason some tax advisers are of the opinion that married couples should make hay while the sun shines, i.e. they should split their dividend income with their spouses while they can.

Preference Shares

The outcome of the Arctic Systems case may have been different if another type of share other than ordinary shares had been involved.

In another tax case (*Young v Pearce*), wives were issued with preference shares that paid income but had very few other rights. The shares did not have voting rights and did not entitle the spouses to receive any payout in the event of the company being sold (other than the original £25 payment for the shares).

All that the preference shares provided was a right to receive 30% of the company's profits as a dividend. The court therefore decided that the preference shares provided wholly or mainly a right to income.

Thus the exemption for gifts between spouses was not available and the settlement rules applied. The wives' dividends were therefore taxed in the hands of their husbands.

Unmarried Couples & Other Family Members

Although HMRC was defeated in the Arctic Systems case, the judges did agree that a settlement had taken place. The taxpayers only won the case thanks to the exemption for gifts between *spouses*.

There is still uncertainty as to where this leaves income-splitting arrangements between other groups of individuals, in particular, *unmarried* couples.

HMRC may take the view that the settlements legislation applies to unmarried couples and other family members, especially where small personal service companies are involved.

However, to date the taxman has not pursued these individuals aggressively so, again, it may be a case of making hay while the sun shines.

To protect against any potential attack the best defence is probably to have both individuals equally involved in the business (a bit of admin or bookkeeping will not suffice, as Mr and Mrs Jones discovered).

HMRC's main concern seems to be personal service companies (IT consultants and other businesses where the profits are generated from one person's services). Larger businesses that have other employees, premises, equipment, etc may be safer because the profits come from various sources, not just one person's work.

Future Danger?

In 2007 draft income shifting legislation was published but fortunately never made it onto the statute books after being widely condemned for being completely unworkable.

That draft legislation essentially sought to prevent business owners from receiving dividends unless they effectively earned them! This would have undermined the whole basis of shareholder capitalism – dividends are supposed to be a reward for being an entrepreneur and setting up or investing in a business.

Although income shifting legislation is on the back burner for now, it could be introduced in the future and could upset some income splitting arrangements.

Dividend Waivers

Dividend waivers are used by company owners who wish to relinquish their rights to dividends. They can be commercially justifiable, for example if a shareholder waives their dividend to protect the company's cash.

To be effective it is necessary to draw up a formal deed which is executed before the dividend is declared or paid.

Company owners have also tried to use dividend waivers to avoid tax by diverting income to their spouse/partner. For example, a higher-rate taxpayer may try to divert a disproportionate share of the company's profit to their spouse/partner who is a basic-rate taxpayer.

HMRC may use the settlements legislation to attack arrangements where shareholders end up with excessive dividends, i.e. more of the company's distributable profit than their shareholding would normally entitle them to. Because dividend waivers involve simply a transfer of income, not assets, they are not protected by the exemption for outright gifts to spouses (see above).

Example

Mrs M owns 80 ordinary shares in M Limited and also has a significant amount of taxable income from other sources. Mr M owns 20 shares and has no other income. The company has retained profits of £50,000. Mrs M waives her right to a dividend and the company then declares a dividend of £2,000 per share. Mr M thus receives a dividend of £40,000, most of which he hopes will be taxed at no more than 8.75%.

HMRC could apply the settlements legislation in this situation. Clearly a dividend of £2,000 per share could not have been paid on all 100 shares, so the waiver enhanced Mr M's dividend.

This would therefore be seen as a 'bounteous arrangement' – it is unlikely Mrs M would have agreed to do the same thing with a third party. £32,000 of the dividend paid to Mr M would therefore be taxed in Mrs M's hands.

Some of the things HMRC will look for when deciding whether to apply the settlements legislation to dividend waivers include:

- Insufficient retained profits to pay the same rate of dividend on all issued share capital.
- Even if there is sufficient profit to pay the same rate of dividend per share for the year in question, there has been a succession of waivers over several years and, in the absence of the waivers, the total dividends payable exceed the company's retained profits.
- Waiving shareholders wish to benefit non-waiving shareholders.
- Non-waiving shareholders pay tax at a lower rate.

In summary, company owners should be careful of entering into arrangements to waive dividends where there is no commercial reason for the waivers and no evidence that the waivers are for non-tax reasons.

Salaries for Spouses/Partners

If your spouse/partner also works for your company they can be paid a salary. Please note, you cannot pay them a salary if they do no work for the company. And you cannot pay them more than is justified for the duties they perform. If you do, the company may be denied tax relief for the expense.

If your spouse/partner is a director then the accompanying legal responsibilities will also justify some remuneration being paid. This factor alone is generally given a lot of weight and will almost always justify a salary up to the level of the personal allowance. However, it remains important for your spouse/partner to be actively carrying out their duties as a director (attending board meetings, reviewing company accounts and other important documents, etc).

If your spouse/partner has no taxable income from other sources, a small salary will be more tax efficient than simply paying them dividends.

Why? Unlike dividends which are paid out of the company's after-tax profits, salaries are a tax deductible expense for the company. In other words, in addition to any *income tax* savings enjoyed by the couple, a salary will also save the company *corporation tax*.

For example, a small salary of £11,908 will currently save a company at least £1,932 in tax, taking into account the small amount of national insurance that is usually payable. The tax savings will be even greater for some companies when the increase in corporation tax is in full force (see Chapter 1).

To avoid national insurance, salary payments should generally be made monthly instead of as a lump sum. If, however, your spouse/partner is a director, the payment can be made as a lump sum because company directors pay national insurance on an annual basis.

Second Jobs

What if your spouse or partner already has income from other sources, e.g. a salary from another job? Is it still tax efficient to get your company to pay them a small salary?

Firstly, it's important to point out that if they work for another employer the employment contract may prevent them working for you as well.

If there is no such restriction, paying your spouse or partner a small national insurance free salary could lead to an overall saving of several hundred pounds in some cases. Why? Because for basic-rate taxpayers the combined tax rate (corporation tax and income tax) for dividend income is currently at least 26%, compared with 20% for salaries.

Thus paying your spouse/partner a salary of, say, £9,100 could lead to an overall saving of around £546 (£9,100 x 6%), providing there is no national insurance payable.

The savings may be much smaller or non-existent in other cases, for example for some higher-rate taxpayers, so it may be necessary to do some calculations specific to your circumstances.

When the corporation tax increase is in full force (see Chapter 1) paying your spouse or partner a salary may become more attractive because that salary may enjoy more corporation tax relief (26.5% or 25%).

Chapter 22

Splitting Income with Your Children

Dividends

It is possible to gift shares in your company to your children. Because they will have their own income tax personal allowance and dividend allowance it may be possible for them to receive tax-free dividends of up to £14,570 each in 2022/23, plus an additional £35,700 taxed at just 8.75%.

However, it is important to point out that this type of tax planning generally only works when *adult* children are involved (i.e. children 18 or older).

Transfers of income to minor children are generally ineffective and the income would be taxed in the parent's hands. This section therefore deals exclusively with adult children.

If you gift shares in the company to your adult children there will potentially be capital gains tax payable, as if you had sold the shares to them for their full market value. However, it may be possible for both the parent and child to jointly elect to hold over the capital gain.

To qualify for holdover relief the company must, generally speaking, be a trading company, although companies carrying on a furnished holiday letting business also qualify.

The safest route is probably to use ordinary shares, which means your children will obtain full ownership and voting rights in respect of their share of the business, not just a right to receive dividends.

There is a potential tax trap for family members who are gifted shares and are also employees of the company. In certain cases, where shares are obtained because of an individual's employment, a gift of shares can be subject to employment income tax charges.

However, there is an exemption where shares are given in the 'normal course of domestic, family or personal relationships'. So in most family companies, where shares are transferred to a spouse/partner or adult children, the transfer should not give rise to any employment tax charges.

There is nevertheless a danger that, in certain circumstances, HMRC may argue that the individuals received shares by virtue of their employment, not because they are family members.

For example, if the individual only receives a small salary from the company (i.e. below market rate) HMRC may have more grounds to argue that the gift was made to increase the individual's remuneration from the company.

If shares are transferred to a family member who is an employee and to other employees who are not family members, this could indicate that the gift was made because of the family member's employment.

On the other hand, if shares are gifted to several family members (some of whom are not employees) this may indicate that the gift was made solely because of the family relationship.

It may be wise in such circumstances to document the reasons for the gift and (as always) obtain professional advice.

Salaries for Children

It's often worth getting your company to employ your children (including your minor children) at certain points in time. The salary payments will be a tax deductible expense for the business, providing the payments can be justified by the duties performed. (In one tax case a son's wages were disallowed because there were no time records or other evidence to justify the payments.)

The income will generally be tax free in the hands of the children, if they're at school, college, or university and have no other taxable income.

A tax deduction coupled with a tax-free receipt is the best possible outcome when it comes to extracting money from your company!

Those aged under 16 can be paid up to £12,570 in 2022/23 with no income tax or national insurance consequences (assuming they have no other taxable income).

Children who are 16 and over are subject to employee's national insurance. The rates and thresholds have been all over the place this year but next year (2023/24) this will be payable at 12% when the annual salary exceeds £12,570.

Employer's national insurance is payable on salaries over £9,100 (unless the company has spare employment allowance). There is no employer's national insurance on salaries of up to £50,270 paid to employees under 21 and apprentices under 25. Note, the exemption is not lost if the employee earns more than £50,270: employer's national insurance is only payable on the excess.

It's important to note the restrictions on the hours and work children can do because this affects how much you can pay them.

Restrictions on Work and Hours

Children are of compulsory school age up to the last Friday in June in the academic year of their 16th birthday. After this they are at the 'mandatory school leaving age' and can apply for a national insurance number and work full time.

Until that time there are restrictions on the hours and types of work that can be carried out. For starters, it is generally illegal to employ children under 13 in any capacity (unless they're involved in acting or modelling).

Other children must not work:

- Without an employment permit if local byelaws require it
- In factories or on industrial sites
- During school hours
- Before 7.00 am or after 7.00 pm
- For more than one hour before school (local byelaws permitting)
- For more than four hours without taking a one hour break
- In occupations prohibited by byelaws/legislation (e.g. pubs)
- If the work will harm their health, well-being or education
- Without having a two week break during the school holidays in each calendar year

More Restrictions on Hours Worked

During term time children under school leaving age can work for no more than 12 hours per week including a maximum of:

- Two hours on school days and Sundays
- Five hours on Saturdays for 13 to 14 year olds; eight hours for 15 to 16 year olds

During school holidays 13 to 14 year olds may work a maximum of 25 hours per week. This includes a maximum of:

- Five hours on weekdays and Saturdays
- Two hours on Sunday

During school holidays 15 to 16 year olds under school leaving age may work a maximum of 35 hours per week. This includes a maximum of:

- Eight hours on weekdays and Saturdays
- Two hours on Sunday

National Minimum Wage & Living Wage

If your children are below the compulsory school leaving age the national minimum wage does not apply. From 1st April 2022 the hourly rates for older children are as follows:

- £9.50   Living wage, 23 and over
- £9.18   21-22
- £6.83   18-20
- £4.81   16-17 if above school leaving age
- £4.81   Apprentice rate

Part 6

Other Profit
Extraction
Strategies

Chapter 23

Loans to Directors

It used to be illegal for companies to make loans to directors. This is no longer the case and loans of any size are now permitted.

With the exception of loans for under £10,000 they generally have to be approved by the company's shareholders.

For most small companies this is obviously not a problem because the shareholders and directors are the same people!

You cannot take a loan from your company for an indefinite period without any tax consequences. If that was possible most company owners would never pay themselves taxable dividends.

The attractiveness of taking a loan from your company is limited by two potential tax charges:

- a 33.75% tax paid by the *company* (the section 455 charge)
- a benefit-in-kind charge paid by the *director*

The section 455 tax charge was increased from 32.5% to 33.75% for new or additional loans made after 5th April 2022. There is no additional charge for loan balances already existing on that date.

Fortunately, it is possible to avoid or mitigate the damage caused by these taxes, if you understand the rules.

The Section 455 Charge

Most small family companies are 'close companies'. A close company is one controlled by five or fewer 'participators'. A close company is also one controlled by any number of participators who are also directors. Broadly, a participator is a shareholder.

If a close company lends money to a participator *the company* will have to pay a 33.75% tax charge on the loan. This is known as the section 455 charge. Failure to pay this charge will result in penalties and interest.

However, there are two reasons why this charge is not as bad as it first appears:

#1 Short-term Loans Escape the Section 455 Charge

The 33.75% tax does not apply if the loan is repaid within nine months of the end of the company's accounting period. This is the normal due date for the company's corporation tax. This means that short-term loans to directors do not attract a company tax charge.

Example
Bill Ltd's accounting period ends on 31st December 2022. The company made a £10,000 loan to Bill, the sole shareholder and director, in July 2022.

Bill repays the loan before the end of September 2023. The company will not have to pay the 33.75% tax charge because the loan was repaid within nine months of the end of the accounting period in which it was made.

Example
The facts are the same as before except only £7,000 is repaid before the end of September 2023. The remaining £3,000 is repaid in October 2024. The company will pay a section 455 tax charge of £1,013 (£3,000 x 33.75%).

#2 The Section 455 Charge is Refundable

Even if the 33.75% tax does end up being paid because the loan is not repaid early enough the tax will be refunded when the loan is repaid.

That's the good news. The bad news is the company will only be repaid nine months after the end of the accounting period in which the loan is repaid. In Bill Ltd's case this means the £1,013 tax will be repaid on 1st October 2025.

Exemption for Minority Shareholders

This exemption isn't much use to most small company owners. Nevertheless it is worth mentioning that there is no 33.75% company tax charge if you own 5% or less of the company's ordinary shares.

There are a number of qualifying criteria:

- Total loans to the individual cannot exceed £15,000
- The individual must work full time in the business

When it comes to the 5% limit you must include shares owned by you, your spouse and other 'associates' (e.g. close relatives).

Although there is no company tax charge on small loans to minority shareholders, there will still be a potential benefit-in-kind charge for the individual.

Benefit-in-kind Charge

If no interest is payable on the loan or if the interest paid to the company is less than the 'official rate', the director will have to pay income tax on the benefit in kind.

The official rate of interest is 2% for the current 2022/23 tax year, so if the interest charged on the loan is less than 2%, a benefit-in-kind charge is payable.

Employer's national insurance is also payable, although there is no employee's national insurance payable by the director.

As far as income tax is concerned, most articles on benefits in kind state that basic-rate taxpayers pay 20% tax and higher-rate taxpayers pay 40% tax.

It's not as simple as that if you're a company owner taking a small tax-free salary and the rest of your income as dividends. The amount of income tax payable on the benefit depends on the level of salary and whether the director has income from other sources such as rental income.

Directors who are higher-rate taxpayers will effectively suffer between 33.75% and 45% tax on the benefit. The lower 33.75% tax rate is payable to the extent that the taxable benefit is covered by the director's personal allowance. The 45% rate then comes into force and is a combination of the 20% tax suffered on the benefit in kind itself and the 25% increase (from 8.75% to 33.75%) in the tax suffered on an equivalent amount of dividend income.

For example, if the loan is for £20,000 and no interest is charged, the director will potentially face the following benefit-in-kind charge as a higher-rate taxpayer:

£20,000 loan x 2% interest x 45% tax = £180

The company will also have to pay class 1A national insurance:

£20,000 loan x 2% interest x 14.53% = £58

The benefit in kind is reduced if interest is paid to the company. For example, if you pay 1.5% interest, the benefit in kind will be calculated using an interest rate of 0.5% (2% less 1.5%). If you pay 2% interest there will be no benefit in kind charge.

Note, however, that the benefit in kind is only reduced if there is a formal obligation to pay interest to the company. For this reason it is probably advisable to have a properly drawn up loan agreement.

If you do pay interest on the loan, the good news is you will be paying the money to your own company, not a bank. However, the company will pay corporation tax on the interest it receives.

It must also be remembered that money inside a company is generally less valuable than money outside a company. If you wish to withdraw the interest back out as a dividend, there is likely to be an income tax charge.

Should Directors Pay Interest?

Let's compare two scenarios:

- An interest-free loan
- Paying interest at the official rate

We will assume that the loan is for £30,000, the official interest rate is 2%, and the director suffers income tax at an effective rate of 45% on any benefit in kind. We will also assume for now that the company pays 19% corporation tax.

#1 Interest-free loan

The benefit-in-kind charge paid by the director will be:

$$£30,000 \times 2\% \times 45\% = £270$$

The national insurance paid by the company will be:

$$£30,000 \times 2\% \times 14.53\% = £87$$

The employer's national insurance is a tax deductible expense, so the net cost would be £71 (£87 less 19% corporation tax relief).

$$\text{Total cost of loan: } £270 + £71 = £341$$

Note too that your accountant will probably also charge a fee to complete a P11D form to report the benefit of an interest-free loan to HMRC.

#2 Interest paid at the official rate

On a £30,000 loan the director will currently pay £600 interest to the company (£30,000 x 2%). The company will pay 19% corporation tax on this interest so the cost will be £114:

$$£600 \times 19\% \text{ corporation tax} = £114$$

Even if the after-tax interest is paid out as a dividend, producing an income tax charge of £164 for a higher-rate taxpayer (£486 x 33.75%), the total tax cost will be £278.

This is a bit less than the cost of an interest-free loan. However, the difference is small so it may be other factors (such as accountancy fees or simplicity) that determine which route is best.

In the above example we assumed that the company pays 19% corporation tax.

Paying interest at the official rate becomes less attractive when the company has a higher corporation tax rate (see Chapter 1).

The Official Rate of Interest

Back in 2009 the official rate of interest was 6.25%. Interest rates have been rising, as we all know, and it's likely the official rate of interest will be increased soon, although we don't know by how much.

If the official rate is increased from, say, 2% to 6%, the tax cost of directors' loans could also triple (whether it's an interest-free loan or interest is paid to the company at the official rate). In other words, loans to directors are likely to become more expensive in future tax years.

The current and previous official rates can be found by typing 'official rate of interest' into Google.

Exemptions from the Benefit in Kind Charge

There are two important exemptions from benefit in kind charges:

- Loans to invest in another company
- Loans for less than £10,000

Note that neither exemption makes any difference to the requirement to pay the section 455 company tax charge. Remember, however, that the company tax charge does not apply to short-term loans (up to 21 months in some cases) and is repayable.

Benefit-in-kind exemption #1
Loans to invest in another company

There is generally no benefit in kind charge on certain *qualifying* loans. A qualifying loan is one where the interest (if interest was charged) would be a tax deductible expense for the director.

An example of a qualifying loan would be one given to an individual so they can acquire an interest in another close company carrying on qualifying activities: namely either trading or letting property to unconnected third parties.

The person borrowing the money must generally hold more than 5% of the ordinary shares in the company in which the money is being invested.

Whether this is the most tax-efficient way to finance a new business venture is, of course, another question altogether, although we will return to this issue later.

Remember that the section 455 company tax charge still applies, unless the loan is repaid within nine months of the end of the accounting period in which it is made.

Benefit-in-kind exemption #2
Loans not exceeding £10,000

There is no benefit-in-kind charge if all of the loans to the director/shareholder total £10,000 or less throughout the tax year.

It is important to understand that any sum due from the director to the company is counted as a 'loan', including goods or services that have been provided to the director but not paid for.

The section 455 corporation tax charge still applies if the loan is not repaid on time. Nevertheless, this exemption currently allows a director/shareholder to take a loan of up to £10,000 for up to 21 months with no adverse tax consequences.

Larger Short-term Loans

By taking a loan for no more than £10,000 and repaying it on time, both the 33.75% section 455 tax charge and the benefit-in-kind charge can be avoided. What if you want to borrow more than the tax-free limit for a short period – how does this compare with paying yourself additional taxable dividends?

Example
Penelope owns Pitstop Hotels Ltd, which has a 31st December accounting date. Penelope normally withdraws a salary of £12,570 and enough dividend income to use up her basic-rate band. It's the beginning of January 2023 and Penelope would like to withdraw some additional money from Pitstop Hotels, over and above her usual salary and dividend income. She needs £13,500 for some home improvements.

If she takes the money as a dividend she will need to withdraw £20,377. There will be an income tax charge of £6,877 payable by 31st January 2024, leaving her with the required £13,500.

Instead she decides to take an interest-free loan of £13,500 from her company on 6th January 2023. Because it's an interest-free loan and the loan is for more than £10,000 she will be subject to a benefit-in-kind charge. (Paying interest to her company at the official rate may be more tax efficient but she decides that an interest-free loan will be simpler).

The loan will also be subject to the 33.75% section 455 tax charge unless it is repaid by the end of September 2024 (nine months after the end of the company's accounting period on 31st December 2023).

She repays the loan on 5th September 2024, after 20 months. The loan falls into the 2022/23 tax year (3 months), the 2023/24 tax year (12 months) and the 2024/25 tax year (5 months). We'll assume the official rate of interest in each of those years is 2%, 4% and 6% respectively (although we have no idea what the actual official rate will be in future tax years).

Penny will face the following income tax charge on the benefit in kind:

2022/23: £13,500 x 2% x 3/12 x 45%   = £30
2023/24: £13,500 x 4% x 12/12 x 45% = £243
2024/25: £13,500 x 6% x 5/12 x 45% = £152
Total   £425

The national insurance paid by the company will be:

2022/23: £13,500 x 2% x 3/12 x 14.53% = £10
2023/24: £13,500 x 4% x 12/12 x 13.8% = £75
2024/25: £13,500 x 6% x 5/12 x 13.8% = £47
Total   £132

The employer's national insurance is a tax deductible expense, so the total net cost to the company would be no more than £107.

The maximum total cost of the loan is therefore: £425 + £107 = £532

To repay the £13,500 loan Penelope withdraws additional dividend income, over and above what she normally takes, of £20,377 during the 2024/25 tax year. The income tax on this additional dividend is £6,877, payable by 31st January 2026.

By taking a loan in 2023 instead of a taxable dividend, Penelope has managed to defer paying income tax of £6,877 for two years.

The maximum total cost is £532. The cost would be significantly lower if the official rate of interest remained at 2%.

Additional points to note:

- If Penelope thinks her marginal income tax rate in 2024/25 may be higher than in 2022/23 she may be better off paying herself a dividend in January 2023 instead of taking a loan. In particular she may have to watch out for the £100,000 personal allowance withdrawal threshold.

- If Penelope can repay the loan out of her regular dividend income taxed at just 8.75% (i.e. without having to withdraw an additional dividend taxed at 33.75%) she may be able to *save* £6,877 income tax, not just defer paying it.

Longer-term Loans

Arguably, one could say it's worth every higher rate taxpayer director borrowing £10,000 from their company. There would be no benefit in kind charge but, as we know, a section 455 charge at 33.75% will arise if the loan is not repaid within nine months of the end of the accounting period in which it is made.

So, if the loan is left outstanding for a longer period, the director has extracted £10,000 from the company at a cost of £3,375.

BUT that's still cheaper than the cost to a higher rate taxpayer of getting a net sum of £10,000 by way of a dividend. To get £10,000 net of tax at 33.75% means taking a dividend of £15,094 and paying £5,094 in income tax: £1,719 more than the section 455 charge.

For an additional rate taxpayer to get a net sum of £10,000 by way of a dividend would mean taking a dividend of £16,488 and paying £6,488 in income tax at 39.35%: £3,113 more than the section 455 charge (the company charge is still at 33.75%, even if the director is an additional rate taxpayer).

Having borrowed £10,000 though, the director needs to be very careful. Even just £1 more borrowed for just one day would lead to a benefit in kind charge for the whole tax year. If the official rate rose to, say, 6%, this could cost a total of up to £337 in combined income tax and national insurance (net of corporation tax relief).

And remember, borrowing will include any goods or services provided to the director but not *immediately* paid for.

Hence, perhaps, if following this strategy, it may be best to leave a little leeway and only borrow, say £9,000.

Greater borrowings (potentially without limit) will enjoy similar benefits if used to invest in a qualifying close company. As we said above, this may not be the best way to finance, or structure, such an investment, but it could well beat taking a dividend.

Example

Dick owns Muttley Ltd, a successful trading company with over £200,000 in surplus cash sitting in its bank account. Together with three friends, Dick is planning to set up a property investment company to be called Pigeon Properties Ltd. Dick and his friends are each going to invest £100,000 in Pigeon Properties Ltd (the investment will be made up of 25 £1 shares and a loan to the company of £99,975, but it will all qualify).

Dick has no other resources available, so he will have to obtain the cash he needs from Muttley Ltd. So far this tax year, he has already taken a salary of £11,908 and dividends of £82,092, giving him taxable income of £94,000. He needs that income (£76,117 net of tax) to fund regular living expenses. Now he needs another £100,000. To get a further net sum of £100,000 in 2022/23, he will need to take a dividend of £168,913, which will suffer income tax as follows:

Cost of lost personal allowance	
Salary becoming taxable £11,908 x 20% =	*£2,382*
Dividend becoming taxable £662 x 33.75% =	*£223*
Dividend pushed into higher rate £11,908 x 25% =	*£2,977*
Tax on additional dividend	
£56,000 x 33.75%	*£18,900*
£112,913 x 39.35%	*£44,431*
Total tax suffered	*£68,913*

On the other hand, if Dick borrows £100,000 from Muttley Ltd, the section 455 charge will amount to just £33,750, saving £35,163 compared with taking a dividend.

Not only can this strategy lead to a massive, immediate saving, it's worth remembering that tax paid under the section 455 charge is ultimately repayable, tax paid on dividend income is not.

In fact, so great is this saving it may sometimes be worth contemplating this type of strategy even when the loan does not qualify for the benefit in kind exemption.

Let's say Dick was not going to invest in a qualifying company, but needed the £100,000 for some other type of investment (perhaps residential rental property owned personally). Let's also say his loan is interest free. For future years, let's assume the official rate rises to 6%, Muttley Ltd is paying corporation tax at 25%, and Dick takes a salary of £12,570 plus dividends of £81,430 to give him the same total taxable income of £94,000 as at present.

The annual benefit in kind on the loan will therefore be £6,000 (£100,000 @ 6%), leading to the following costs:

Income tax
Benefit in kind £6,000 x 20% =   £1,200
Dividend pushed into higher rate £6,000 x 25% = £1,500

Employer's national insurance £6,000 x 13.8% =   £828
Corporation tax relief thereon £828 x 25% =   (£207)

Total annual cost   £3,321

In this example, it will take eleven years before the cumulative annual cost of the loan exceeds the initial saving of £35,163.

Furthermore, assuming Dick eventually repays the loan and hence Muttley Ltd recoups the £33,750 section 455 charge, it will take 21 years before the cumulative annual cost exceeds the tax he would have suffered if he had taken a dividend.

As we have seen, for higher rate taxpayers, taking loans from your company can be a cheaper option than taking dividends. Where money is borrowed to make investments outside the company, and thus can reasonably be expected to ultimately be repaid, such a strategy may make sense.

However, borrowing long term from your own company simply to fund regular living expenses is not generally a good idea, due to the ultimate costs that could arise if the loan eventually has to be written off (see further below). Furthermore, if the company runs into financial difficulty, its creditors will be able to force you to sell personal assets in order to repay your loan.

Large loan balances also carry a risk of legal challenge, as it is questionable whether the director is fulfilling their duty to act in the best interests of the company: unless a market rate of interest is being paid and the company could not have obtained a better return by investing the funds elsewhere.

Loans to Directors – Other Issues

Loans to Family

You cannot necessarily avoid the section 455 tax charge and benefit-in-kind charge by making loans to family members.

For example, both the section 455 charge and the benefit-in-kind charge apply to loans to spouses and children of the director/shareholder and other close relatives. The section 455 charge also applies to loans to business partners.

The charges do not apply to loans to friends and some more distant relatives BUT you will incur the taxman's wrath if the benefit of the loan passes back to you or a close relative.

Loan Written Off

If the loan is formally released or written off by the company, the amount is likely to be treated as a deemed dividend for income tax purposes.

In most instances, the amount released will also be subject to employer's national insurance, like a benefit in kind.

This treatment was confirmed in the case of Stewart Fraser Ltd, which involved a write off of loans by a close company to an employee shareholder. The loan write offs were treated as distributions taxable on the employee and HMRC successfully argued that national insurance was also payable by the company.

Because of this national insurance cost you may wish to consider declaring a dividend to settle the debt, providing the company has sufficient distributable reserves. One drawback of this is a dividend would have to be paid to all shareholders pro rata.

A loan written off in these circumstances will not be deductible for corporation tax purposes. Any section 455 tax charge paid is, however, refunded to the company if the loan is released or written off. The safest course of action may be to ensure that any loan is always repaid, wherever possible, rather than written off.

Paperwork

Although it's simple in small companies to obtain shareholder approval for loans, it's important to get the paperwork right. There should be a proper loan agreement with written documentation outlining the nature of the loan, the company's liability and the amount and purpose of the loan.

The shareholders should then grant their approval at a meeting or by written resolution, again with all the appropriate documentation. Shareholder approval is not required for loans of up to £10,000, although it is good practice to continue to produce the same paperwork, where possible, as this may provide more certainty as to the tax treatment of the borrowed money.

Financial Reporting Standard 102 (FRS 102)

A recent financial reporting standard (FRS 102) may affect the accounting treatment of directors' loans in certain circumstances.

Where interest is not charged at a market rate the loan may have to be discounted in the company's accounts. For example, if the market interest rate is 5% and an interest-free loan of £100,000 is made to a director and is repayable after three years, the present value of the loan is £86,384:

$$£100,000/(1.05 \times 1.05 \times 1.05) = £86,384$$

The initial shortfall of £13,616 would be treated as a 'distribution'.

The tax treatment does not, however, follow the accounting treatment. The section 455 charge is still based on the total amount of the loan and the director's taxable benefit will be calculated in the way described earlier in this chapter.

To avoid the complexities of FRS 102, tax commentators suggest that it should be specifically recorded that directors' loan accounts are repayable on demand or to make sure that a market rate of interest is charged.

Of course, it's only an accounting adjustment, and there's no tax cost involved, but it is a nuisance. And one indirect consequence is that the deemed distribution (e.g. £13,616 in our example) reduces the company's distributable profits available for paying dividends.

Loan Recycling

To prevent directors simply repaying loans before the section 455 charge is payable, and then taking a new loan out straight away (known as 'bed and breakfasting'), there are some additional rules:

The 30 Day Rule

Relief from the section 455 charge is denied if:

- A shareholder makes repayments totalling £5,000 or more to the company and within 30 days...
- new loans totalling £5,000 or more are made to the same person or their associates

For this rule to apply, the original loan and repayment can take place in the same or different accounting periods. The new loan must be in a subsequent accounting period to the original loan.

It's important to point out that the 30-day rule does not apply where the loan is repaid using amounts that give rise to an income tax charge, for example where a taxable dividend is declared and credited to the director's loan account.

Example 1
During accounting period 1 there is a loan outstanding of £6,000. Two days before the end of the accounting period £6,000 is repaid. Three days into accounting period 2 a new £6,000 loan is taken. The repayment will be matched with the new loan, not the old loan. The loan from accounting period 1 is treated as still outstanding and will be subject to the section 455 tax charge if not repaid.

Example 2

C Ltd is a close company in which Jim is a shareholder. C Ltd's accounting period ends on 31st March 2023. On 25th March 2023, Jim borrows £15,000 from C Ltd. If the loan is not repaid within nine months of the end of the accounting period, C Ltd must pay a 33.75% section 455 tax charge (£5,063).

On 1st December 2023, a dividend of £9,000, which is chargeable to income tax, is declared by C Ltd and credited to Jim's loan account. On the same day, Jim repays the remaining £6,000 of his loan. On 10th December 2023, Jim borrows £3,500 from the company. On 15th December 2023, Jim borrows a further £2,000.

The section 455 tax charge is calculated as follows:

- £9,000 was repaid by applying a chargeable dividend towards the loan. This is ignored when it comes to applying the 30 day rule. The remaining £6,000 that Jim repays exceeds the £5,000 minimum repayment under the 30-day rule.

- Nine and 14 days later respectively (i.e. within 30 days) Jim withdraws a further £5,500 (£3,500 + £2,000) which is also in excess of the £5,000 limit for new loans.

- The new loans (£5,500) are less than the repayments (£6,000). Relief from the section 455 tax charge is denied on the lesser amount of £5,500, resulting in a tax charge of £1,856. Only the real repayment of £500 is recognised.

The Arrangements Rule

This rule applies even if the new borrowing takes place after 30 days. Relief from the section 455 charge will be denied if:

- Prior to repaying the loan, the total amount owed by the shareholder to the company is £15,000 or more, and
- At the time of the repayment, arrangements had been made for new loans of £5,000 or more to replace the amounts repaid.

The relief denied is the lower of the amount repaid and the new loan. 'Arrangements' are not defined and HMRC will give the term a wide meaning.

Once again, the arrangements rule does not apply if the loan is repaid with a taxable dividend or bonus. In other words, if a loan account is credited with a taxable dividend this will be treated as a valid loan repayment.

Example

Brigitte owes her company Bard Ltd £25,000 which she borrowed on 1st June 2022 during the accounting period ending 30th June 2022.

After the end of the accounting period, Brigitte takes a 45-day loan from the bank for £25,000 and uses it to repay the loan to her company. 40 days after repaying her company, Brigitte takes a new loan of £30,000 from her company and uses it to repay the bank.

There is a significant risk HMRC will argue that, at the time she repaid her company, Brigitte had made arrangements to withdraw a new amount from her company (to repay the bank), so the original loan will be treated as not repaid. Thus the section 455 charge will become payable on the initial £25,000 loan, unless a further repayment is made.

What is a Valid Income Tax Charge?

As mentioned above, the anti-avoidance rules do not apply if the amount repaid gives rise to an income tax charge in the hands of the director-shareholder.

This will be the case if a loan is repaid by means of a dividend credited to the director's loan account which is included as income on the director's tax return (or where a bonus is paid subject to PAYE before being credited to the director's loan account).

According to HMRC, if a dividend is first paid out in cash and the money is then paid back into the company and credited to the director's loan account, the exemption does not apply.

HMRC also contends that, if the director owns the business premises and the company pays them rent, the exemption does not apply to rent credited to the director's loan account.

Chapter 24

Rental Income: Better than Dividends

Many company owners own their business premises *personally* and the company pays them rent.

Paying yourself rent is often more tax efficient than paying yourself a higher salary. Like salaries, rental payments are a tax deductible expense (providing the rent does not exceed the market rent). But, unlike salaries, there is no national insurance cost.

Following recent increases in dividend tax rates, rental income is also more tax efficient than dividend income and is becoming even more attractive for those whose companies face higher corporation tax rates (Chapter 1).

Of course, there are also non-tax reasons why you may wish to pay yourself rental income instead of withdrawing dividends from your company. For starters, to pay dividends the company must have sufficient distributable profits. There is no such requirement when it comes to paying rent.

Secondly, with rental income it is relatively straightforward to pay yourself a fixed monthly amount throughout the year, for example by setting up a direct debit from your company bank account to your personal bank account. This could be helpful if you have to personally pay various costs associated with the property, especially mortgage interest.

With rental income there is no requirement to continually do all the paperwork that often accompanies dividends, for example holding directors' board meetings and shareholder meetings.

How much better off could you be by paying yourself rental income instead of dividends? It all depends on your personal circumstances, for example how much taxable income you have and the amount of tax deductible mortgage interest you have.

Example – Basic-rate Taxpayer

Warren is a company owner and a basic-rate taxpayer. He personally owns the property out of which the company operates but the company currently doesn't pay him any rent. He does not have any tax deductible mortgage interest to offset.

During the current 2022/23 tax year he decides to pay himself a small salary of £9,100 (see Chapter 19). He also has other taxable income which uses up the balance of his £12,570 income tax personal allowance. He withdraws the rest of the company's profits as dividends.

Let's say he gets the company to pay him rental income of £10,000 per year. After paying income tax at 20% he will be left with £8,000.

If the company had not paid him rent it would have had an extra £8,100 at most to pay dividends (£10,000 profit less at least 19% corporation tax). Warren would have been left with £7,391 at most after paying 8.75% income tax.

By getting the company to pay him rent Warren is better off by at least £609. This is because, for basic-rate taxpayers, the combined tax rate on dividends is currently around 26% at least, compared with 20% for rental income.

Example 1 – Higher-rate Taxpayer

The facts are exactly the same except Warren is a higher-rate taxpayer. If he gets the company to pay him rental income of £10,000, after paying income tax at 20% he will be left with £8,000.

However, his rental income will use up £10,000 of his basic-rate band which means £10,000 of his dividend income will be taxed at 33.75% instead of 8.75%, resulting in additional tax of £2,500. Overall Warren will be left with £5,500 (£8,000 - £2,500).

If the company had not paid him any rental income, it would have been left with an extra £8,100 at most to pay out as dividends and Warren would have been left with £5,366 after paying income tax at 33.75%.

Rental income is still more tax efficient than dividends but in this example the saving could be very small – perhaps just £134 on £10,000 of rental income. If Warren's company has a higher marginal corporation tax rate, the saving will be slightly greater, although still not really significant as far as the current, 2022/23 tax year is concerned.

In other cases, however, higher-rate taxpayers could save considerably more tax by paying themselves rental income:

Example 2 – Higher-rate Taxpayer

This time we'll assume that Warren's premises are more substantial and he gets the company to pay him rental income of £37,700. Along with his salary and other non-dividend income this will take him up to the £50,270 higher-rate threshold. After paying 20% tax on his rental income he will be left with £30,160 of this income.

His rental income will use up his entire £37,700 basic-rate band, which means £35,700 of his dividend income will be taxed at 33.75% instead of 8.75%, resulting in additional tax of £8,925 (it's £35,700 and not £37,700 because of his £2,000 dividend allowance for 2022/23).

Overall Warren will be left with £21,235 (£30,160 - £8,925) from his rental income of £37,700.

If the company had not paid him £37,700 of rental income, it would have been left with an extra £30,537, at most, of after-tax profit to pay out as dividends. Warren would then have been left with £20,231 after paying income tax at 33.75%.

Warren is at least £1,004 better off by paying himself rental income.

After the Corporation Tax Increase

Once the corporation tax increase begins to affect the company (see Chapter 1) the tax savings enjoyed from rental income will be greater. This will apply to most companies, except those with annual profits of less than £50,000. Whereas rental income will enjoy corporation tax relief, dividends will be paid out of profits that have been taxed at up to 25% or 26.5%, compared with 19% previously.

If we assume that Warren's company in the above example has a future marginal corporation tax rate of 26.5%, he could end up £2,877 better off by paying himself rental income in future tax years.

In the meantime, since rent is a periodic cost (see Chapter 1), the effective overall rate of corporation tax relief on rental income paid to a director in 2022/23 will generally be as set out in Appendix B.

Mortgage Interest and Other Property Expenses

Many company owners who personally own their business premises will also have a mortgage over those premises on which they personally pay the interest. These interest payments can be offset against your rental income, effectively making some or all of it 'tax free'.

Note that, although tax relief on mortgage interest for residential property has been reduced (see Chapter 20), mortgages used to buy commercial properties are unaffected.

Most company owners will instinctively realise that it would be foolish not to receive rental income if they also have mortgage interest to set off (or other tax-deductible property expenses). Tax-free rental income has to be better than a taxable dividend!

Example 3 – Higher-rate Taxpayer

Warren has a salary and other income of £12,570, is a higher-rate taxpayer and has tax deductible mortgage interest of £5,000. If he gets the company to pay him rental income of £10,000, he'll have a taxable rental profit of £5,000. After paying income tax at 20% he will be left with £4,000 (£10,000 - £5,000 interest - £1,000 tax).

His taxable rental income will use up £5,000 of his basic-rate band which means £5,000 of his dividend income will be taxed at 33.75% instead of 8.75%, resulting in additional tax of £1,250. Overall Warren will be left with £2,750 (£4,000 - £1,250).

If the company had not paid him any rental income, it would have been left with an extra £8,100 at most to pay out as dividends (assuming 19% corporation tax) and Warren would have been left with £5,366 after paying income tax at 33.75%. After paying his interest costs Warren would be left with just £366.

Overall, Warren is £2,384 better off paying himself rental income.

After the Corporation Tax Increase

Once the corporation tax increase begins to affect his company, Warren will again be even better off paying himself rental income. If we assume his company has a future marginal corporation tax rate of 26.5%, he will end up £2,881 better off in future tax years by paying himself rental income instead of a dividend.

Summary

The above examples illustrate that it is often more tax efficient to get your company to pay you rent instead of dividend income.

Rental income is most tax efficient to the extent that you have tax deductible costs to offset, such as mortgage interest.

The savings vary considerably from case to case so it is essential to do your own number crunching.

The potential tax savings will be even higher when the increase in corporation tax begins to affect your company.

Business Asset Disposal Relief (BADR)

Although you may be able to save income tax by paying yourself as much rental income as possible, there is one reason why you may prefer to get your company to pay you a below-market rent.

If you sell your business, you may be able to claim Business Asset Disposal Relief ('BADR'), which means you may be able to pay capital gains tax at just 10%.

Trading premises can also qualify for BADR, even if you own them personally. But you cannot claim the relief if your company has paid you a full market rent (although rent paid for periods before 6th April 2008 is ignored). If your company pays you a rent that is lower than the market rent, or if you owned the property before April 2008, then a partial claim can usually be made.

If BADR is not available when you dispose of your premises you will be subject to capital gains tax at the normal rates for commercial property. Higher-rate taxpayers pay 20% capital gains tax and 10% tax is payable to the extent your basic-rate band is not used up by your income.

So it's possible that, even without BADR, company owners will be able to benefit from a 10% tax rate on at least some of their capital gains by making sure they don't have much taxable income in the year they sell their trading premises.

Furthermore, since the lifetime maximum cumulative claim for BADR by any individual has been reduced to just £1m, many company owners will exhaust their potential relief on the sale of the company itself, so that there is none remaining for the gain on their business premises: in which case, there is no disadvantage in paying yourself a full market rent.

Capital Allowances

Company owners who also own the company's business premises personally may be entitled to claim capital allowances on part of the cost of the property. However, where less than full market rent is charged, the company owner can only claim a suitable proportion of the available capital allowances. For example, if the rent charged equates to 75% of a full market rent, 75% of the available allowances may be claimed.

This means the income tax advantages of paying yourself full market rent may be even greater than we have seen so far: and this may be enough to outweigh any potential loss of Business Asset Disposal Relief.

For further details of the capital allowances available on business property owned personally see the Taxcafe guide *'How to Save Property Tax'*.

Chapter 25

Pay Yourself Tax-free Interest Income

If your company owes you money you can make it pay you interest. In some cases the interest will be both a tax deductible expense for the company and tax free in your hands – the best case scenario when it comes to extracting money from your company.

In this situation extracting interest income may be more tax efficient than other types of income, including dividends.

How can interest income be tax free? For starters, interest is not subject to national insurance. As for income tax, there is a 0% 'starting rate band' for up to £5,000 of savings income.

There's also a personal savings allowance which shelters up to £1,000 of interest income from tax if you're a basic-rate taxpayer and £500 if you're a higher-rate taxpayer (additional-rate taxpayers do not benefit from the personal savings allowance).

In Chapter 20 we were looking at company owners with income from *other sources*, including interest from investments. In this chapter we're looking at a different type of interest income: interest that comes out of your own company.

The £5,000 Starting Rate Band

Not everyone can benefit from the 0% starting rate. It's designed to benefit those with very low income. Hence the £5,000 starting rate band is reduced if you have any *taxable non-savings income*.

Non-savings income includes income from employment, self-employment, pensions and rental properties. Crucially, it does not include dividend income.

Furthermore, thanks to the personal allowance, the first £12,570 of non-savings income you receive is effectively not taxable and thus cannot reduce the £5,000 starting rate band (unless your total income exceeds £100,000).

For example, if you have a salary of £12,570 this year and no other income apart from dividends, you won't have any taxable non-savings income and can receive £5,000 of tax-free interest.

You may also be able to receive up to £1,000 of additional tax-free interest thanks to the personal savings allowance.

But if you have a salary of £12,570 and rental income of more than £5,000, your rental income will eat up your entire starting rate band, so none of your interest income will be tax-free under the 0% starting rate.

You may, however, be able to receive up to £1,000 of tax-free interest thanks to the personal savings allowance.

The £5,000 starting rate band is not given in addition to the basic-rate band – it is part of the basic-rate band. In other words, if you have £5,000 of interest income your basic-rate band will be reduced by £5,000.

This means some of your dividend income may be pushed into the higher-rate tax bracket.

This may reduce the attractiveness of extracting interest income from your company but may not eliminate the benefit altogether.

The Personal Savings Allowance

The personal savings allowance (also known as the savings nil rate band) operates separately from, and in addition to, the starting rate band. This means some company owners will be able to pay themselves up to £6,000 of tax-free interest per year.

The personal savings allowance is especially useful to company owners who cannot use the starting rate band because they have too much non-savings income, e.g. rental income.

They can typically extract £1,000 (basic-rate taxpayers) or £500 (higher-rate taxpayers) of tax-free interest from their companies.

Lending to Your Company

There are lots of circumstances in which company owners may lend money to their companies. For example, it may be a new company that needs some cash to get started or a well-established company that needs money to buy some new equipment.

In some cases company owners lend money to their companies indirectly, for example when a dividend is declared but the cash is not withdrawn immediately, perhaps because the company owner wants to reinvest it to help the business grow.

The Mechanics of Extracting Interest Income

There is no requirement for a director to charge interest on a loan account with their own company but, if they do, it must not exceed a reasonable commercial rate.

If the company pays more than a commercial rate the excess payment could be treated as salary income and subject to income tax and national insurance.

Interest paid to a director on their loan account will usually be an allowable expense for the company, providing the money is used for business purposes. The interest will therefore provide corporation tax relief.

Although your interest income may ultimately be tax free, the company will have to deduct income tax (at 20%) and pay this to HMRC quarterly, using form CT61 (which can be requested online). If this results in a tax overpayment, you can reclaim the excess through your self-assessment tax return. The company should also issue you an annual interest certificate.

While interest can be a very tax efficient way to extract money from your company, the additional reporting duties and payments may put some company owners off.

How Much Tax Can You Save?

This will depend on *how much* and what *type* of income you earn.

Example 1
Basic-Rate Taxpayer, No Taxable Non-Savings Income

Gillian is a company director with salary and other non-savings income (e.g. rental income) of £12,570. She has £15,000 of dividend income. She charges her company £5,000 interest for a substantial loan she made to help it buy new equipment. Interest is at a commercial rate.

The interest will be a tax deductible business expense, saving the company at least £950 corporation tax (£5,000 x 19%). Gillian has no taxable non-savings income so all of her interest income will be tax free, being covered by the £5,000 starting rate band (although the company will initially have to withhold 20% tax and pay this to HMRC).

If instead Gillian decided to NOT pay herself interest, the company would have an extra £5,000 of taxable profit. After paying at least £950 corporation tax there would be an extra £4,050 at most that could be paid out as dividends taxed at 8.75%, leaving Gillian with £3,696.

The potential tax saving is at least £1,304.

Example 2
Higher-Rate Taxpayer, No Taxable Non-Savings Income

As before Gillian has £12,570 of salary and other non-savings income and £5,000 of interest from her company. However, this time she has dividend income of £50,000 which means she pays 33.75% tax.

Gillian can enjoy £5,000 of tax-free interest income but because the starting rate band is part of the basic-rate band an additional £5,000 of her dividends will be taxed at 33.75% instead of 8.75%, resulting in additional tax of £1,250. So effectively Gillian receives £3,750 after tax.

If she did not pay herself interest, the company would have an extra £5,000 profit. After paying at least £950 corporation tax there would be an extra £4,050 at most to pay out as dividends, leaving her with £2,683 at most after tax.

For a higher-rate taxpayer with no taxable non-savings income the potential saving is £1,067 (£3,750 - £2,683).

Example 3
Basic-Rate Taxpayer, No Starting Rate Band Available
This time Gillian has £17,570 of salary and rental income, £5,000 of interest income and £15,000 of dividend income.

Because she has £5,000 of taxable non-savings income (£17,570 - £12,570 personal allowance) she will have no starting rate band available. However, thanks to the personal savings allowance, £1,000 of her interest income will be tax free and the rest will be taxed at 20%, leaving her with £4,200.

If Gillian did not pay herself interest, the company would have an extra £5,000 of taxable profit. After paying at least £950 corporation tax there would be an extra £4,050 at most that could be paid out as dividends taxed at 8.75%, leaving her with £3,696.

So in this case Gillian is at least £504 better off paying herself interest. Not only is £1,000 of her interest income tax free, the remaining £4,000 is taxed at just 20% (remember the total combined tax rate on dividend income is currently at least 26% if you are a basic-rate taxpayer).

Example 4
Higher-Rate Taxpayer, No Starting Rate Band Available
This time Gillian has £17,570 of salary and rental income, £5,000 of interest income and £50,000 of dividend income. Once again she will have no starting rate band available. However, thanks to the personal savings allowance, £500 of her interest income will be tax free and the rest will be taxed at 20%, leaving her with £4,100.

An additional £5,000 of her dividend income will be taxed at 33.75% instead of 8.75%, resulting in an additional income tax charge of £1,250. So effectively Gillian ends up with £2,850 after tax.

If instead she had decided to not pay herself interest, the company would have an extra £5,000 of taxable profit. After paying at least £950 corporation tax there would be an extra £4,050 at most that could be paid out as dividends, leaving her with £2,683 at most after tax.

So in this case Gillian is just £167 better off paying herself interest.

The tax saving in this last example is quite marginal, especially considering the company will have to deduct 20% tax from the interest it pays to Gillian and she can only recover the excess over her true, final liability when she submits her tax return.

However, this saving will increase in future years if the company has annual profits of more than £50,000, and could reach as much as £415 (see further below regarding the impact of the corporation tax increase).

Making the Most of Your Personal Allowance

If you pay yourself a salary of £9,100 and do not have any rental income or other non-savings income, you will have spare personal allowance of £3,470 (£12,570 - £9,100) to set off against your interest or dividends.

In Chapter 20 we saw how you can save tax by allocating your spare personal allowance to your dividend income rather than your interest income (if your interest is tax free anyway).

In that chapter we were focusing on interest income from investments but the same principle applies when you extract interest income from your own company.

Example 5
Higher-Rate Taxpayer, Spare Personal Allowance
Roisin's company pays her a salary of £9,100 and she extracts the remaining profits as dividends totalling £50,000. She has no other income and therefore has spare personal allowance of £3,470 to use against her dividends. She ends up with after-tax income of £52,996.

Let's now assume Roisin receives £5,000 of interest from her company (which also reduces the amount of profit that can be distributed as dividends).

*If her spare personal allowance of £3,470 is set against her **interest income** she will end up with after-tax income of £53,759 – £763 more than before.*

*But if her spare personal allowance is set against her **dividend income** she will end up with £54,063 – an additional £304.*

Overall Roisin ends up £1,067 better off by extracting £5,000 of interest from her company but the maximum saving is only achieved if she allocates her personal allowance correctly.

After the Corporation Tax Increase

Getting your company to pay you interest instead of dividends will become even more attractive when the corporation tax increase begins to affect your company.

Once the corporation tax increase is in full force, dividends will be paid out of profits that may have already suffered corporation tax of 25% or 26.5%, whereas an interest payment will enjoy full corporation tax relief.

For example, for Gillian in Example 2 the potential saving could rise from £1,067 to £1,315.

In the meantime, for payments of interest during the 2022/23 tax year, since interest is a periodic cost (see Chapter 1), the effective rate of corporation tax relief will generally be as set out in Appendix B.

Tax-free Loan Repayments

Apart from the beneficial tax treatment of interest income, it's worth pointing out that some or all of the outstanding balance on a director's loan account can be paid out tax free at any time.

Having such an amount 'banked' inside your company that can be withdrawn tax free at any time could prove useful, for example if the director unexpectedly requires additional money that would be taxed heavily as a salary or dividend.

The only potential cost of making loan repayments is where the director is claiming qualifying loan interest on amounts borrowed to invest in the company. Let's say, for example, a director borrowed £100,000 and then loaned that sum to their own company. Provided the company was carrying on a qualifying business (trading or letting property to unconnected third parties will qualify), the director can claim the interest paid on their personal borrowing for income tax purposes (it can be set against any personal income, not just against interest income).

As long as the company continues to owe the director at least £100,000, they may continue to claim full income tax relief for their personal interest cost. However, if the company repays part of the director's loan so that the balance falls below £100,000, the director's qualifying loan interest claim must be restricted accordingly.

Having said that, losing some of the tax relief for the director's personal interest costs will almost certainly be a lot cheaper than the income tax suffered on additional dividends taken out of the company instead of a loan repayment.

Note that qualifying loan interest is subject to an annual cap, which is generally the greater of £50,000 or 25% of the director's total income for the year. That's usually enough for most people though. For further details, see the Taxcafe guide *'Using a Property Company to Save Tax'*.

Summary

Some company owners may be able to save over £1,000 by getting their companies to pay them interest.

The potential tax saving is a lot smaller if there is no starting rate band available, for example if the taxpayer has a significant amount of salary income or rental income.

For many taxpayers the additional tax paperwork will nullify the tax savings: although this burden can be significantly reduced by making a single, annual interest payment.

Finally, it's important to remember that the interest you charge your company must be at no more than a commercial rate. However, in most cases, your loan to the company will be unsecured and for no fixed term. Hence it will be more akin to an overdraft than a mortgage or personal loan and the question of what constitutes a commercial rate can be judged in that context.

Chapter 26

Charitable Donations: You or the Company?

Who should donate to charity: you or your company?

In this chapter we'll focus on the tax benefits and drawbacks of both types of donation, although *non-tax* factors may be more important.

For example, charitable donations by your company could enhance its reputation and good standing in the community which in turn could help its business.

Donations by Your Company

Charitable donations are a tax deductible expense for corporation tax purposes. So if your company donates £100 its taxable profits will be reduced by £100, saving it at least £19 corporation tax.

The company can also enjoy tax relief when it gives money to community amateur sports clubs, a list of which can be obtained by entering 'community amateur sports clubs registered with HMRC' into a search engine like Google.

No gift aid declaration is necessary for company donations (see below for more on gift aid declarations).

Nevertheless you should still obtain documentation from the charity to support the donation, just as you would for any other business expense.

Charitable donations cannot create or increase a trading loss. If the donation exceeds the company's taxable profit, the excess will not enjoy any corporation tax relief and cannot be carried forward to the next year.

Donations do not enjoy automatic corporation tax relief if there are strings attached, for example a condition that the charity will buy goods from the company (or anyone connected with the company). However, where the donation was clearly intended to benefit the company's business, the cost may still be allowable as a regular business expense, like advertising.

Companies don't have to donate money, they can also donate equipment, stock (the goods they sell), or employees' time.

If a company donates equipment (e.g. furniture and computers) on which capital allowances have been claimed the disposal value used in the capital allowances calculation is zero. Normally when a business gives away an asset on which capital allowances have been claimed the disposal value is the market value of the asset.

If a company donates its trading stock it can claim the cost of the goods as an expense for corporation tax purposes.

If the company is VAT registered it will need to account for VAT on the items given to charity. However, you can apply VAT at the zero rate if the charity will sell, hire out or export the item donated. This means you can still reclaim the VAT on the cost of the stock donated.

If a company lends an employee to a charity the employee's salary can still be claimed as a business cost for corporation tax purposes.

Grassroots Sports

A corporation tax deduction is available for contributions to grassroots sports, even where the beneficiary is not a registered charity.

The rules allow companies to deduct all contributions to grassroots sports through recognised sport governing bodies, and deductions of up to £2,500 annually for contributions made directly to grassroots sports, without the involvement of a qualifying sports body.

Donations by You Personally

If you make a charitable donation of, say, £80 the charity can claim £20 gift aid. Essentially what the charity is doing is reclaiming from HMRC the 20% basic-rate tax you will typically have paid on £80 of after-tax income.

The charity will require you to make a gift aid declaration. This entails stating that you have paid sufficient tax to cover the basic-rate tax the charity reclaims.

It is important that you are actually liable for the tax the charity reclaims. The tax can be either income tax or capital gains tax (but not national insurance).

For example, a company owner with a salary of £11,908 and dividend of £25,000 will face an income tax bill of £1,955 in 2022/23.

If that company owner makes an £8,000 charitable donation, the gift aid rules require that the donor has paid tax of £2,000. The company owner will therefore have to make up the shortfall of £45.

Higher-rate Taxpayers

Higher-rate taxpayers who make charitable donations can claim higher-rate tax relief when they submit their tax returns.

Example
Melinda, a company owner who takes most of her income as dividends, donates £80 to a charity. The gift aid on the donation is £20, resulting in a gross donation of £100.

Melinda's basic-rate band is extended by £100 which means she will pay 8.75% tax instead of 33.75% tax on an additional £100 of her dividend income. This will save her £25 income tax.

In summary, Melinda has effectively made a £100 donation with a net cost to her of £55. The basic-rate tax relief goes to the charity, the higher-rate tax relief goes to the person making the donation.

Protecting Child Benefit & Personal Allowance

Your family's child benefit is gradually taken away when the highest earner in the household has adjusted net income of more than £50,000. All the child benefit will be withdrawn when that person's income exceeds £60,000.

Your personal allowance is also gradually taken away when your adjusted net income exceeds £100,000. All of your personal allowance is withdrawn when your income exceeds £125,140 in 2022/23.

Like pension contributions, gift aid donations reduce your adjusted net income and can therefore be used to increase your personal allowance or protect your family's child benefit payments, in addition to enjoying higher-rate tax relief.

Example

Hassan is a company owner with salary and dividend income of £110,000. He donates £4,000 to his favourite charity and the gift aid on the donation is £1,000, resulting in a gross donation of £5,000. As a result his adjusted net income is reduced by £5,000 from £110,000 to £105,000. This in turn increases his personal allowance by £2,500.

If Hassan has taken a salary of £9,100 and the rest of his income as dividends, his £4,000 donation will save him £2,266 in income tax, meaning the net cost to him is only £1,734. If he has taken a salary of £11,908, his income tax saving will be £2,375 and the net cost of his donation will be just £1,625: that's more than £3 for the charity for every £1 it costs Hassan.

Carrying Back Donations to the Previous Tax Year

You can claim tax relief on donations a year early if you like. For example, you can claim tax relief for donations you have made during the current 2022/23 tax year when you submit your tax return for 2021/22.

Understandably, you can only claim tax relief for donations made between 6th April 2022 and the date you file your 2021/22 tax return, and the return must be filed on time (i.e. by 31st January 2023 if filed online).

This option to carry back donations is attractive if you want the tax relief sooner or if you were a higher-rate taxpayer during the previous tax year but you are not certain whether you will be a higher-rate taxpayer this year.

When you come to submit your 2021/22 tax return you will know for certain your taxable income for that year and thus how much tax relief you will obtain.

Similarly, carrying back donations may be attractive if your income in the previous 2021/22 tax year was in the £50,000-£60,000 bracket (child benefit withdrawal) or the £100,000-£125,140 bracket (personal allowance withdrawal).

In these cases you may enjoy extra tax relief on your charitable donations if you do not expect your income to fall into those tax brackets this year.

Note that only specific donations may be carried back and not an arbitrary sum: for example, if you made a single net donation of £800 (£1,000 gross), you can either carry it back or not, you cannot carry back, say, £400.

By contrast, if you had made four separate donations of £200 each (even if to the same charity) you could carry back any combination of those donations totalling £200, £400, £600, or £800, thus giving you far greater flexibility.

For this reason, regular, small donations will offer more opportunities to optimise your tax position.

Company versus Personal Donations

In this section we will compare the tax relief enjoyed by companies on their charitable donations with the tax relief enjoyed by individuals.

Example – Basic-rate taxpayer
Beric's company has £1,000 in its bank account which he would like to give to charity. If the company makes the donation it will enjoy corporation tax relief so the whole £1,000 can be paid directly to the charity with no further tax consequences.

If instead Beric decides to make the donation personally, the company will pay at least 19% corporation tax, leaving £810 at most to pay out as additional dividend income.

Let's say Beric holds onto £10 and gives £800 to the charity. The taxman will add £200 of gift aid, leaving the charity with the same amount – £1,000.

But that's not the end of the matter: Beric will still have to pay 8.75% tax on his £810 dividend – £71. Beric is worse of by about £60 (£71 less the £10 of dividend income he held onto).

Thus, if you're a basic-rate taxpayer, for every £1,000 that ends up with the charity you will have to pay an additional 6% in tax.

In this case a company donation is clearly more tax efficient than a donation made personally by the company owner.

Example – Higher-rate taxpayer
This time we'll assume Beric is a higher-rate taxpayer. If the company makes the donation it can pay £1,000 directly to the charity. Alternatively Beric can pay himself additional dividend income of up to £810, hold onto £10 and give £800 to the charity. The taxman will add £200 of gift aid, resulting in the same donation of £1,000.

Again, that's not the end of the matter. Beric still has to pay income tax on the additional dividend.

With a gross donation of £1,000, Beric's basic-rate band will be increased by £1,000. This means the £810 dividend will be taxed at just 8.75%, not 33.75%, so the tax will be £71.

Furthermore, an additional £190 of his other dividend income will also be taxed at 8.75% instead of 33.75%, saving him an extra £48.

All in all a £1,000 donation made by the company owner is only £13 more expensive than a donation made by the company:

£71 income tax - £48 higher-rate relief - £10 saved dividend = £13

In this case a company donation is again more tax efficient than a contribution made personally by the director but the difference is small.

Because the saving is so small it will probably be other factors that determine whether the company or the individual makes the donation.

Example Revisited – Personal Allowance Withdrawal

Previously, we saw that Hassan was able to make a gross donation of £5,000 to his favourite charity at a net cost to him of only £1,734, or perhaps even just £1,625.

However, it's worth considering whether this was the best strategy for him to follow. Assuming his company still has a corporation tax rate of 19% this year, if it had made the £5,000 donation to the charity, this would have reduced Hassan's dividend income by £4,050, thus in turn significantly reducing his income tax bill.

Let's compare the two scenarios based on the assumption that Hassan takes a salary of £9,100 and the rest of his income as dividends:

Personal Donation

Total income	£110,000
Income tax suffered	£22,876
Charitable donation	£4,000
Net income remaining	£83,124

Company Donation

Total income	£105,950
Income tax suffered	£22,920
Net income remaining	£83,030

In this example, the company owner would be slightly worse off if the charitable donation was made by the company instead of by them personally. But it's pretty marginal with an overall difference of just £94.

After the Corporation Tax Increase

Some companies will eventually enjoy up to 25% or 26.5% tax relief on their charitable donations, compared with 19% previously.

In such cases company donations will become even more attractive than donations made personally out of dividend income that has been more heavily taxed.

Some company owners may consider postponing charitable donations until the corporation tax increase is in full force, so that more tax relief can be enjoyed.

A company that will have a marginal tax rate of 26.5% will be able to enjoy up to £75 more tax relief for every £1,000 of charitable donations it postpones. A company which will have a marginal tax rate of 25% will enjoy up to £60 of additional tax relief.

However, the company may have to wait a while to enjoy the maximum tax relief. For a company with a January to December accounting period, only donations made from January 2024 onwards will enjoy up to 26.5% tax relief, although donations made between January and December 2023 will enjoy up to 24.65% tax relief (a charitable donation is not a periodic cost, so the marginal tax rate applying is as set out in Appendix A in this case).

Some company owners may be willing to postpone making donations for this amount of time; others may feel that their favoured charities require help sooner.

As for someone like Hassan, if his company's marginal corporation tax rate is 24.65% when the donation is made, he will be slightly better off if the company makes the donation: but it's still pretty marginal.

Chapter 27

Pension Contributions: Better than Dividends

Following the latest increase in dividend tax rates in April 2022, some company owners may be thinking about paying themselves smaller dividends and getting their companies to make bigger pension contributions instead.

When their company's corporation tax rate increases, some company owners may find it even more appealing to make pension contributions instead of paying themselves additional dividend income. This is because dividends will be paid out of profits that have been more heavily taxed.

By contrast, when the corporation tax rate increases many companies will enjoy more tax relief on any pension contributions they make for their directors and employees.

At the time of writing many companies are enjoying 19% tax relief on their pension contributions but this will rise to 26.5% for those with profits between £50,000 and £250,000 and 25% for companies with profits in excess of £250,000.

If such a company has profits of £100,000 it will currently save £1,900 corporation tax by making a pension contribution of £10,000. When the company's marginal rate of tax increases to 26.5% it will save £2,650 tax.

There are several reasons why pension contributions are currently an attractive alternative to dividends and may become even more attractive when corporation tax increases:

- Like salaries, company pension contributions enjoy corporation tax relief. In other words, they're a tax deductible business expense.

- Unlike salaries, there is no national insurance on the income you eventually withdraw from your pension.

- When you eventually withdraw money from your pension, 25% can be taken tax free.

- Pension income is taxed at the 'regular' income tax rates, typically 20% or 40%. By contrast, for companies currently paying 19% corporation tax, the combined tax rate on dividend income is around 26% for basic-rate taxpayers and 46% for higher-rate taxpayers. When corporation tax increases these combined tax rates will rise to approximately 32% and 50% respectively for owners of companies with profits in excess of £250,000. Similar rates will be payable by many owners of smaller companies.

- When you start withdrawing income from your pension, you could find yourself in a lower tax bracket than you are now (many retirees are basic-rate taxpayers). This means you could end up paying income tax at just 20%.

Putting all this together, it's possible that you could ultimately pay income tax on your pension withdrawals at an overall effective rate of just 15%.

By contrast, you may face a combined tax rate that is possibly two to three times higher if the same money is paid out as dividend income.

There is, of course, a major drawback with pensions: your money is locked away until you are 55 (rising to 57 in 2028). Nevertheless, when you do reach the minimum retirement age you can make unlimited withdrawals.

Another drawback with pensions is you are potentially exposed to any future increase in income tax rates. Essentially your savings are at the mercy of future governments.

Having said this, we do believe that pension contributions are still worth making in many cases.

Example – Higher-rate Taxpayer
Before Corporation Tax Increase
Lesleyanne is a company owner and a higher-rate taxpayer (i.e. her taxable income is more than £50,270).

Let's say she is trying to choose between taking an additional £1,000 of the company's profit as a dividend and getting the company to invest £1,000 in her self-invested personal pension (SIPP).

With a dividend the company will first pay corporation tax at 19% (£190), leaving £810 to distribute. Lesleyanne will then pay income tax at 33.75%: £273. The total combined tax rate on the dividend is roughly 46%.

By contrast, a company pension contribution will enjoy corporation tax relief so the whole £1,000 will go straight into Lesleyanne's SIPP. Ignoring investment growth (it doesn't affect the outcome), when she eventually withdraws the money from her pension the first £250 will be tax free and the remaining £750 will be subject to income tax.

If Lesleyanne is a basic-rate taxpayer when she retires in the future she will pay 20% income tax (£150), leaving her with £850 overall. Thus her effective overall tax rate will be 15%.

If Lesleyanne is a higher-rate taxpayer when she retires (for example, if she ends up with a significant amount of rental income from buy-to-let properties) she will effectively pay 40% tax on her taxable pension income (£300), leaving her with £700 overall. Thus the effective tax rate on her pension withdrawals will be 30%.

If Lesleyanne does not have much income from other sources when she retires (except perhaps for her state pension), it's also possible that some of her pension withdrawals will be covered by her income tax personal allowance and therefore tax free. Although this is a distinct possibility for many retirees we will ignore it for the remainder of this chapter so as not to overstate the potential benefits of pensions.

In summary, Lesleyanne's choice is between paying tax at roughly 46% on her additional dividend income and paying tax at 15% or possibly 30% on her pension withdrawals.

Example – Higher-rate Taxpayer
After Corporation Tax Increase

Let's say that after the increase in corporation tax is in full force Lesleyanne's company makes profits of approximately £100,000 and she is once again trying to choose between the same additional dividend and pension contribution.

With a dividend the company will face a marginal corporation tax rate of 26.5% which means it will pay £265 tax, leaving £735 to distribute. Lesleyanne will then pay income tax at 33.75%: £248. The total combined tax rate on the dividend will be roughly 51%.

With a company pension contribution the whole £1,000 will go straight into Lesleyanne's SIPP. The effective tax rate on her pension withdrawals will be either 15% if she is a basic-rate taxpayer when she retires or 30% as a higher-rate taxpayer.

In summary, Lesleyanne's choice will be between paying tax at roughly 51% on her additional dividend income and paying tax at 15% or possibly 30% on her pension withdrawals.

What these examples show is that, for company owners who have not yet built up significant pension savings, a company pension contribution is currently an extremely attractive alternative to additional dividend income and will become even more attractive when the corporation tax increase is in full force.

Of course, one must never lose sight of the fact that your pension savings are placed in a locked box until you are at least 55. So a company pension contribution is only an attractive alternative to a dividend if you have already withdrawn enough money from your company to cover your living costs.

In the above example we have assumed that the company will have a marginal tax rate of 26.5% after the increase in corporation tax. If its profits are greater than £250,000 it will face a marginal tax rate of 25%. In this case Lesleyanne's choice will be between paying tax at roughly 50% on her additional dividend income and paying tax at 15% or possibly 30% on her pension withdrawals.

Are company pension contributions attractive if you're a basic-rate taxpayer (i.e. if your taxable income is less than £50,270)? Let's find out:

Example – Basic-rate Taxpayer
Before Corporation Tax Increase
Poppy is a company owner and a basic-rate taxpayer. She too is trying to choose between taking £1,000 of the company's profit as a dividend and a £1,000 company pension contribution.

With a dividend the company will first pay corporation tax at 19% (£190), leaving £810 to distribute. Poppy will then pay income tax at 8.75%: £71. The total combined tax rate on the dividend is roughly 26%.

With a company pension contribution the whole £1,000 will go straight into Poppy's SIPP. As with Lesleyanne, the effective tax rate on her pension withdrawals will be either 15% if she is a basic-rate taxpayer when she retires or 30% if she is a higher-rate taxpayer.

In summary, Poppy's choice is between paying tax at roughly 26% on her additional dividend income and paying tax at 15% or possibly 30% on her pension withdrawals.

Example – Basic-rate Taxpayer
After Corporation Tax Increase
If the company's profits do not exceed £50,000 in the future it will continue to pay corporation tax at 19% and the outcome will be the same as the above example.

With a dividend, if the company has profits in the £50,000-£250,000 bracket it will face a marginal corporation tax rate of 26.5% which means it will pay £265 tax on the £1,000 of profit, leaving £735 to distribute. Poppy will then pay income tax at 8.75%: £64. The total combined tax rate on the dividend will be roughly 33%.

In summary, Poppy's choice will be between paying tax at roughly 33% on her additional dividend income and paying tax at 15% or possibly 30% on her pension withdrawals.

What this example shows is that, if you are a basic-rate taxpayer, a company pension contribution is currently a reasonably attractive alternative to additional dividend income and will become even more attractive when corporation tax increases.

However, pension contributions will not be very attractive if Poppy ends up wealthier in retirement and becomes a higher-rate taxpayer. This could happen if, for example, she inherits or accumulates a significant amount of assets and the income takes her over the higher-rate threshold before she starts withdrawing money from her pension.

Periods Straddling the Date of Change

The above examples all use the 19% corporation tax rate that currently applies to many companies or rates that will apply after the increase is in full force.

However, we also have to consider those rates that apply to accounting periods that straddle 1st April 2023, the date the corporation tax rate increases. Some companies are already in this situation and are therefore already partly affected by the corporation tax increase, others will be soon.

Pension contributions in these years will potentially enjoy more than 19% tax relief but not quite as much as when the corporation tax increase applies for the whole year.

Example 1

Three Trees Ltd has an accounting period that runs from 1st August to 31st July and has taxable profits of approximately £200,000 per year. The company faces the following marginal corporation tax rates:

- *August 2021 to July 2022   19%*
- *August 2022 to July 2023   21.51%*
- *August 2023 to July 2024   26.5%*

If the company made any pension contributions before 31st July 2022 it will have enjoyed 19% tax relief. Any contributions it makes between 1st August 2022 and 31st July 2023 will enjoy up to 21.51% tax relief. Any contributions made from 1st August 2023 onwards will enjoy up to 26.5% tax relief.

Example 2

Four Firs Ltd has an accounting period that runs from 1st January to 31st December and has taxable profits of approximately £200,000 per year. The company faces the following marginal corporation tax rates:

- *Year ended 31st December 2022   19%*
- *Year ended 31st December 2023   24.65%*
- *Year ended 31st December 2024   26.5%*

If the company makes pension contributions before 31st December 2022 it will enjoy 19% tax relief. Any contributions between 1st January 2023 and 31st December 2023 will enjoy up to 24.65% tax relief.

Any contributions made from 1st January 2024 onwards will enjoy up to 26.5% tax relief.

(See the Taxcafe guide *'The Company Tax Changes'* for a full discussion of how marginal corporation tax rates are calculated.)

Pension contributions a company makes on behalf of an owner/director are not generally periodic costs (see Chapter 1), so the rate of corporation tax relief applying will usually be as set out in Appendix A, based on the company accounting period in which the contribution is made. This is the basis for the tax relief described in the examples above.

However, if contributions are made in monthly instalments throughout the 2022/23 tax year, the effective rate of corporation tax relief will be as set out in Appendix B.

These effective rates may also apply if the contribution is made under a contractual commitment between the director and the company, although this depends on the period the contribution is meant to cover (if it covers the 2022/23 tax year, use the rates in Appendix B, if it covers the company's accounting period, use the rates in Appendix A for the period it covers).

Most pension contributions made on behalf of an owner/director are single large lump sums and are not part of any contractual commitment, so we will usually be looking at the marginal tax rates in Appendix A, as further illustrated by the examples above.

Postponing Pension Contributions

Some may be wondering whether it is worth postponing or reducing pension contributions until their company's corporation tax rate increases, so that more tax relief can be enjoyed.

(Note, here we are talking about voluntary pension contributions, typically for the directors, rather than compulsory ones due under auto-enrolment.)

A company with profits of £50,000-£250,000 will eventually face a marginal rate of 26.5% and may be able to enjoy £75 of additional tax relief for every £1,000 of pension contributions it postpones. A company with profits of more than £250,000 may be able enjoy up to £60 of additional tax relief.

It's certainly worth considering postponing contributions but it should be pointed out that this strategy is not without its risks and practical problems.

For starters, the company may have to wait quite some time to enjoy the maximum tax relief. Take a company with accounting periods that run from January to December. Only pension contributions made from January 2024 onwards will enjoy up to 26.5% tax relief, although contributions made between January and December 2023 will enjoy up to 24.65% tax relief.

Some company owners may be willing to postpone making contributions until these dates; others may prefer to make more steady contributions.

One reason why it may be worth making pension contributions sooner rather than later is that cash kept inside a company is arguably more vulnerable to commercial risk than cash stored away in a pension.

Another reason is that it is possible that changes could be made to the pension contribution rules that make it harder to make bigger catch-up contributions. For example, at present the annual allowance is £40,000 which means your company can make contributions of up to £40,000 per year on your behalf. It's also possible to make use of any unused annual allowance from the three previous tax years.

But what if the annual allowance is reduced to, say, £20,000 or less? That could make it more difficult for some company owners to receive catch-up contributions.

Furthermore, rumours are always circulating that tax relief on pension contributions will be reduced at some point in the future. We don't know if these rumours have any substance and how any changes would affect company pension contributions.

In summary, postponing or partly reducing pension contributions may produce greater tax savings but you will have to keep your eyes open for changes to pension tax relief that may scupper your plans. (On this point, there were no proposals regarding any changes to pension tax relief in the Autumn Statement on 17th November 2022. However, while this is reassuring, it does not represent a guarantee that there will be no such changes in future.)

Auto-Enrolment

In recent years the Government has rolled out a system of compulsory pensions called auto-enrolment. Essentially it's an extra tax on employers.

Only employees earning more than £10,000 and aged from 22 to state pension age need to be *automatically* enrolled into a pension. Some older and younger employees and those who earn less than £10,000 also have certain workplace pension rights.

According to the Pension Regulator a company does not have any automatic-enrolment duties when:

- It has just one director, with no other staff,
- It has a number of directors, none of whom has an employment contract, with no other staff, or
- It has a number of directors, only one of whom has an employment contract, with no other staff

A contract of employment does not have to be in writing. However, according to the Pension Regulator, if there is no written contract of employment, or other evidence of an intention to create an employer/worker relationship between the company and the director, it will not argue that an employment contract exists.

If a director does not have an employment contract they do not need to be assessed for automatic enrolment. If a director has a contract of employment and is not the only person working for the company under an employment contract, they are not exempt. Depending on their age and earnings, they may then qualify for automatic enrolment.

However, unlike other employees, the company may choose not to enrol a director who qualifies for automatic enrolment. If the company chooses not to enrol the director, the director still has the right to opt in or join a pension.

If the company decides not to enrol an employed director who is eligible for automatic enrolment, and it has no other eligible staff, it does not have to set up a pension scheme. However, it will need to make a 'declaration of compliance'.

Chapter 28

Pension Contributions: You or the Company?

In the previous chapter we showed that company pension contributions can be an attractive alternative to dividends. However, company directors can also make pension contributions *personally*, so a key question is: *"Who should make the contributions: the director or the company?"*

Company Owner Pension Contributions

When you make pension contributions *personally* (as opposed to getting your company to make them) the taxman will top up your savings by paying cash directly into your pension. For every £80 you invest the taxman will put in an extra £20.

Why £20? Your contributions are treated as having been paid out of income that has already been taxed at 20%, the basic rate of income tax.

The company that manages your pension plan – usually an insurance company or SIPP provider – will claim this money for you from the taxman and credit it to your account.

So whatever contribution you make personally, divide it by 0.80 and you'll get the total amount that is invested in your pension pot (your gross pension contribution).

Example
Peter is a company owner who takes most of his income as dividends. He invests £800 in a self-invested personal pension (SIPP). The taxman will top up his pension with £200 of basic-rate tax relief which means he'll have £1,000 in his pension pot: £800/0.80 = £1,000.

If Peter is a higher-rate taxpayer he can also claim higher-rate tax relief when he completes his tax return. This is given by increasing his basic-rate band by the amount of his gross pension contribution.

Peter's gross pension contribution is £1,000 so his basic-rate band will be increased by £1,000. This means £1,000 of his dividend income will be taxed at 8.75% instead of 33.75%, i.e. a 25% saving. Thus, Peter's higher-rate tax relief is: £1,000 x 25% = £250.

In total Peter will enjoy £450 of tax relief (£200 basic-rate relief plus £250 higher-rate tax relief). Peter's total tax relief is 45% of his £1,000 gross pension contribution.

Company Directors with Small Salaries

To obtain tax relief on your pension contributions they have to stay within certain limits:

* **Earnings.** Contributions made by you *personally* must not exceed the greater of £3,600 (gross), or your 'relevant UK earnings'. Earnings include your salary, bonus and taxable benefits in kind but do NOT include your dividends.

* **The £40,000 Annual Allowance.** Total pension contributions by you and your company must not exceed £40,000 per year, although it is possible to carry forward any unused annual allowance from the three previous tax years. The annual allowance is reduced if your 'adjusted income' exceeds £240,000 (see Chapter 17).

For a company director taking a salary of, say, £9,100 (see Chapter 8) the maximum personal pension contribution that can be made with tax relief in 2022/23 is therefore £9,100.

This is the maximum *gross* contribution. The director would personally invest £7,280 (£9,100 x 80%) and the taxman will top this up with £1,820 of basic-rate tax relief for a total gross contribution of £9,100.

For a company director taking a salary of, say, £11,908, the maximum gross pension contribution is £11,908. The director would personally invest £9,526 (£11,908 x 80%) and the taxman will top this up with £2,382 of basic-rate tax relief for a total gross contribution of £11,908.

Directors who want to make bigger pension contributions personally have to pay themselves bigger salaries. However, this may not be an attractive option because a bigger salary may be subject to employer's national insurance (at 14.53% this year) or employee's national insurance (at 12.73%) or both.

Company Pension Contributions

As a company owner you can also get your company (your employer) to make pension contributions on your behalf. Company pension contributions are always paid *gross* (there is no top up from the taxman) but the company will normally enjoy corporation tax relief on the payment. For example, a company currently paying 19% corporation tax can make a pension contribution of £10,000 and enjoy £1,900 tax relief.

Note, you do not need a dedicated company pension scheme to make company pension contributions. Most firms that offer SIPPs allow your company to pay directly into your pension (although these plans may not be qualifying schemes for auto-enrolment purposes).

How much can your company contribute? Unlike the contributions that you make personally, the company's contributions are NOT restricted by the size of your salary.

In other words, the company can make a pension contribution that is bigger than your salary. However, there are other restrictions on company contributions:

- Total pension contributions by you and your company must not exceed the annual allowance (typically £40,000) although you can carry forward any unused allowance from the previous three tax years.

- The company may be denied corporation tax relief on any pension contributions made on behalf of directors, if the taxman views them as 'excessive' (see below).

Corporation Tax Relief on Pension Contributions

Unlike the pension contributions that you make personally, tax relief for company pension contributions is not automatic.

Company contributions will only be a tax deductible expense for corporation tax purposes if they are incurred wholly and exclusively for the purposes of the business.

There is a danger that HMRC will deny corporation tax relief for 'excessive' pension contributions. In practice this is relatively rare.

When determining whether company pension contributions qualify for corporation tax relief, HMRC will look at the total remuneration package of the director. The total package (including salary, pension contributions and other benefits in kind) must not be excessive relative to the work the individual carries out and his or her responsibilities.

Relevant factors may include:

- The number of hours you work, your experience and your level of responsibility in the company.
- The pay of unconnected employees in your company and other companies who perform duties of similar value.
- The pay required to recruit someone to take over your duties.
- The company's financial performance.

Extra care may be necessary in the event of a large one-off company pension contribution.

It may be sensible to document the commercial justification (for example, strong recent financial performance of the company) in the minutes of a directors' board meeting and hold a shareholders' meeting to approve the contribution.

In some cases, when a company is making pension contributions on behalf of all employees, including directors, of more than £500,000 in total, it may be necessary to spread tax relief for the excess over a number of years. These spreading rules will obviously not affect most small companies.

Although the risk that your company will be denied corporation tax relief may be small, it is important to stress that, when it comes to company pension contributions, unlike contributions made by individuals, there is no cast-iron guarantee that the company will enjoy tax relief.

That's why we would recommend speaking to a tax adviser before your company starts making significant contributions.

Pension Contributions: You or the Company?

Using a couple of case studies we will now compare company pension contributions with pension contributions made personally by company owners to see which is most tax efficient.

Case Study 1 – Basic-rate Taxpayer

Eva owns Cassidy Ltd. She is a basic-rate taxpayer and pays herself a salary of £11,908 this year (2022/23) and takes the rest of her income as dividends.

She also decides to use £1,000 of the company's pre-tax profit to fund a pension contribution. If Cassidy Ltd makes the contribution it can pay £1,000 directly into Eva's SIPP and the amount will be a tax deductible expense.

Alternatively Eva can pay herself a dividend to fund a pension contribution she makes personally. We'll assume the company currently pays 19% corporation tax on the £1,000 profit leaving Eva with £810 to take as dividend income.

Eva holds onto £10 and invests £800 in her SIPP. The taxman will add £200 of basic-rate tax relief, leaving her with the same amount in her pension – £1,000.

But that's not the end of the matter: Eva will still have to pay 8.75% tax on her £810 dividend – roughly £70.

Eva is worse off by £60: £70 less the £10 of saved dividend income.

Thus, if you're a basic-rate taxpayer, for every £1,000 that ends up in your pension you may have to pay an additional 6% in tax. In this case a company pension contribution is clearly more tax efficient than a contribution made personally by the director.

Other Important Points

If Eva wants more than £11,908 invested in her pension, making the contribution personally will be even more expensive.

She would have to pay herself a bigger salary and this could result in a significant amount of national insurance becoming payable. This is because, to enjoy tax relief, any pension contribution you make personally cannot exceed the greater of £3,600 (gross) or your earnings (i.e. salary).

The additional salary would typically attract 12.73% employee's national insurance and 14.53% employer's national insurance (unless the company has spare employment allowance).

Case Study 2 – Higher-rate Taxpayer

This time we'll assume Eva is a *higher-rate taxpayer* and again wants to make a £1,000 pension contribution.

If Cassidy Ltd makes the contribution it can pay £1,000 directly into Eva's SIPP. Alternatively Eva can pay herself an £810 dividend, hold onto £10 and invest £800 in her SIPP. The taxman will add £200 of basic-rate tax relief, resulting in the same gross pension contribution of £1,000.

Again, that's not the end of the matter. Eva still has to pay income tax on the additional dividend.

With a gross pension contribution of £1,000, Eva's basic-rate band will be increased by £1,000. This means the £810 dividend will be taxed at just 8.75%, not 33.75%, so the tax is roughly £70.

Furthermore, an additional £190 of her other dividend income will also be taxed at 8.75% instead of 33.75%, saving her an extra £48.

All in all, a £1,000 pension contribution made by the director is £12 more expensive than a contribution made by the company:

£70 income tax - £48 extra relief - £10 saved dividend = £12

In this case a company pension contribution is again more tax efficient than a contribution made personally by the director but the difference is small. Because the saving is so small it will probably be other factors that determine whether the company or the individual makes the pension contribution.

Other Important Points

Note that if Eva wants to enjoy full higher-rate tax relief on a gross pension contribution of £11,908 (i.e. equal to her salary), she must have at least £11,908 of dividend income above the higher-rate threshold (income of at least £62,178 in 2022/23).

If Eva wants to make a pension contribution bigger than £11,908 personally she will have to take a bigger salary and this may result in a significant amount of national insurance becoming payable.

When Personal Contributions Are Attractive

Making pension contributions personally is still worth considering in some situations. Take the example of a director who unexpectedly finds themselves with income of £120,000, which means most of their personal allowance will be withdrawn.

Let's also say the director has received a salary of £9,100 this year. If they make a gross pension contribution of £9,100 they will enjoy full income tax relief on the contribution. Furthermore, their adjusted net income will fall by £9,100 which means £4,550 of their personal allowance will be clawed back, saving them even more tax.

Potentially, the saving in this scenario could be as much as £4,323, reducing the cost of their net £7,280 contribution to just £2,957. That's over £9,000 in your pension at a cost of less than £3,000!

Lifetime ISAs

Those aged 18 to 39 can open a Lifetime ISA which can be used to save for a first home or for retirement.

Up to £4,000 per year can be invested and receives a 25% Government bonus. So if you put in £4,000, the Government will add £1,000. This is the same as the basic-rate tax relief enjoyed on pension contributions.

It is possible to continue making contributions up to age 50. This means you can invest a total of up to £128,000 between age 18 and 50 with a Government bonus of up to £32,000.

Unlike a pension, your savings are not locked up inside a Lifetime ISA. However, if you withdraw money before reaching age 60, for any reason other than to buy your first home, there will be a 25% early withdrawal charge. This will claw back all of the Government bonus, plus an additional 6.25% of the amount you invested.

Lifetime ISA versus Company Pension Contribution

The Lifetime ISA is an attractive alternative to saving in a pension if you are a basic-rate taxpayer. Like pensions they attract a top up from the Government but, unlike pensions, ALL the money you take out will be tax free.

Let's say a company owner who is a basic-rate taxpayer is trying to decide between a £1,000 company pension contribution and using a dividend to fund a Lifetime ISA contribution.

A £1,000 pension contribution will attract corporation tax relief so the whole £1,000 will go directly into the company owner's pension.

If the same money is used to pay a dividend to fund a Lifetime ISA contribution, and assuming the company currently pays 19% corporation tax, £810 will be left to pay out. After paying 8.75% income tax the company owner will be left with around £739 to invest in a Lifetime ISA. Adding the Government bonus the company owner will end up with £924 in the Lifetime ISA.

When the company owner reaches age 60, all withdrawals from the Lifetime ISA will be tax free, whereas only 25% of the money withdrawn from the pension will be tax free (although they can get it slightly earlier). The rest will possibly be taxed at just 20% if they are a basic-rate taxpayer.

If we ignore investment growth to keep the example simple (it doesn't affect the outcome), with a Lifetime ISA the company owner will end up with £924; with a pension they will end up with just £850 after tax.

Thus, if you're a basic-rate taxpayer, your retirement income could be 9% higher with a Lifetime ISA

What about higher-rate taxpayers? Once again a £1,000 pension contribution will attract corporation tax relief so the whole £1,000 will go directly into the company owner's pension.

If the same money is used to pay a dividend to fund a Lifetime ISA contribution, and assuming the company currently pays 19% corporation tax, £810 will be left to pay out. After paying 33.75% income tax the company owner will be left with £537 to invest in their Lifetime ISA. Adding the Government bonus the company owner will end up with £671 in their Lifetime ISA.

When the company owner reaches age 60, all withdrawals from the Lifetime ISA will be tax free, whereas only 25% of the money withdrawn from the pension will be tax free. The rest could be taxed at just 20% if they are a basic-rate taxpayer at that point (most retirees end up as basic-rate taxpayers).

Ignoring investment growth again, with a Lifetime ISA the company owner will end up with £671; with a pension they will end up with £850 after tax.

Thus, your retirement income could be 27% higher with a <u>pension</u>.

However, if the company owner is a higher-rate taxpayer when they retire (e.g. if they have a lot of income from other sources, such as rental property) they will end up with £700 from a pension, compared with £671 from a Lifetime ISA. The difference is small, so the investment decision will probably be based on other factors in this scenario.

Finally, it's also important to remember that you can only invest £4,000 per year in a Lifetime ISA (with an additional £1,000 bonus from the Government), compared with the maximum gross pension contribution of £40,000 per year. Furthermore, you can only open a Lifetime ISA if you're under 40 years of age and it's only possible to continue making contributions up to age 50.

After the Rise in Corporation Tax

Company pension contributions will become even more attractive as companies become subject to higher corporation tax. Some companies are already in this situation and are partly affected by the corporation tax increase. Let's look at another couple of case studies to see why.

Case Study 3 – Basic-rate Taxpayer

During the 2024/25 tax year Eva has £1,000 of pre-tax profit in Cassidy Ltd that she would like to use to fund a pension contribution. We'll assume her company has a marginal tax rate of 26.5%.

If Cassidy Ltd makes the contribution it can pay £1,000 directly into Eva's SIPP.

Alternatively, Eva can use that same £1,000 to pay herself a dividend to fund a pension contribution that she makes personally. The company will pay 26.5% corporation tax leaving the company £735 to pay out as a dividend.

Eva will also have to pay income tax of £64 on the dividend (at 8.75%), leaving her with around £670 to invest in her pension. The taxman will add £168 of basic-rate tax relief (at 20%), resulting in a total gross pension contribution of £838.

In summary, Eva's pension contribution will be over 16% smaller if she decides to make it personally.

Case Study 4 – Higher-rate Taxpayer

This time we'll assume Eva is a *higher-rate taxpayer* and again has £1,000 of pre-tax profit in Cassidy Ltd that she would like to use to fund a pension contribution.

If Cassidy Ltd makes the contribution it can pay £1,000 directly into Eva's SIPP. Alternatively Eva can pay herself a £735 dividend and invest it in her SIPP. The taxman will add £184 of basic-rate tax relief, resulting in a gross pension contribution of £919.

With a gross pension contribution of £919, Eva's basic-rate band will be increased by £919. This means the £735 dividend will be taxed at just 8.75%, not 33.75%, so the tax will be roughly £64.

Furthermore, an additional £184 of her other dividend income (£919 less £735) will also be taxed at 8.75% instead of 33.75%, providing additional tax relief of £46.

All in all, Eva will end up with 8% less money in her pension if she decides to make the contribution personally and she will pay an additional £18 of income tax on her £735 dividend.

£64 income tax - £46 extra higher-rate relief = £18

Lifetime ISA versus Company Pension Contribution After the Rise in Corporation Tax

Let's say a company owner who is a basic-rate taxpayer and whose company has a marginal tax rate of 26.5% is trying to decide between a £1,000 company pension contribution and using a dividend to fund a Lifetime ISA contribution.

A £1,000 pension contribution will attract corporation tax relief so the whole £1,000 will go directly into the company owner's pension. When the company owner retires he or she could end up with £850 after tax (first 25% tax free, remainder taxed at 20%).

If the same money is used to pay a dividend to fund a Lifetime ISA contribution, the company will pay 26.5% corporation tax leaving £735 to pay out. After paying 8.75% income tax the company owner will be left with £671 to invest in a Lifetime ISA. Adding the Government bonus the company owner will end up with £839 in the Lifetime ISA, all of which can eventually be withdrawn tax free

Thus, if you're a basic-rate taxpayer, a company pension contribution could leave you around 1% better off than a Lifetime ISA.

Because the difference is so small the investment decision will probably be based on other factors.

What about higher-rate taxpayers? Once again a £1,000 pension contribution will attract corporation tax relief so the whole £1,000 will go directly into the company owner's pension.

When the company owner retires they could end up with £850 after tax if they are a basic-rate taxpayer at that time (first 25% tax free, remainder taxed at 20%). If they are a higher-rate taxpayer they could end up with £700 (first 25% tax free, remainder taxed at 40%).

If the same £1,000 is used to pay a dividend to fund a Lifetime ISA contribution, the company will pay 26.5% corporation tax leaving £735 to pay out.

After paying 33.75% income tax the company owner will be left with £487 to invest in their Lifetime ISA. Adding the Government bonus the company owner will end up with £609 in their Lifetime ISA, all of which can be withdrawn tax free.

Thus, if you're a basic-rate taxpayer when you retire your retirement income could be 40% higher with a pension.

If you're a higher-rate taxpayer when you retire, your retirement income could be 15% higher.

Contributions in the 2022/23 Tax Year

As explained in Chapter 27, company pension contributions made on behalf of a director are not generally a periodic cost. Hence, when comparing a company pension contribution with paying out dividends to fund either personal pension contributions or Lifetime ISA contributions, the appropriate marginal corporation tax rate to use is as set out in Appendix A.

Summary

Company pension contributions are currently more tax efficient than contributions made personally by directors.

The additional saving is currently quite small if the director is a higher-rate taxpayer.

If you want to make a pension contribution bigger than your existing company salary it is usually more tax efficient to get the company to make the contribution, rather than pay yourself a bigger salary which may have a significant national insurance cost.

The increase in corporation tax will, in many cases, make company contributions even more attractive than contributions made personally.

Tax relief for company pension contributions is not automatic – tax relief could be denied if the contributions are viewed as excessive, although this is rare in practice.

A Lifetime ISA is currently a fairly attractive alternative to a company pension contribution if you are a basic-rate taxpayer. Company pension contributions may be a more attractive alternative if you are a higher-rate taxpayer.

When corporation tax increases, Lifetime ISAs and company pension contributions may produce a similar outcome if you are a basic-rate taxpayer. Company pension contributions may become even more attractive for many higher-rate taxpayers.

Chapter 29

Putting Property into a Pension

In Chapter 24 we explained that company owners who own their business premises personally can get the company to pay them rent and this may be an attractive alternative to dividends.

Some company owners also use a SIPP or other pension plan to hold their business premises and in this chapter we'll take a look at the benefits and drawbacks of this alternative.

Note that you can put *commercial property* into a pension but not residential property.

Holding business property in a pension has a number of benefits:

- **Tax-free rent**. There's no income tax payable by you on the rent your business pays into your pension. The rent is also a tax deductible expense for the business.

- **No capital gains tax**. When a property held inside a pension is sold there is no capital gains tax payable.

- **Inheritance tax exemption**. Assets held in a pension generally fall outside your estate for inheritance tax purposes.

Although the ability to roll up rental income tax free inside a pension is enticing, you must never lose sight of the fact that all the money you eventually withdraw from your pension, over and above your 25% tax-free lump sum, will be subject to income tax.

If you are a higher-rate taxpayer at present but expect to be a basic-rate taxpayer when you retire, it's possible the rental income will ultimately be much less heavily taxed by going the pension route.

Similarly, although property held inside a pension can be sold without incurring capital gains tax, when you eventually withdraw the capital gain most of it (75%) will be subject to income tax.

If you are a basic-rate taxpayer when you retire you will pay 20% tax and if you are a higher-rate taxpayer you will pay 40% tax.

By contrast, if you sell commercial property that you own personally you will be subject to capital gains tax. Commercial property benefits from the lower 20% CGT rate and it's possible some of the gain will be taxed at just 10% if your basic-rate band isn't used up by your other income. Some of the gain may also be covered by your annual exemption, although this is due to fall from its current, 2022/23 level of £12,300 to just £6,000 in 2023/24 and then a measly £3,000 thereafter.

In some cases a sale of business premises owned personally will qualify for Business Asset Disposal Relief. If so, a tax rate of 10% may apply to the whole gain, although the relief will be restricted if your company has paid you rent at any time since 6th April 2008.

Business premises held inside your pension do not have to be sold when you retire. If your own business ceases to occupy the property, the property can remain in your pension and be rented out to someone else and the rent will roll up tax free in your pension.

Although property held inside your pension may fall outside your estate for inheritance tax purposes, in most cases the family members that inherit your pension pot will have to pay income tax on any money they subsequently withdraw.

By contrast, if you own your business premises personally, the property may qualify for business property relief (100% inheritance tax exemption if you are a sole trader, 50% if the property is used by your partnership or company).

Finally, when it comes to tucking away money inside a pension we must never lose sight of the fact that you will not be able to get your hands on any of the money until you are at least 55 (rising to 57 in 2028).

Clearly there are benefits to holding business property inside a pension but it is by no means a 'no brainer'. There are benefits but also drawbacks and each case would have to be decided on its merits with help from a professional.

Funding the Property Purchase

The purchase of a business property by a pension can be funded in several ways. Typically you will use your existing pension savings, topped up with fresh contributions (including company pension contributions).

It is also possible for your pension fund to borrow money but only up to 50% of its net assets. For example, if you have pension savings of £100,000 an additional £50,000 can be borrowed.

Some pension providers allow a part share in a property to be acquired by the pension plan, with the balance owned outside the pension.

Several individuals can also pool their pension savings to collectively buy a property.

Transferring Existing Property

If you already own the property you can sell it to your SIPP and this may allow you to release a sizeable amount of cash from your pension savings.

Transferring an existing property into a pension is likely to result in capital gains tax becoming payable if the property has risen in value since you bought it.

Commercial property benefits from the lower 20% CGT rate and some of the gain may be taxed at just 10%. Part of the gain may be tax-free thanks to the annual exemption although, as discussed above, this is being drastically reduced over the next couple of years. It is unlikely Business Asset Disposal Relief would be available in such cases.

A sizeable capital gains tax bill may put off many existing property owners going down the pension route but others may still be tempted by the prospect of receiving a large cash payment out of their pension savings.

The transfer may also result in a stamp duty land tax bill and VAT may also be payable in certain circumstances, although a VAT refund can usually be claimed.

Those who are considering going this route may want to take action soon (i.e. by 5th April 2023) as the forthcoming reductions in the annual exemption will lead to increased CGT costs thereafter.

In Specie Contributions

Properties have also been transferred into pensions as *in specie* pension contributions, with the member claiming income tax relief. *In theory* a property worth, say, £100,000 would be transferred into the pension scheme with the scheme administrator claiming £25,000 of basic-rate tax relief to add to the member's pension pot and the member themselves claiming higher-rate tax relief when they submit their tax return.

In specie contributions are no longer permitted by most pension firms following a clamp down by HMRC because of perceived abuse. In a recent case, the Upper Tribunal ruled that tax relief was not available on an in specie contribution of shares and some in the pensions industry fear HMRC may now attempt to reclaim millions of pounds of tax relief on past in-specie contributions.

Costs and other Formalities

Not all pension providers deal with property purchases so you may need to transfer your existing pension to a specialist provider.

When your property is held inside a pension your business will have to be treated just like any other tenant, with no special favours, which means rent will have to be paid at a full market rate come hell or high water.

If rent is not paid this will be treated as an unauthorised payment by your pension and HMRC may levy a charge of 40% on you personally and a charge of up to 40% on the pension itself.

Property SIPPs are also much more expensive to run than those that only allow you to invest in traditional 'stocks and shares'. Initial set up costs include legal fees, surveyor fees, lenders fees and fees to the pension company managing your SIPP. Fees will also have to be paid for regular rent revaluations and a third party property manager may have to be appointed to collect the rent from your company.

Chapter 30

Sell Your Business and Pay 10% Tax!

One of the most tax-efficient ways to grow your wealth is to build up a successful company and then sell it. This allows you to convert heavily taxed income into a less heavily taxed capital gain.

Many company owners who receive dividends have a marginal income tax rate of 33.75%. Those with income over £150,000 have a marginal tax rate of 39.35% and those with income between £125,140 and £150,000 will be joining them next year.

But when you sell a company and receive a cash lump sum, which replaces all of this heavily taxed income, you could end up paying just 10% tax thanks to Business Asset Disposal Relief (previously known as Entrepreneurs Relief, which was a much better name).

The lifetime limit used to be £10 million of capital gains per person. But in the March 2020 Budget the Government slashed this to £1 million with immediate effect (from 11th March 2020).

The announcement could have been a lot worse. There were fears in some quarters that the relief would be abolished altogether. And because it applies on a per person basis, couples can still enjoy £2 million of capital gains taxed at 10%.

Business Asset Disposal Relief is, however, no longer very attractive to serial entrepreneurs, who build up and sell many businesses during their careers. Many will have already exhausted their £1 million allowance.

Even if you have no immediate plan to sell your company or wind it up, it's still a good idea to have a basic understanding of the Business Asset Disposal Relief rules. There are certain things you need to check and do *before* you take any action.

However, if you are denied the relief all is not lost. You could end up paying capital gains tax at 20% instead of 10%, but that's still a lot more attractive than the top tax rates for dividends.

Qualifying for Business Asset Disposal Relief

Company owners are entitled to Business Asset Disposal Relief when they sell their shares or wind up the company. The main qualifying criteria are:

- The company must be your 'personal company' which, generally speaking, means you must own at least 5% of it (but matters can get more complicated – see below)
- You must be an officer or employee of the company
- The company must be a 'trading' company

Each of these rules must be satisfied for at least *two years* before the company is sold or wound up.

Where the company has ceased trading each of the rules must be satisfied for at least two years before it ceases trading. The disposal of the company must then take place within three years after trading has stopped.

Like many CGT reliefs, qualifying furnished holiday letting businesses are treated as trading for the purposes of Business Asset Disposal Relief.

Selling a Recently Incorporated Business

If you have only recently incorporated your business, you don't have to own the shares of the newly formed company for two years. The period you owned the unincorporated business is added to the period you own the company shares in this situation.

Transferring Shares to Your Spouse/Partner Etc

You do, however, have to be wary of transferring shares to your spouse within two years of selling the company. Transfers to spouses are exempt from capital gains tax and your spouse can then claim Business Asset Disposal Relief when the business is sold, but they personally must satisfy the necessary conditions outlined above in their own right. This generally means the transfer must have taken place at least two years before selling the company for the spouse to qualify for Business Asset Disposal Relief.

Spouse transfers weren't always necessary when the lifetime limit for the relief was £10 million but are probably more important now that it is just £1 million. Many company owners also transfer shares to their spouse to reduce the income tax payable on dividends.

Similar principles apply to transfers to an unmarried partner or other adult family member; although a holdover relief claim will be necessary (see Chapter 21).

What is a Personal Company?

As stated above, to qualify for Business Asset Disposal Relief the company must be your personal company. This means you must own at least 5% of the ordinary share capital and have at least 5% of the voting rights.

HMRC was concerned that ordinary shares encompass a very broad range of share arrangements, including those where the shareholders have restricted rights to dividends and the company's assets.

As a result, you must now also meet at least one of the following two conditions to qualify for Business Asset Disposal Relief:

- You must be entitled to at least 5% of the profits available for distribution and at least 5% of the assets available for distribution if the company is wound up, or
- In the event of a disposal of all the ordinary share capital of the company, you would be entitled to at least 5% of the disposal proceeds

According to the Government, *"These changes improve the effectiveness of [the relief] by ensuring that claimants disposing of shares have a minimum economic stake in the company. The government considers this to be more characteristic of entrepreneurial activity."*

Initially the Government introduced just one additional condition (the first bullet point above). However, several expert tax commentators pointed out this would have prevented owners of alphabet shares (common in many small family companies) from claiming the relief.

For example, where a company has A and B shares and a different rate of dividend can be declared on each type, it could be argued that neither type of shareholder is entitled to at least 5% of the profits available for distribution: because there is no dividend entitlement until the dividends are declared.

As a result the second condition was tagged on. This allows the company owner to instead enjoy Business Asset Disposal Relief if they are entitled to at least 5% of the proceeds when the company is sold.

What is an Officer?

Company officers include non-executive directors and company secretaries, so you don't even have to work full-time at the company to qualify for Business Asset Disposal Relief.

What is a Trading Company?

To qualify for Business Asset Disposal Relief, the company must be a trading company. HMRC regards the following as non-trading activities:

- Holding investment property, including property for letting (except qualifying furnished holiday lets, as mentioned above)
- Holding shares or securities
- Holding surplus cash

If there is substantial non-trading activity you could be denied Business Asset Disposal Relief. HMRC generally regards non-trading activities to be substantial where either non-trading income or non-trading assets exceed 20% of the totals for the company as a whole. However, this test is only a rule of thumb and does not have any statutory basis. It must be remembered that, in cases of dispute, it is for the courts to decide the matter, not HMRC. For further analysis of this issue and the current legal position established in court, see Chapter 1.

Nonetheless, it remains the fact that if just 20% of the assets or income of the company are not trading assets or income, you may be denied Business Asset Disposal Relief when you sell your shares.

In this context, it is worth pointing out that business goodwill is a trading asset and should be taken into account, even if its value is not reflected on the company's balance sheet.

If your company doesn't own investment property or invest in other companies, the most serious danger is holding too much cash. In the early days of what was then Entrepreneurs' Relief, many people were concerned that excessive amounts of cash could result in the company losing its trading status and hence the relief (now Business Asset Disposal Relief) could be taken away.

However, more recent case law has placed far less emphasis on surplus holdings of cash than HMRC seemed to think was appropriate. After all, the legislation only talks about substantial non-trading *activity*: and there is not much activity involved in simply holding cash!

Remember, case law now tells us that non-trading activities will only be regarded as substantial if they are of material or real importance in the context of the company's activities as a whole (see Chapter 1).

So if, for example, a company has a trading business whose total net assets are worth £700,000, plus surplus cash of £300,000 which is simply being held in a bank account and not actively invested then, while that cash amounts to 30% of the company's assets, it is clearly not a substantial activity and the company remains a trading company.

Nevertheless, while the 20% used as a benchmark by HMRC has no legal substance, and were it to relate purely to a holding of cash, they would be laughed out of court, there *would* still come a point when the cash held by a company came to be so significant that it threatened the company's trading status.

So, this brings us to the question of when is cash surplus? Let's say a company has £500,000 in its bank account. That's a lot of cash. But if that company buys £1 million of trading stock every month, the cash is only covering two weeks' supplies. It is therefore simply working capital, it is not surplus cash, and is part of the assets of the trade.

But larger holdings of cash proportionate to the size of the company's trading activities will eventually become surplus to the requirements of the company's business. Eventually, a large enough cash holding will begin to pose a risk.

However, even such large holdings should not be a problem if you can prove the cash was required for business purposes, for example as part of a well-documented expansion plan.

Like many aspects of tax law, this issue is something of a grey area and, in cases of doubt, professional advice is recommended. (And, despite all we have said, any holding that represents more than 20% of the company's assets will always cast some degree of doubt.)

If the company really does have a substantial amount of surplus cash that cannot be justified for business reasons, it may be necessary to extract it at least two years in advance to prevent the company's trading status being challenged on a sale of the company's shares.

You then have to weigh up the potential costs and benefits: the benefit being a CGT rate of 10% instead of 20% on a gain of up to £1 million (per person); the cost being the income tax on any additional dividends.

Business Premises – 'Associated Disposals'

Many business owners purchase business premises *personally* and rent them to their company. The good news is Business Asset Disposal Relief is available when 'associated' assets like these are sold. The bad news is many company owners will not qualify!

The asset will only qualify for Business Asset Disposal Relief if you also make a 'material disposal' of shares in your company. The stake being disposed of must generally be at least 5%.

It is possible to claim Business Asset Disposal Relief on an associated disposal even if the stake in the business is sold or gifted to a family member, for example an adult child.

However, there must also be no 'share purchase arrangements' in place at the time of disposal. This rule is designed to prevent you from taking back your stake in the business after the property has been sold and Business Asset Disposal Relief has been claimed.

To qualify for Business Asset Disposal Relief the 'associated' asset must have been in use in the business for at least two years. The asset must also have been held for at least three years to qualify.

The relief is also restricted if you've received any payment for the use of the property since 5th April 2008 (e.g. if your company has paid you rent).

Where the property was acquired after 5th April 2008 and a full market rent was received throughout the period of its use in the company's trade, no Business Asset Disposal Relief is available.

Where the property was acquired at an earlier date or rent was charged at a lower rate there will be a partial restriction in the relief.

As we saw in Chapter 24, getting your company to pay you rent is an attractive alternative to dividends, especially when the company owner (who owns the property) has expenses that can be deducted from the rent for tax purposes, such as mortgage interest.

Another advantage of charging your company rent is so that capital allowances can be claimed on the qualifying fixtures in the property. If a market rent is not charged the property owner will not be treated as having a proper 'property business', which is necessary for them to make a full capital allowances claim (although a partial claim is possible where a lower level of rent is charged).

For newer properties, or those that have recently undergone improvements, the owner may also be able to claim the Structures and Buildings Allowance (see the Taxcafe guide *'How to Save Property Tax'* for details). Again, the claim is restricted if the owner charges less than a full market rent.

In summary, company owners who own their business premises personally have to weigh the benefits of Business Asset Disposal Relief against the benefits of paying themselves rental income. The reduction in the relief's lifetime limit from £10 million to £1 million has made paying rent more attractive than previously.

Winding Up Your Company

It is not always possible to sell your company shares to a third party. Buyers are often fearful of acquiring companies outright for fear of taking on any unknown liabilities. Instead they often prefer to buy the assets (e.g. premises, goodwill, stock and customer lists).

The disadvantage of an asset sale such as this is the double tax charge: The company will pay corporation tax on the proceeds and you will pay tax (income tax or capital gains tax) when you extract the after-tax proceeds.

Providing you meet the qualifying criteria, Business Asset Disposal Relief is still available if you wind up your company following an asset sale and extract the cash as a capital distribution.

There are generally two ways to wind up a company:

* Dissolution under the Companies Act
* Voluntary liquidation under the Insolvency Act

With a *dissolution* capital gains tax treatment is only possible if the total distributions are less than £25,000. Where the total distributions exceed £25,000 they are taxed as dividends, possibly at 33.75% or 39.35%.

A *voluntary liquidation* ensures that payments to shareholders are treated as capital distributions for capital gains tax purposes. However, voluntary liquidation requires the appointment of a licensed insolvency practitioner with fees running to many thousands of pounds in some cases (the fees may be less if the company's affairs are simple and its main asset is cash).

To qualify for Business Asset Disposal Relief the capital distribution must be made within three years of the cessation of trading.

The following criteria must be met for the two years before cessation of trading:

* The company must be your 'personal company' (see above)
* You must be an officer or employee of the company
* The company must be a 'trading' company (see above)

As discussed above, in some cases a large surplus cash balance (a non-trading asset) already held in the company before the sale, or cessation, of the business, may throw in doubt the ability to claim Business Asset Disposal Relief.

It goes without saying that in all cases where a winding up of the company is to be carried out, professional advice should be obtained to ensure the desired tax treatment of the distributions.

The Anti-Phoenixing Rule

The anti-phoenixing rule means a distribution made when winding up a company will sometimes be taxed as a dividend. This is to prevent company owners continually winding up companies and starting new ones to enjoy the lower capital gains tax rates.

The rule applies where *all* of the following conditions are met:

- **Condition A & B**. The individual holds at least 5% of the ordinary share capital and voting rights immediately before the winding up and the company is a close company at some point in the two years before the winding up

- **Condition C**. Within two years after the distribution the company owner carries on the same or a similar trade or activity to the company being wound up

- **Condition D**. It is reasonable to assume that the main purpose or one of the main purposes of the winding up is to avoid income tax

With regards to Condition C, it makes no difference whether you operate as a sole trader or through a partnership or new company in which you have at least a 5% interest or through a connected person (e.g. your spouse or another close relative).

The test is clearly very subjective and it is feared it could catch many innocent situations, for example where a company owner retires, winds up their company and a year later decides to take on a few clients or do some work for a family member involved in the same trade.

It is also feared that Condition D could be applied broadly. For example, HMRC could argue that if a company owner decides not to pay surplus funds out as dividends prior to the winding up, there is as an 'arrangement' to reduce income tax.

HMRC provided the following examples which were intended to allay these fears and explain when the rules will apply:

Example 1

Mr A has been the sole shareholder of a company which carries on the trade of landscape gardening for 10 years. Mr A decides to wind up the business and retire. Because he no longer needs a company he liquidates the company and receives a distribution in a winding up. To subsidise his pension, Mr A continues to do a small amount of gardening in his local village.

Conditions A to C are met, because gardening is a similar trade or activity to landscape gardening. However, when viewed as a whole, these arrangements do not appear to have tax as a main purpose. It is natural for Mr A to have wound up his company because it is no longer needed once the trade has ceased.

Although Mr A continues to do some gardening, there is no reason why he would need a company for this, and it does not seem that he set the company up, wound it up and then continued a trade all with a view to receive the profits as capital rather than income.

In these circumstances, Mr A's distribution in the winding up will continue to be treated as capital.

Example 2

Mrs B is an IT contractor. Whenever she receives a new contract, she sets up a limited company to carry out that contract. When the work is completed and the client has paid, Mrs B winds up the company and receives the profits as capital.

Again, conditions A to C are met because Mrs B has a new company which carries on the same or a similar trade to the previously wound up company. Here, though, it looks like there is a main purpose of obtaining a tax advantage. All of the contracts could have been operated through the same company, and apart from the tax savings it would seem that would have been the most sensible option for Mrs B.

Where the distribution from the winding up is made in these circumstances, the distribution will be treated as a dividend and subject to income tax.

Example 3

Mrs C is an accountant who has operated through a limited company for three years. She decides that the risk involved with running her own business is not worth her effort, and so decides to accept a job at her brother's accountancy firm as an employee. Her brother's firm has been operating for eight years. Mrs C winds up her company and begins life as an employee.

Conditions A to C are met because Mrs C is continuing a similar activity to the trade that was carried on by the company. She is continuing it as an employee of a connected party, triggering Condition C.

But looking at the arrangements as a whole it is not reasonable to assume that they have tax advantage as a main purpose, so Condition D will not be met. Mrs C's company was incorporated and wound up for commercial, not tax, reasons; although she works for a connected party it is clear that the other business was not set up to facilitate a tax advantage because it has been operating for some time.

In these circumstances, the distribution from the winding up will continue to be treated as capital, absent any other considerations.

Transaction in Securities

HMRC can also use the so-called 'transaction in securities' rules to attack distributions when a company is wound up if it thinks the main reason for the liquidation is to save income tax.

The transaction in securities rules are contained in vague legislation that can be used to convert capital gains into income subject to the dividend tax rates if HMRC takes the view that income has been incorrectly extracted as a capital gain.

This introduces a second obstacle for business owners who wish to liquidate their companies. Hence, given the wide-ranging nature of the transaction in securities legislation, most tax advisers recommend obtaining pre-transaction clearance from HMRC. While the liquidation of a long-standing company after it has ceased trading, or sold its business assets to a third party, will seldom be challenged, it is better to be safe than sorry.

The transaction in securities rules cannot apply if there is a simple, straightforward, genuine third-party sale of company shares, even if one of the main reasons for the sale is to save tax.

Overdrawn Directors Loan Accounts

When a director owes their company money, the overdrawn loan account is an *asset* of the company. When there is a members' voluntary liquidation, it is common practice to distribute this asset to the shareholders *in specie* (i.e. not as a cash payment).

In other words, instead of the director repaying the company and receiving the cash back as a liquidation distribution in his capacity as a shareholder, the distribution is handled as a paper transaction.

In the past the distribution of the director's loan account during a liquidation was treated as a capital distribution and taxed at just 10% if the company owner was entitled to Business Asset Disposal Relief.

Apparently HMRC is now taking the approach that such distributions are subject to income tax at the dividend tax rates (i.e. at up to 39.35%).

For this reason several expert tax commentators recommend that directors with overdrawn loan accounts should pay back their loans to the company before the company enters liquidation.

Conclusion

There is some uncertainty amongst tax professionals as to how the various anti-avoidance measures will be applied in practice when a company is liquidated.

Where capital gains treatment is in doubt it may make sense to pay actual dividends over several tax years, rather than making a single large distribution when you wind up the company.

Adopting a phased approach to the withdrawal of profits from your company may allow you to enjoy the 8.75% tax rate that applies to basic-rate taxpayers, rather than the 33.75% or 39.35% tax rates that apply to higher and additional-rate taxpayers.

Adopting this strategy over several tax years could allow a significant amount of cash to be extracted from the company, especially when the amounts taxed at 8.75% can be doubled up in the case of a company owned by a couple.

A Final Note on Business Asset Disposal Relief

Business Asset Disposal Relief is complicated and constantly changing. This chapter is by no means a definitive guide.

There are various quirks in the legislation that we have deliberately ignored for simplicity's sake but could see the relief denied in certain circumstances. For this reason anyone who wants to benefit from Business Asset Disposal Relief should seek advice from a tax professional with experience in this area.

Chapter 31

Employee Ownership Trusts

In the previous chapter we saw how, thanks to Business Asset Disposal Relief, company owners can pay just 10% capital gains tax when they sell their businesses.

Many company owners have heard about Business Asset Disposal Relief but did you know that you can also sell your company TAX FREE to something called an employee ownership trust?

With an employee ownership trust the company ends up being owned by a trust for the benefit of employees generally (shares are not earmarked for individual employees).

Note, employee ownership trusts are not to be confused with the much discredited use of employee benefit trusts to give employees interest-free loans that were supposedly tax free.

The capital gains tax relief for the sale of company shares to employee ownership trusts was introduced in the 2014 Finance Act and therefore has the Government's blessing.

A typical business sale would take place as follows:

- An employee ownership trust is established.

- Shares in the company are sold to the trustees of the employee ownership trust. An independent valuation will be required so that the correct market value is used.

- The trust does not need to have any money to buy the company. The purchase consideration will typically take the form of a debt owed to the original shareholders.

- The company will then gift its earnings to the employee ownership trust to pay off the original owners over a number of years. These gifts of earnings are not an allowable expense for corporation tax purposes, so money will need to be retained by the company to settle its corporation tax bills.

- Payments from the employee ownership trust to the original owners will be exempt from capital gains tax, providing various conditions are met (see below).

- The employees will only be indirect owners of the company and will therefore not receive dividends. Instead the trustees of the employee ownership trust can arrange for bonuses to be paid by the company. Annual cash bonuses of up to £3,600 per employee are allowed free from income tax (but not national insurance).

Qualifying Requirements

There are, of course, a number of conditions that have to be satisfied to qualify for the tax benefits:

- The company must be a trading company or the holding company of a trading group

- The trustees of the employee ownership trust must provide benefits to all eligible employees on the same terms. It is, however, possible to distinguish between employees based on their levels of pay, length of service and hours worked.

- The trustees of the employee ownership trust must acquire at least 51% of the company and thus have a controlling interest. Up to 49% of the shares can, however, remain in direct ownership.

- The directors can remain at the company following the sale. However, the number of continuing shareholders (and any other 5% participators) who are directors or employees (or persons connected to them, such as close relatives) must not exceed 40% of the total number of employees. So if a company has five employees only two of them can be the original shareholders. This is to show that there has been a genuine change of ownership in the business. This condition must also be met for one year before the sale of the business.

It is possible for the capital gains tax relief to be clawed back if a disqualifying event occurs in the same tax year that the employee ownership trust acquires shares in the company or in the following tax year.

The original owners will then be subject to capital gains tax under the normal rules, as laid out in the previous chapter.

If any of the conditions for CGT relief are breached in a later tax year it is the trustees who will be liable for capital gains tax. The capital gains tax bill will be calculated using the original owners' base cost in the shares.

Employee ownership trusts are supposed to be long-term ownership vehicles but it is possible that the 51% controlling interest requirement could be breached if, for example, the trustees decide to sell shares in the business to a third party on the basis that the offer is in the interest of the beneficiaries of the employee ownership trust.

The sale of the business to the employee ownership trust must not be for tax avoidance purposes and could fall foul of the so-called 'transactions in securities' rules if one of the main purposes is to obtain a tax benefit.

For this reason several tax commentators recommend obtaining advance clearance from HMRC to ensure that the payments from the trustees to the original owners will not be treated as disguised dividends.

Of course, selling to an employee ownership trust will not appeal to all business owners. In particular, many will be put off by the potentially long delay receiving payment for their sale of the business. If the company starts making losses the employee ownership trust may be unable to pay the original owners.

Apart from the tax benefits, selling to an employee ownership trust is also seen as a useful way to solve succession issues, where there are no family members willing to carry on with the business and the owners are unwilling to sell to a competitor or third party with all the hassle this may involve.

Part 7

Salary & Dividends: Practical Issues & Dangers

Chapter 32

How to Avoid the Minimum Wage Rules

If you take a small salary from your company (for example, £9,100, £11,908 or £12,570) there is a danger of falling foul of the national living wage (NLW).

Where wages are too low, HMRC will force the company to make up the shortfall. Bigger wage payments may result in bigger national insurance bills for both the company and the director.

There is also a penalty equivalent to 200% of the unpaid wages with a maximum penalty of £20,000 per worker. Those found guilty will also be considered for disqualification from being a company director for up to 15 years.

However, the key point to note about the NLW is that it only applies to directors who have a contract of employment.

Due to the informal set up in many small companies, there may be some uncertainty as to whether an employment contract exists between the director and the company (employment contracts do not need to be in writing).

However, it is generally accepted amongst the tax profession that if you do not issue yourself with an explicit contract of employment the minimum wage regulations will not apply.

This means you should be able to continue paying yourself a small salary, even if it is less than the national living wage.

However, risk averse company owners (those worried about potential penalties) should consider paying themselves enough salary to satisfy the minimum wage regulations.

National Living Wage Rates

The national living wage applies to those aged 23 and over. From April 2022 the rate is £9.50 per hour.

If you spend, say, 35 hours per week actively managing your business, the total salary due for 2022/23 will be: 35 x 52 weeks x £9.50 = £17,290.

Such a salary could result in unwelcome national insurance charges.

The national insurance payable on this salary by the director would be £685 and £1,190 would be payable by the company (possibly £0 if the company has spare employment allowance).

Of course, every case is different and some directors will be able to argue that they spend fewer hours actively managing the business.

Although it may seem that the best strategy is to simply not have a contract of employment, there may be other reasons why having such a contract is important.

Note that directors are exempt from the national living wage with respect to hours spent performing their duties as directors: as distinct from hours spent managing the business. In a small company, this can often be a difficult distinction to draw. But if, for example, the company owner appointed their spouse/partner as a director, but that spouse/partner did no other work for the company apart from fulfilling their duties as director, then the NLW would not apply in their case.

Family Members Who Aren't Directors

It is possible that some family members will be employees of the company but not directors. These individuals are subject to the national minimum wage or living wage for all hours spent working in the business. The exemption for members of your own household does not apply where the employer is a company.

However, it is possible that, if they only work part time, the salary that must be paid to them will still be within the typical optimal amounts of £9,100, £11,908 or £12,570.

Chapter 33

Is My Salary Tax Deductible?

One of the benefits of getting your company to pay you a salary is that the amount will normally be a tax deductible expense and reduce the company's corporation tax bill.

There is no automatic right to corporation tax relief. The amount paid has to be justified by the work carried out for the business and the individual's level of responsibility.

While this may not be an important issue for company owners who work full time in the business and pay themselves a small salary, it may be important if you start paying salaries to other family members, in particular those who only work part time.

The question of whether your employment income will attract corporation tax relief may also become an issue if you decide to pay yourself a large one-off bonus. Factors that may determine whether a salary or bonus payment is tax deductible include:

- The number of hours worked in the business
- The individual's legal obligations and responsibilities (e.g. directors' duties)
- The pay received by the company's other employees
- The pay received by employees at other companies performing similar roles
- The company's performance and ability to pay salaries/bonuses.

In the case of large one-off bonus payments made only to the company's directors/shareholders it may be necessary to document the commercial rationale for the payment to show that the payment is justifiable. This can be done in the minutes of a directors' board meeting. It may also be advisable to record the approval of any bonus in the minutes of a shareholders' meeting.

Chapter 34

Salary vs Dividends: Non-Tax Factors

Most of this guide focuses on choosing the most tax efficient *level* of income and the most tax efficient *mix* of income (i.e. salary versus dividends).

However, when it comes to withdrawing money from your company there are lots of other non-tax factors that may need to be considered. This chapter provides a short overview of some of the issues but is not definitive.

Cashflow and Working Capital Needs

When deciding how much income you withdraw from your company you must consider the cashflow and working capital requirements of the business.

It would naturally be irresponsible to pay yourself a large bonus or dividend if this affects the company's ability to carry on its business.

If you prefer to retain the cash in your company, it may be possible for a dividend to be declared but not paid out. The dividend can simply be credited to the director's loan account and withdrawn at a later date when it is more convenient.

Income tax will still be payable on any dividends declared but not paid.

Dividends & Company Insolvency

Dividends should not be declared when the company is insolvent or if the payment of those dividends will render the company insolvent.

Dividends that are deemed illegal may have to be repaid, even if this results in the director being made bankrupt or being forced into an individual voluntary arrangement (IVA).

Director's Ability to Borrow

If you take a small salary and the rest of your income as dividends there is a possibility that this will affect your ability to borrow money personally.

Some lenders may only be interested in the level of your salary and ignore your dividends, being unfamiliar with this sort of pay structuring.

Other lenders, on the other hand, will look at the complete picture and will look at your recent tax returns and the company's most recent accounts when assessing your ability to repay a loan.

Effect on Share Value

The value of a company is usually based on a multiple of its after-tax profits. A small minority shareholder's stake, however, is often valued according to the dividend history of the company. A consistent or steadily increasing annual dividend may enhance the value of the shares.

Company's Profitability

The payment of a large salary or bonus will depress the company's profits. This may affect the company's ability to borrow.

It could also affect the amount received in the event of a sale of the company or its underlying business: although more sophisticated buyers will generally discount actual payments to directors and substitute a market rate when valuing the company's shares or business goodwill.

Government Support

It's worth remembering that during the covid pandemic, one of the groups that received very little support from the government was small company directors paying themselves a small salary.

While sole traders and business partners were able to claim grants under the Self-Employed Income Support Scheme and regular employees could get most of their pay through the furlough scheme, all a small company director could claim was a proportion of their salary and then *only if* they stopped work in their business.

Those following the small salary/large dividend route received very little support (although their companies may have received some support if they had business premises). Perhaps this was the government's revenge for years of tax savings.

The worst of the pandemic is behind us now (we hope) but there is always the risk of something similar happening again one day, so it's worth remembering what happened this time!

Chapter 35

Paying Salaries & Dividends: Profits & Paperwork

Salaries – Real Time Information

Employers have to report salary payments to HMRC under the Real Time Information (RTI) regime. Under real time information, employers are required to submit a Full Payment Submission (FPS) to HMRC at the same time or before each payment is made to a director or employee.

The idea is to make sure the right amount of tax is paid at the right time. Under the previous system, employers generally only had to report payroll information to HMRC at the end of the year.

Under RTI the directors' own salaries could result in additional payroll costs (for example, in small husband and wife companies or 'one man band' companies, where the only salaries paid are those of the directors themselves).

Where the directors receive small salaries, it may be cheaper and easier to register with HMRC as an annual scheme and pay salaries as a single annual lump sum (for example, in March just before the end of the tax year).

With annual schemes an FPS is only expected in the month of payment and HMRC only has to be paid once a year. However, it is only possible to register as an annual scheme if all employees are paid annually at the same time.

Once a business is registered as an annual scheme, an Employer Payment Summary (EPS) is not required for the 11 months of the tax year where no payments are made to the directors. Schemes not registered as annual schemes have to make monthly submissions, even if no salaries are paid.

An additional problem may arise where directors withdraw cash from their companies and only later decide how these payments are to be treated (for example, as salaries or dividends).

Where the director's loan account is overdrawn, an amount withdrawn and subsequently designated as salary could result in a late filing penalty under RTI.

When directors withdraw money from their companies it is essential to decide up front the nature of the payment (salary, loan, dividend, reimbursement of expenses etc) and to have evidence supporting that decision.

For example, where a director borrows money from the company, the terms of the loan should be set out in writing. Withdrawals by directors that cannot be categorised might be treated as earnings by HMRC unless the company can prove otherwise.

The only potential exception to these stringent requirements is where the director is simply drawing from a director's loan account which is in credit (the company owes them money). In these cases withdrawals can usually be safely debited to the loan account (provided it does not then become overdrawn) and then a salary, dividend, etc, might later be declared and credited to the loan account to re-establish the balance. The supporting evidence still has to be there, but there is a little more time to sort things out.

Dividends

Distributable Profits

Under the Companies Act a company cannot legally pay a dividend unless it has sufficient distributable profits to cover it.

A company's distributable profits are its accumulated realised profits, less accumulated realised losses. This information can generally be found in the company's most recent annual accounts.

It is not necessary for the company to actually make a profit in the year the dividend is paid, as long as there are sufficient accumulated profits (after tax) from previous years.

So all is not necessarily lost if your company has been experiencing difficult trading conditions in recent times. As long as there are sufficient distributable profits from previous years, it may be possible to continue paying dividends.

Where the most recent annual accounts do not show sufficient profits, interim or management accounts can be prepared with more up to date information. This may be useful if business conditions have improved since the last accounts were prepared.

It's also important to remember that directors have a duty to promote the company's success, protect its assets and take reasonable action to ensure that the company can pay its debts.

If future trading losses are expected, this is a factor that should be taken into account when considering the cash flow implications of any proposed dividend.

Thus, even if the most recent set of accounts show that there are sufficient distributable profits, the directors must take account of any change in the company's financial position since the accounts date and consider whether the company will remain solvent after any proposed dividend is paid. The key point is that directors must act honestly and reasonably at all times.

Before paying any dividends it is probably wise to speak to your accountant to check whether the company does indeed have sufficient distributable profits.

If the company does not have sufficient distributable profits to cover its dividend payments, the dividends will be illegal and the shareholder will be liable to repay the company.

Dividend Formalities & Paperwork

If the proper formalities are not observed, it is possible that HMRC will try to tax dividends as employment income. To help avoid any such challenge it is essential to ensure that dividends are properly declared and you have the supporting paperwork to prove it. This includes:

- Holding a directors' board meeting to recommend the dividend payment (with written minutes to prove the meeting took place)
- Holding a general meeting of the company's members (i.e. shareholders) to approve the dividend payment (with written minutes to prove the meeting took place).
- Issuing a dividend confirmation to each shareholder.

See Appendix C for sample documentation.

Some commentators also argue it is not advisable to declare dividends monthly because this will look more like salary income, especially if the above formalities are neglected.

A better alternative would be an infrequent dividend credited to the director's loan account which can then be drawn down throughout the year.

Paying a dividend towards the end of the tax year, when it may be easier to work out how much income tax will be payable, is possibly best in timing terms. If a dividend is paid at the beginning of the year and income from other sources (for example, rental income) turns out to be higher than expected, the company owner could end up paying tax at a higher rate on their dividend income.

Interim versus Final Dividends

A final dividend must be recommended by the directors and endorsed by a shareholders' meeting. For tax purposes the dividend is treated as paid on that date (unless a later date is specified).

Interim dividends can be authorised at the discretion of directors and are recognised for tax purposes only when they are paid, for example by crediting the director's loan account.

Chapter 36

Dividends Taxed as Earnings and Other Potential Dangers

Back in 2013, HMRC managed to get something called the general anti-abuse rule (GAAR) onto the statute books. As the name implies, the rule is aimed at blocking abusive tax arrangements. An arrangement is considered abusive if it cannot reasonably be regarded as a reasonable course of action: commonly referred to as the double reasonableness test.

Clearly this is very subjective, but HMRC has sought to reassure us there is a high threshold for showing that tax arrangements are abusive:

"In respect of any particular arrangement there might be a range of views as to whether it was a reasonable course of action: it is possible that there could be a reasonably held view that the tax arrangements were a reasonable course of action, and also a reasonably held view that the arrangement is not a reasonable course of action. In such circumstances the tax arrangements will not be abusive for the purposes of the GAAR."

An indicator that tax arrangements are not abusive is if they were established practice when entered into and HMRC indicated its acceptance of that practice at the time.

On the other hand, tax arrangements may be abusive if, for example, the tax result is different to the real economic result, such as tax deductions or tax losses significantly greater than actual expenses or real economic losses.

If you think all of the above is a bit vague, you are not alone. Even the best tax brains in the land don't know what this test means in practice. When legislation contains words like 'reasonable' and 'abusive' you know you have to be on your guard!

The question for us in this guide is: could the anti-abuse rule ever be used to attack 'normal' or 'mainstream' tax planning carried out by small company owners, such as taking small salaries and large dividends?

Thankfully, most tax experts are confident that well-established, conventional tax planning will not be attacked by HMRC using the GAAR. Instead the focus is on 'aggressive' or 'artificial' tax avoidance schemes.

This view is backed up by HMRC guidance, which says the following about small company dividends:

"Just as it is essential to understand what the GAAR is targeted at, so it is equally essential to understand what it is not targeted at. To take an obvious example, a taxpayer deciding to carry on a trade can do so either as a sole trader or through a limited company whose shares he or she owns and where he or she works as an employee. Such a choice is completely outside the target area of the GAAR, and once such a company starts to earn profits a decision to accumulate most of the profits to be paid out in the future by way of dividend, rather than immediately paying a larger salary, is again something that should in any normal trading circumstances be outside the target area of the GAAR."

Phew! So, routine tax planning carried out by small company owners when extracting money from their company as tax efficiently as possible is safe from the GAAR... but what about case law?

There have been some tax cases which demonstrate there is a potential danger that dividends paid to a director/shareholder could, in some circumstances, be vulnerable to a national insurance liability and possibly a full PAYE charge.

It is unlikely that these decisions will ever affect small family companies with simple share structures, but it's worth us taking a look at them as they illustrate the courts' attitude to this area of tax planning.

P A Holdings: PA Holdings switched from a conventional bonus arrangement to a more intricate structure whereby an employee benefit trust was funded by the company, which in turn awarded preference shares to employees. These preference shares duly paid a dividend after which they were redeemed.

The company and its employees argued that the dividends should be taxed as dividends using dividend tax rates and without any PAYE or national insurance implications.

By contrast, HMRC took the view that the dividends simply amounted to earnings and that the normal PAYE and national insurance payments should have been deducted from them and accounted for to HMRC.

The Court of Appeal decided that the dividends were indeed earnings for employment and should therefore suffer deductions of income tax at source through PAYE. Both employers and employees national insurance deductions should also have been made. PA Holdings initially decided to appeal to the Supreme Court but later threw in the towel.

Uniplex (UK) Ltd: Uniplex was sold a scheme aimed at giving employees dividend income instead of remuneration, issuing different classes of share to each employee. This type of arrangement is generally known as alphabet shares.

The scheme failed as it was not implemented as planned. However, the First Tier Tribunal judge added that the scheme, even if implemented correctly, might still have failed.

Practical Implications

The practical implications relate to the boundary between normal dividend payments and those which, under the PA Holdings/Uniplex case principles, would be treated as employment earnings and hence attract income tax and national insurance deductions through PAYE. For instance in PA Holdings the First Tier Tribunal said:

"if something is paid out as a distribution by a company to an investing shareholder then the issue of derivation may arise if the shareholder is also an employee. The facts may show that the derivation of a dividend from a share may not be related to earnings because the acquisition and ownership of the share was not related to earnings or more generally to the status of the individual as an employee of the company".

In Uniplex, the First Tier Tribunal said:

"The PA Holdings case is authority for the proposition that payments from a party other than the employer can be from an employee's employment" and *"It may well have still been the case that the full amount would have been taxable because employees had given no consideration for the payment other than their services"*

What all this demonstrates is that there can come a point where dividends paid to an employee-shareholder could be vulnerable to a national insurance liability, and possibly a full PAYE charge.

However, both these cases involved complex tax avoidance schemes: a million miles from the normal, routine tax planning whereby a small company owner structures the payments they take from their company in the most tax efficient way.

Most tax advisers would argue the aggressive tax planning undertaken by PA Holdings (trying to change bonuses into dividends for a large chunk of employees) is entirely different to the profit extraction model of most small companies.

As yet, the simple salary versus dividend planning we have examined throughout most of this guide, where we are concerned only with payments to one or more shareholder/directors, each of whom holds a sizeable stake in a company with only one class of share capital, would not appear to be threatened by the decisions in the more complex cases examined above.

Nonetheless, there is a fear among some more cautious advisers that cases like these might one day be seized upon by HMRC as having created a wider precedent which they can apply to any employer that pays dividends to its staff.

The most vulnerable are those that use tax planning HMRC may view as aggressive. We already know some of their main targets. Those we would class as **'Close to Extinction'** include:

- Large scale contrived arrangements where dividends are created for tax avoidance purposes (as in *PA Holdings*).

- 'Alphabet' share arrangements, where different classes of shares (A, B, C, etc) have no substantive rights other than to dividends and are used to share profits in a way that relates to the amount of work carried out in the business (by substituting dividends for salaries or bonuses).

These contrived arrangements have probably had their day and there is a strong risk that dividends paid under these circumstances will be taxed as employment income. In short, we wouldn't touch these types of schemes with a bargepole.

Beyond these, there are other arrangements which we would view as being on the *'Endangered Species'* list, including:

- Alphabet share arrangements or other shares that have no capital or voting rights, used to divert income to spouses/partners or other family members with lower income tax rates. These arrangements are highly likely to fall foul of the settlements legislation.

- Directors' loans that are written off and taxed as dividends.

- Dividend waivers that are used to divert income to other shareholders, for example where a director waives their own dividends so that their spouse/partner can receive more income. HMRC succeeded in challenging dividend waivers in the case of *Donovan & McLaren v HMRC*.

- Situations where previous salaries paid to minority shareholders have been reduced in favour of dividends.

While these arrangements might still work in some cases, we would urge anyone considering using them to proceed with extreme caution and to seek independent professional advice (independent of whoever is recommending them to you).

Back to Normal

The sixty-four thousand dollar question is: where does all this leave the average small company owner taking a small salary and the rest of their income as dividends?

At the time of writing, it would appear the vast majority of small companies are not under any threat of attack, but this state of affairs could change in the future. The small salary/big dividend tax planning technique may not continue to produce the same savings company owners are currently able to enjoy indefinitely. There is a danger, no matter how small, that HMRC may try to tax your dividends as earnings at some point in the future.

Some tax advisers recommend taking a salary slightly larger than the 'optimal' amounts, so that at least some income tax and national insurance is paid by the director. Some even argue that if you are currently taking a salary larger than the 'optimal' amounts listed in Chapter 8 you should not reduce it.

However, there are still many tax advisers who are content to continue with the current, long-standing tax planning technique, where the most optimal salary is taken each year, until such time as there is an actual change in the law which puts a stop to it.

Remember, HMRC do not make tax law, they only administer it. It's only judges and politicians who can change the law: now isn't that comforting!

Chapter 37

Personal Service Companies

If your company is classed as a personal service company, many of the tax planning opportunities available to other company owners may not be available, for example, the ability to take dividends that are free from national insurance.

Personal service companies often have to operate the infamous 'IR35' regime which means the company may be forced to calculate a notional salary for the director/shareholder. This deemed income will be subject to PAYE and national insurance.

Essentially, HMRC may ignore the company set up and treat most of the company's income as employment income.

Which Companies Are Affected by IR35?

This is where it all becomes a bit of a grey area (which is why professional advice is essential!)

A personal service company is, generally speaking, a firm that receives all or most of its income from services provided by the director/shareholder personally.

Often the work will be carried out for just one client, often for a long period of time, and the client will probably only want the personal services of the company owner (hence IR35 often applies to 'one man band' companies).

Essentially HMRC is looking for cases of 'disguised employment'. In other words, ignoring the fact that there is an intermediary company, the relationship is more like that of an employer and employee rather than the kind of relationship that exists between independent self-employed business owners and their clients.

Where such 'disguised employment' exists, the company must generally apply the IR35 regime to the payments received from that client – effectively treating most of those payments as if they were salary paid to the director/shareholder.

A typical situation which might be caught under the IR35 rules is where the individual resigns as an employee and then goes back to the same job but working through their own personal service company.

However, it's all very subjective with a long line of legal cases adding to the confusion.

Personal service companies can be found in many different business sectors: the most cited example is IT consultants. They also came under the media spotlight in recent times when it was disclosed that some BBC presenters had been operating as 'freelancers' via personal service companies, when many would argue that they are in fact nothing but employees of the BBC.

Recent Changes

Since 2017, new 'off-payroll' legislation has applied to employers in the public sector. The same legislation has applied to larger *private sector* employers since April 2021.

Under these new rules the onus is on the employer to assess the contractor's employment status and pay income tax and national insurance where there appears to be an employment relationship.

Small organisations are exempt from this legislation. Where small businesses take on contractors through an intermediary, the responsibility for applying the IR35 rules stays with the contractor.

A business will generally be treated as small if it satisfies two or more of the following requirements:

- Annual turnover does not exceed £10.2 million
- Assets not more than £5.1 million
- No more than 50 employees

In his infamous September 2022 'Mini Budget', former Chancellor Kwasi Kwarteng proposed doing away with this off-payroll legislation. However, this proposal has itself been scrapped, so the legislation will remain in force.

IR35 and the off-payroll legislation are beyond the scope of this guide.

Part 8

More Tax Planning Ideas

Chapter 38

How to Pay Less CGT by Postponing Dividends

The main capital gains tax ('CGT') rates were reduced in April 2016:

- From 18% to 10% Basic rate taxpayers
- From 28% to 20% Higher rate taxpayers

Sadly, the 18% and 28% rates still apply to gains arising on disposals of *residential* property.

Where the individual is entitled to Business Asset Disposal Relief (previously called Entrepreneurs Relief), the gain is taxed at 10%. This relief is generally only available when you sell or wind up a trading business (furnished holiday letting businesses may also qualify). In other cases, the CGT rate depends on how much income you've earned during the tax year.

In the absence of Business Asset Disposal Relief, the maximum amount of capital gains that you can have taxed at 10% or 18% during the current tax year is £37,700. This is the current level of the basic-rate tax band.

Basic-rate taxpayers pay 10% less CGT than higher-rate taxpayers. This means the basic-rate tax band can save each person £3,770 in CGT this year: £37,700 x 10% = £3,770.

Postponing Dividends

If you expect to realise a large capital gain, for example by disposing of a buy-to-let property, you may be able to save some tax by making sure the disposal takes place during a tax year in which your taxable income is quite low.

In this respect, company owners can manipulate their incomes more easily than regular employees, sole traders or business partners. The company itself can keep trading and generating profits but the company owner can make sure very little of these profits are extracted and taxed in his or her hands.

Example

Richard, a company owner, sells his second home in March 2023, realising a gain of £50,000 after deducting all buying and selling costs. Deducting his annual CGT exemption of £12,300 leaves a taxable gain of £37,700.

Richard hasn't paid himself any dividends during the current tax year and decides to postpone paying any so that his £37,700 capital gain is taxed at 18% instead of 28%. This simple piece of planning saves Richard £3,770 in CGT.

Note that Richard can still pay himself a tax-free salary of up to £12,570 to utilise his income tax personal allowance. The income tax personal allowance does not interfere with the CGT calculation.

In fact, as we saw in Chapter 8, Richard may be better off paying himself a smaller salary of £9,100 or £11,908 plus a small tax-free dividend to use up his remaining personal allowance.

For example, if Richard takes a salary of £11,908, he can take a dividend of £662 without affecting his CGT bill. However, taking the further £2,000 of tax-free dividend covered by his dividend allowance for 2022/23 would still use up part of his basic rate band and lead to a £200 increase in CGT.

Limitations

Although postponing dividends could help you pay less CGT, it's probably not worth doing this unless you can withdraw the postponed dividends in a future tax year and pay no more than 8.75% tax. If you take a bigger dividend in a later tax year, and end up paying 33.75% income tax, you may end up worse off overall.

Example continued

In the above example Richard postponed taking a dividend of £37,700 to free up his basic-rate band and pay 18% CGT.

If during 2023/24 he takes an additional dividend of £37,700, on top of his usual salary and maximum dividend taxed at 8.75%, he will pay additional income tax of £12,724 (£37,700 x 33.75%). However, if he had taken that income in 2022/23 he would have paid income tax of £3,124 – so he ends up paying £9,600 more income tax.

He saved £3,770 in CGT in 2022/23 but pays an additional £9,600 in income tax in 2023/24. Overall Richard is £5,830 worse off.

Future Tax Years

This type of planning may become more valuable in future due to the reductions in the annual CGT exemption: to £6,000 in 2023/24 and £3,000 in subsequent years. However, what these reductions also mean is it may be unwise to postpone capital gains which would otherwise arise this year: or at least the benefit of doing this will be reduced.

Let's go back to Richard in our example. Let's say he's already taken enough dividends to make him a higher rate taxpayer for 2022/23, so he postpones both the sale of his second home (to after 5th April 2023) and the dividends he would otherwise take in 2023/24 (to after 5th April 2024).

Having £37,700 of his gain taxed at 18% instead of 28% will save him £3,770, as before. However, the delay to his property sale will mean £6,300 of his gain is taxed at 28% instead of being covered by his annual exemption: that will cost him £1,764. So his overall net saving is just £2,006: probably not worth it when you consider the risks inherent in delaying a property sale.

Note that, to postpone a sale for CGT purposes, it is necessary to postpone the date of unconditional contract, not just the date of completion. See the Taxcafe guide *'How to Save Property Tax'* for further details.

Chapter 39

Emigrating to Save Tax

Possibly the most drastic step you can take to save tax is leave the country. By becoming non-UK resident you may be able to avoid both capital gains tax (when you sell your company) and income tax (if you want to withdraw big dividends).

Capital Gains Tax ('CGT')

In the past it was possible to go and live in certain countries for just one year and completely avoid CGT. This was a fantastic loophole, especially when CGT was levied at rates of up to 40%.

Unfortunately that loophole was closed and most UK taxpayers who move abroad temporarily to avoid CGT will be taxed when they return if their period of non-UK residence lasts less than five years.

With a CGT rate of just 10% applying to many company sales (where Business Asset Disposal Relief applies), many company owners would be unwilling to exile themselves from the UK for five years just to increase their bank accounts by 10%.

Moving abroad is an expensive and time-consuming business and these costs would eat into your tax savings.

Having said this, the reduction in the lifetime allowance for Business Asset Disposal Relief from £10 million of gains to just £1 million of gains means that many business owners will now pay the higher 20% CGT rate when they sell their companies.

If you plan to emigrate one day anyway, this is all academic. You may be able to live in the country of your dreams **and** reduce your tax bill at the same time.

However, emigration isn't always what it used to be. UK CGT may still be charged on all or part of the gain on the sale of your company after you become non-UK resident if UK property (land and buildings) accounts for 75% or more of the company's total gross asset value. The charge applies to the increase in value arising after 5th April 2019. For further details, see the Taxcafe guide *'Using a Property Company to Save Tax'*.

Income Tax

Where a company has built up significant distributable profits it was possible in the past to withdraw these profits as tax-free dividends during a short period of non-UK residence.

This tax planning opportunity is no longer available following the introduction of some anti-avoidance rules.

Income from 'closely controlled companies' (most small companies) will be taxed if the recipient becomes UK resident again after a temporary period of non residence of five years or less.

This anti-avoidance rule does not apply to dividends paid out of post-departure profits, i.e. profits built up while you are non-UK resident.

It is not meant to apply to employment and self-employment earnings or regular investment income, e.g. dividends from stock market companies and bank interest.

Furthermore, the anti-avoidance rule will only apply where an individual has been UK resident in four or more of the seven tax years prior to the tax year in which they become non-resident.

While it may no longer be possible to avoid income tax by becoming non-UK resident for a short period, this tax planning strategy may still work for genuine emigrants who decide to leave the UK permanently.

Becoming Non-UK Resident

It used to be the case that you could generally establish, or maintain non-UK resident status by making sure you never spent more than 90 days in the UK in any tax year. That's still a reasonable rule of thumb in many cases but there is now far more that needs to be considered.

A statutory residence test is now used to determine whether or not you are UK resident in any particular tax year.

The test is complex to say the least and includes rules which can seem quite arbitrary at times. For example, I once had to tell my daughter that she couldn't stay at her mother's house (my ex-partner) beyond a certain date as she would then lose her non-UK resident status and be liable for UK income tax on the salary she had earned in Dubai earlier in the same tax year. Honestly, I'm not making this up!

Anyway, suffice to say, if you intend to emigrate to avoid or reduce UK taxes, it's essential to get professional advice.

Professional advice should also be obtained in your new intended country of residence, as becoming resident in another country will expose you to their taxes: you don't want to end up 'jumping out of the frying pan and into the fire!'

For more information on the statutory residence test see the Taxcafe guide *'Tax Planning for Non-Residents & Non Doms'*.

Chapter 40

Venture Capital Trusts (VCTs)

One of the easiest ways to cut your income tax bill is by investing in a venture capital trust (VCT). Venture capital trusts are funds that invest in small unquoted companies, including companies quoted on the Alternative Investment Market (AIM).

VCT investments provide 30% income tax relief, so if you invest £10,000 your income tax bill will be cut by £3,000.

An investment of roughly £10,413 is required to wipe out the entire income tax bill of a company owner who pays themselves income of £50,270 in 2022/23.

Example

Leanne, a company owner, pays herself a salary of £11,908 and dividend of £38,362 in 2022/23 – a total of £50,270. Her salary is tax free in her hands, as is £2,662 of her dividend income (being covered by the remainder of her personal allowance and the dividend allowance). She stands to pay 8.75% income tax on the remaining £35,700 dividend: £3,124.

Leanne has a significant amount of money tucked away in a bank savings account. So before the end of the tax year she withdraws £10,413 and invests it in a venture capital trust. This reduces her income tax for the year by £3,124 (£10,413 x 30%). When she submits her tax return for 2022/23 she will not have any income tax to pay and will not have to make any payments on account (see Chapter 5).

A VCT can also be used to head off an unexpectedly high tax bill:

Example

Tony owns a catering company and a number of rental properties. Just before the end of the tax year he works out that his taxable rental profit will be higher than expected. He took a dividend from his company early in the tax year but only now realises that an additional £12,000 of this income will be taxed at 33.75% instead of 8.75%, producing an unexpected tax bill of £3,000. Tony decides to invest £10,000 in a VCT. This will provide income tax relief of £3,000, wiping out the higher-rate tax he otherwise would have had to pay.

There are some other points to note about VCT income tax relief:

- The maximum investment is £200,000 per tax year, so the maximum initial tax saving is £60,000.

- The 30% up-front tax relief is available only if your income tax bill for the year is high enough. So if you invest £10,000, your maximum tax relief is £3,000. But if your tax bill is only £2,000, your tax relief will be limited to £2,000.

- VCTs provide income tax relief only. They do not reduce your capital gains tax or national insurance.

- You can no longer defer capital gains tax from the sale of property or other assets by investing in a VCT.

VCTs also offer two further tax benefits: tax-free dividends and tax-free capital gains.

ISAs also offer tax-free dividends and capital gains so tax-free VCT dividends, in particular, will be most appealing to company owners who are higher-rate taxpayers or additional-rate taxpayers and max out their ISA allowance each year.

These taxpayers would normally pay 33.75% tax or 39.35% tax on any additional dividend income they receive outside a VCT or ISA.

A lot of the return from a VCT investment will often come in the form of dividends.

VCTs vs ISAs & Pensions

What makes VCTs more attractive on paper than other tax shelters like ISAs and pensions is the double tax relief: when you put your money in AND when you take it out.

Pensions provide tax relief when you put your money in but your withdrawals are taxed. You can withdraw 25% of your fund as a tax-free lump sum when you retire but you have to pay income tax on everything else.

ISAs, by contrast, allow you to make tax-free withdrawals of income and capital gains but do not provide any up-front tax relief for your initial contributions. An exception is the Lifetime ISA which provides a 25% Government bonus and allows tax-free withdrawals. However, you cannot open one if you're 40 or older and the maximum investment is £4,000 per year.

So venture capital trusts offer the best of both worlds and are arguably one of the most generous tax shelters available. Even if you only receive back your original money after five years, with no capital gains or dividends, you will still have enjoyed a return of around 7.5% per year, thanks to the initial tax relief.

VCTs may also appeal to those who have already made the maximum investment allowed in ISAs and pensions.

VCT Drawbacks

Five Year Minimum

The first catch with VCTs is you have to invest for a minimum period of five years; otherwise you will lose the income tax relief.

Pensions can be even more restrictive depending on your age: you cannot touch your money at all until you reach age 55 at least. With ISAs you can withdraw your money tax free at any time.

With the new and more generous Lifetime ISA withdrawals before age 60 attract a penalty (unless you use the money to buy your first home).

A traditional ISA is therefore the only tax shelter that comes with no strings attached and is arguably the best investment for those who want easy access to their money.

Small, Risky Companies

The second and most important catch with VCTs is they have to invest most of your money in the smallest and arguably most risky companies. This, after all, is why the Government created such a generous tax shelter in the first place: it wants to encourage investment in small but potentially high-growth companies.

With pensions and ISAs, on the other hand, you can invest in the biggest blue chip companies, as well as small companies, corporate bonds and cash.

VCTs have to put at least 80% of the money they raise in 'qualifying' companies. The remaining money can be invested in pretty much anything, including bigger companies and other less risky investments.

Companies are no longer allowed to use the money they raise from VCTs to acquire other existing businesses (they're supposed to use it to grow organically). VCTs are also prohibited from investing in management buy-outs (MBOs). These were a particularly lucrative source of returns in the past.

There are other investment rules and if a VCT doesn't comply it could lose its special tax status which means investors may have to pay back the income tax relief they received. This almost happened to one well-known fund in recent times.

The investment rules basically mean VCTs have to invest most of the money they raise in small (usually privately-owned) firms. VCTs generally also have to invest in relatively young companies that have not been selling for more than seven years (10 years if the company is defined as 'knowledge-intensive'). Small, young businesses are arguably the riskiest.

Having said this, if you take part in a fund raising by a large established VCT you will end up owning shares in a fund that also has an established portfolio of companies, some of which may be quite large and profitable businesses. For example, looking at the 10 biggest holdings in a sample fund, the Hargreave Hale AIM VCT, many have a market capitalisation of over £100 million.

If a VCT with a portfolio worth £80 million raises a further £20 million from investors (including you), 80% of your shareholding will be in the existing holdings, some of which may be more established companies, and only 20% in new investments.

Illiquid Investments

A major drawback of VCTs is their lack of liquidity. The trusts themselves are quoted on the London Stock Exchange but you may struggle to sell your shares at a decent price when the five-year period is up. Why? Because the 30% income tax relief – the only reason most people invest in venture capital trusts – is only available on *new* VCT shares.

Investors who buy 'second-hand' VCT shares are entitled to tax-free dividends but the all-important 30% tax refund is denied. For this reason, there are very few people willing to buy VCT shares from exiting investors.

Some VCTs do, however, offer to buy back shares from investors who wish to exit. This will typically be at a discount to net asset value of, for example, 5% to 10%.

Previously, some VCTs offered a buy-back facility that allowed investors to sell back their shares and buy new ones in the same VCT with another round of income tax relief. VCTs are no longer able to carry out these enhanced share buybacks that offer a fresh round of income tax relief.

Investors are also not able to obtain a second round of income tax relief if they sell their VCT shares and invest in a new issue of shares in the same fund within six months.

Higher Charges

VCTs have higher charges than more mainstream investment funds such as unit trusts and OEICs. Initial charges can be as much as 5%, whereas most traditional investment funds have no initial charges these days when you invest through one of the big investment platforms such as Hargreaves Lansdown. However, discounts on VCT investments are generally available when you invest through a platform.

Annual management fees are in the region of 2% per year or more, also higher than the charges levied by mainstream funds. There may also be a performance fee.

These initial and ongoing charges, coupled with the fact that you may have to eventually sell your investment at a discount, mean that a significant portion of your initial income tax relief (possibly over half) could be swallowed up by additional charges.

Our View of VCTs

It's important not to invest in VCTs solely for the tax savings. You must want to invest in small companies. Some readers may feel that they already have ample exposure to small companies... namely their own!

For those who do want to invest in small companies, investing in a VCT with 30% income tax relief may be more attractive than investing in a regular small company fund, especially for those who have already made the maximum permitted investment in ISAs and pensions.

VCTs are typically associated with year-end tax planning: steps you take just before the end of the tax year to head off an unwelcome tax bill. However, in recent times demand for some of the best VCT offers has outstripped supply and it has been essential to invest well before the end of the tax year on 5th April.

The minimum investment period is five years but a longer time horizon is arguably necessary because of the inherent riskiness of this type of investment. Company owners who have volatile income and are not comfortable with having their savings locked up for at least five years should arguably steer clear of VCTs.

Although a VCT investment could be a useful way to cut your income tax bill it should also be remembered that the easiest way for company owners to avoid unwanted income tax bills is by paying themselves smaller dividends!

Financial advice may be necessary to help you decide whether to invest and what type of VCT to buy.

Finally, note that there is currently a 'sunset clause' in place in relation to the income tax relief offered by VCT schemes which means this will cease to exist from 6th April 2025. In the November 2022 Autumn Statement the Government stated that it remains supportive of Venture Capital Trusts and sees the value of extending them in the future.

Marginal Corporation Tax Rates

Year Ending	Small Profits Rate	Marginal Rate	Main Rate
31-Mar-2023 or earlier	n/a	n/a	19.000%
30-Apr-2023	19.000%	19.616%	19.493%
31-May-2023	19.000%	20.253%	20.003%
30-Jun-2023	19.000%	20.870%	20.496%
31-Jul-2023	19.000%	21.507%	21.005%
31-Aug-2023	19.000%	22.144%	21.515%
30-Sep-2023	19.000%	22.760%	22.008%
31-Oct-2023	19.000%	23.397%	22.518%
30-Nov-2023	19.000%	24.014%	23.011%
31-Dec-2023	19.000%	24.651%	23.521%
31-Jan-2024	19.000%	25.288%	24.030%
29-Feb-2024	19.000%	25.865%	24.492%
31-Mar-2024	19.000%	26.500%	25.000%

Subject to the rules for associated companies (see Chapter 1), the small profits rate will apply to companies making profits of £50,000 or less; the marginal rate will apply to profits between £50,000 and £250,000; and the main rate will apply where profits exceed £250,000.

These marginal rates represent the effective rate of tax relief on one-off or annual payments made during the company accounting period listed above, where those payments are not recognised on a time apportionment, or periodic basis in the company's accounts.

Corporation Tax Relief on Periodic Costs in 2022/23

Company Year End	Small Profits Rate	Marginal Rate	Main Rate
30-Apr	19.000%	19.565%	19.452%
31-May	19.000%	20.045%	19.836%
30-Jun	19.000%	20.402%	20.122%
31-Jul	19.000%	20.671%	20.337%
31-Aug	19.000%	20.834%	20.467%
30-Sep	19.000%	20.880%	20.504%
31-Oct	19.000%	20.832%	20.466%
30-Nov	19.000%	20.671%	20.337%
31-Dec	19.000%	20.413%	20.130%
31-Jan	19.000%	20.048%	19.838%
29-Feb	19.000%	19.572%	19.458%
31-Mar	19.000%	19.000%	19.000%

Subject to the rules for associated companies (see Chapter 1), the small profits rate will apply to companies making profits of £50,000 or less in the accounting period that straddles 1st April 2023; the marginal rate will apply where the profits of that period are between £50,000 and £250,000; and the main rate will apply where profits exceed £250,000.

The level of profit made in the previous accounting period will have no effect on the effective rate of tax relief.

These effective rates apply to payments made monthly, or to payments that are made annually, but recognised on a time apportionment basis in the company's accounts.

Appendix C

Sample Dividend Documentation

1. Directors' Board Meeting Minute

BOARD MINUTE

Minutes of a Meeting of Directors of Winging It Ltd held at 13 Fluky Road, Charmedtown, ZZ1 1AA on 31st March 2023.

Present: Mr AB Happy – Director
Mrs CD Go – Director
Mr EF Lucky – Director

In attendance: Mr G Downcast – Company Secretary

Motions:
1) The directors noted the company's excellent trading results for the year ended 31st December 2022.
2) It was recommended that the company pay a dividend of £2.50 per ordinary share out of the profits for the year ended 31st December 2022, to be paid on 1st April 2023.
3) No other motions.

Signed _____   Date _____
(Mr AB Happy)

Notes (Not Part of the Minute)
The minutes of a directors' board meeting should:
a) Show who is present.
b) Include enough information to show how directors reasonably came to reasonable decisions.
c) Include details of any conflicts of interest or abstainment from voting.
d) Be signed by a director present at the meeting.
e) Be retained with the company's statutory records.

Regarding point (a) above, a quorum may need to be present for the meeting to be valid. This depends on the company's own constitution as set out in its Articles of Association.

2. Member's General Meeting Minute

GENERAL MEETING OF MEMBERS

Minutes of an Extraordinary General Meeting of the Ordinary Shareholders of Winging It Ltd held at 13 Fluky Road, Charmedtown, ZZ1 1AA on 31st March 2023.

Present: Mr AB Happy – Ordinary Shareholder
               Mrs CD Go – Ordinary Shareholder
               Mr EF Lucky – Ordinary Shareholder

In attendance: Mr G Downcast – Company Secretary

Motions:
1) The members, all being present, agreed to accept the short notice period for the meeting.
2) The members approved the recommendation of the directors that the company pay a dividend of £2.50 per ordinary share for the year ended 31st December 2022. Payment to be made on 1st April 2023.
3) No other motions.

Signed _____   Date _____
       (Mr AB Happy)

3. Dividend Confirmation

Dividend Confirmation

Winging It Limited
13 Fluky Road, Charmedtown, ZZ1 1AA

Ordinary shares of £1 each

Mr AB Happy   1st April 2023
1 Blessed Street
Charmedtown
ZZ2 1XY

Payment of the final dividend in respect of the year ended 31st December 2022, at the rate of £2.50 per share on the ordinary shares registered in your name on 31st March 2023 is enclosed herewith.

H. Godwinson, Company Secretary

Shareholding	Dividend Payable	Payment Number
10,000	£25,000.00	12

This dividend confirmation should be kept with your tax records.